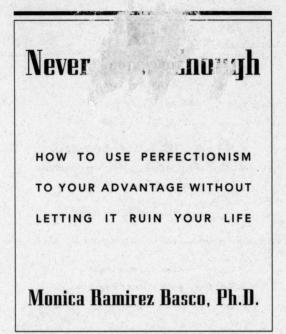

Never Good Enough

HOW TO USE PERFECTIONISM

TO YOUR ADVANTAGE WITHOUT

LETTING IT RUIN YOUR LIFE

Monica Ramirez Basco, Ph.D.

A Touchstone Book
Published by Simon & Schuster
New York   London   Sydney

TOUCHSTONE
Rockefeller Center
1230 Avenue of the Americas
New York, NY 10020

Copyright © 1999 by Monica Ramirez Basco

First Touchstone Edition 2000

TOUCHSTONE and colophon are registered trademarks of Simon & Schuster, Inc.

Designed by Jenny Dossin
Manufactured in the United States of America

7   9   10   8   6

The Library of Congress has cataloged the Free Press edition as follows:

Basco, Monica Ramirez.
Never good enough : freeing yourself from the chains of
perfectionism / Monica Ramirez Basco.
p.   cm.
Includes index.
1. Perfectionism (Personality trait) 2. Perfectionism
(Personality trait)—Case studies. 3. Cognitive therapy.
I. Title.

BF698.35.P47B27   1999   98-31575
155.2'32—dc21   CIP

ISBN-13: 978-0–684–84963–8
ISBN-10:   0–684–84963–1
ISBN-13: 978-0–684–86293–4 (Pbk)
ISBN-10:   0–684–86293–X (Pbk)

To my parents who have always been satisfied
with me no matter what I have done

CONTENTS

Acknowledgments *ix*

Preface *xi*

1 Are You a Perfectionist? *1*

2 The Two Faces of Perfectionism *36*

3 Schemas That
Underlie Perfectionism *66*

4 Challenging Your Beliefs *91*

5 Automatic Thoughts
and Thinking Errors *110*

6 Beating Oversimplification *133*

7 Adjusting Your Expectations *162*

8 Perfectionism and
Getting Along With Others *186*

9 Living With Perfectionists *219*

10 Making Changes That Last *250*

Appendix: Where to Call for Help *265*

Index *269*

ACKNOWLEDGMENTS

I would like to thank Kitty Moore for her encouragement and support, which helped me get started in writing this book, and Philip Rappaport of Free Press, for his careful reading and helpful suggestions. I would also like to thank Jesse H. Wright, M.D., Ph.D., for his creative ideas and helpful feedback, and Fastword, for their technical assistance. I am especially grateful to my colleagues, staff, and friends for their eye for perfection. I have been the direct beneficiary of each of these person's efforts to get it "just right," to please me, to go the extra mile to create wonderful experiences to share with me, and to set an example of hard work and motivation. My husband deserves a great deal of thanks for his tolerance of my telling stories about him throughout this book. I would also like to thank my children for their patience while I experiment with my efforts to be a good parent. They have been very tolerant of my imperfections.

I had the idea for this book when, after years of treating people for depression, marital problems, anxiety, eating disorders, and other difficulties, I realized that many of my patients and friends spend an excessive amount of time trying to be the perfect person—worker, parent, child, student, spouse. It seemed to me that people were struggling with some kind of perfectionism without being aware of what was really bothering them or that there was something they could do about it. This book is intended to help people that fall into two general categories. The first group struggles with the idea that they or their actions are not good enough. Although they may seem successful to others, deep down inside, they think that there is something wrong with them, that they are flawed, stupid, ugly, or unwanted. They are afraid to make mistakes and risk humiliation, and are particularly concerned with what others think about them. These inwardly focused perfectionists hide what they believe are their incompetencies by working very hard, but still fear that at some point, someone will figure out that they are not what they seem to be.

The second group, which includes people who are frustrated by the way that others seem to do their jobs, whether at home or in the workplace are called outwardly focused perfectionists. In their opinion, the people around them neither care about doing a good job, nor take pride in their performance. This is particularly frustrating when their coworkers, children, or spouses reflect badly on them. Sometimes these perfectionists feel that they would be better off doing a job themselves rather than having to clean up after the sloppy work of others. This frustration with others can cause tension or conflict in relationships and can add extra burden to their own lives. In reality, many people have characteristics of both types depending on the situation. For example, someone you know may feel the anxiety associated with inwardly focused perfectionism at work, but feel more like an outwardly focused perfectionist in her relationships with others.

When inwardly focused perfectionists come to me for treatment they do not usually say, *"I'm a perfectionist. Can you help me?"* Instead, they say that they feel like failures. Often they are depressed. They try hard, do their best, but in their hearts they feel that they will never be good enough. They will never get it right. Not feeling good enough is painful for people. Sometimes it is called low self-esteem. Sometimes it is called a negative self-image.

Outwardly focused perfectionists come to treatment for different reasons. Sometimes they are frustrated with the people in their world, feel a of loss of control over their lives or their family, or feel angry that things in their lives are not turning out the right way. Sometimes they are brought to treatment by family members who report strain in the relationship and poor communication, blaming the perfectionist for being too rigid, too demanding, unforgiving, or intolerant of others.

In working with both types of perfectionists, I have found that Cognitive-Behavior Therapy (CBT) can help to combat the idea that they are not good enough. CBT is based on the cognitive model for treating depression and other psychological difficulties that was developed by Dr. Aaron T. Beck, an internationally recognized scholar from the University of Pennsylvania. With some coaching, people have learned to recognize and understand when perfectionism is helpful in their lives and when it causes problems for them or for those they love. They have learned to use perfectionism to their advantage, for example in the workplace, without making them feel miserable when perfection is not attained. Rather than being driven by the belief that they must be perfect and disappointed when they are not, CBT methods help people to gain a more accurate view of themselves, their world, and others.

Although being a perfectionist can be painful, it is fixable. That is, there are some ways to change your thinking or your actions that help reduce the pain and allow you to achieve your goals. It's not magic. It is a change in the way you view yourself and the way you view others in your world. Throughout this book I will share with you several different ways to make the best of your perfectionism without letting it ruin your life.

Never Good Enough includes step-by-step instructions and exercises for gaining a better understanding of why you think you are never good enough and for making positive changes that will improve your self-esteem. This book can be useful for people who are already involved in therapy, particularly cognitive-behaviorally oriented therapies or are thinking about starting therapy. Although the exercises will be helpful to people with more debilitating levels of perfectionism, such as those with obsessive-compulsive disorder, obsessive-compulsive personality disorder, or eating disorders, they are geared toward the individual who has moderate trouble with perfectionism.

This book walks you through the cognitive-behavioral treatment of perfectionism, beginning in Chapter 1 with an explanation of perfectionism and why it can cause problems in your life. Several self-assessment exercises are provided to help you decide if you are a perfectionist and to recognize your own perfectionistic behaviors and ideas. Chapter 2 will help you examine the ways in which perfectionism helps you and hurts you. The areas or circumstances in which perfectionism causes you stress or difficulties will become targets for change. The cognitive-behavioral approach to controlling perfectionism is based on the idea that underlying beliefs or schemas influence your perceptions of yourself ("I'll never be good enough"), your world ("If I make a mistake I'll be rejected"), your future ("If I can get it perfect I will finally be accepted") and other people ("No one else cares about doing a good job. I'm better off doing it myself"). Schemas guide your choice of actions and greatly influence your emotional reactions to stressful events. However, for perfectionists, these beliefs are often inaccurate or incomplete. Chapter 3 reviews some common perfectionistic beliefs or schemas and Chapter 4 provides exercises for evaluating their accuracy or applicability in your life. With this new perspective you can decide to hold on to your old ideas, change or update them, or you can learn to apply your perfectionistic standards only to situations when they are helpful and to turn them off when they are not helpful.

Chapter 5 covers common misperceptions and misinterpretations that leave people feeling angry, distressed, and frustrated when stressful events occur. Among these "thinking errors" is "oversimplification," the tendency to see things in a black-and-white or all-or-nothing way. Chapters 6 and 7 help readers gain a clearer and more accurate view of themselves and others by examining the shades of gray between the extremes. These chapters provide exercises for defining more realistic goals and expectations as well as assessing your current progress toward those goals.

Chapters 8 and 9 focus on how perfectionism may be affecting your interactions with others at home and at work. If the title of this book caught your eye because no matter what you do, it is never good enough for someone else in your life, that person may be a perfectionist. If you are looking for ways to get along better with this person you will want to pay particular attention to these chapters. While Chapter 8 covers common interpersonal problems associated with perfectionism, Chapter 9 provides tips for your loved ones on how they can respond to your perfectionism in a more productive way. Chapter 10 provides some guidance on how to make these exercises work in your everyday life and how to make changes that last.

Because it is possible to experience the advantages of perfectionism while minimizing, as much as possible, the disadvantages, this book will help you learn how to use perfectionism to your advantage without letting it ruin your life.

1

ARE YOU A

PERFECTIONIST?

Susan had been working frantically for the last month trying to get her end-of-the-year books in order, keep the business running, and plan a New Year's Eve party for her friends and her clients. A few of her friends who have been supportive of Susan's interior design business were going to bring along some potential clients. Susan's home is a reflection of her talent as a designer, so she wanted to make some changes to the formal dining room before the party that she thought would be particularly impressive. It all came together in time for the party and the evening seemed to be going well, until her assistant, Charles, asked her if Mrs. Beale and Mr. Sandoval, two important clients, had arrived. Mrs. Beale had a small antique shop in town and had referred Susan a lot of business over the past two years. Mr. Sandoval was a member of the local Chamber of Commerce and had shown interest in Susan's business.

Susan felt like her head was about to explode when she realized that she had forgotten to invite them to the party.

"Oh no, I completely forgot. How could I be so stupid? What am I going to do? They'll no doubt hear about it from someone and will assume I omitted them on purpose. I am such an idiot. I may as well kiss the business good-bye. When the word gets out, no one will want to refer to me again."

"Susan, don't you think you may be overreacting a little." Charles tried to be supportive, but deep down inside he was glad he hadn't been the one to make such an awful mistake.

For the rest of the night she held her breath waiting for her other clients to ask about Mrs. Beale and Mr. Sandoval. What would she say? That she was a thoughtless numbskull who neglected to invite a former client who referred a substantial amount of business to her each year? Even worse, what will she say when Mrs. Beale and Mr. Sandoval confront her with her rudeness. Ten different excuses ran through her mind, but she ultimately chose to avoid them and their wrath.

Susan is an inwardly focused perfectionist. Although it can help her in her work, it also hurts her when she is hard on herself and finds error completely unacceptable. Like many people, she worries about what others will think of her and her business. However, in Susan's case her errors lead to humiliation, distress, sleepless nights, and withdrawal from others. She has trouble letting go and forgiving herself because, in her mind, it is OK for others to make mistakes, but it is not OK for her to make mistakes. This book was written to help people like Susan stop beating themselves up and, instead, make the most of their skills as a perfectionist.

Tom is an outwardly focused perfectionist. He feels OK about himself, but he is often disappointed in and frustrated with others who seem to always let him down. Quality control is his line of work, but he cannot always turn it off when he leaves the office. Tom drove into his garage to find that there was still a mess on the workbench and floor that his son, Tommy, had left two days ago.

He walked through the door and said to his wife in an annoyed tone of voice, "I told Tommy to clean up his mess in the garage before I got home."

"He just got home himself a few minutes ago," his wife defended.

"Where is he now? He better not be on the phone." Tom went to his son's room only to find Tommy on the phone with his girlfriend. Tom could feel himself tensing up. "Get off the phone and go clean up that mess in the garage like I told you."

"Yes, sir." Tommy got off the phone, knowing that a lecture was coming.

Tom cannot understand why his son cannot follow simple instructions. It seems like every day there is something new. He doesn't listen, his wife doesn't take care of things on time, and the burden usually falls on him. There is always an excuse. Even when they do their parts it usually isn't good enough and they don't seem to care. It is so frustrating for Tom sometimes that he does the job himself rather than ask for help, just so he doesn't have to deal with their procrastination and excuses.

Tom's type of perfectionism causes him problems in his relationships with others because he is frequently frustrated by their failure to meet his expectations. When he tries to point this out in a gentle way, it still seems to lead to tension, and sometimes to conflict. He has tried to train himself to expect nothing from others, but that strategy doesn't seem to work either. He needs some new ideas for coping with his frustration and for how to deal with the people in his life who seem to continually let him down.

This book will help you to identify, evaluate, and change the underlying beliefs that affect your management of stressful events and your interactions with others, particularly those who leave you thinking that either you or they are not good enough. The first goal will be to gain a better understanding of how thinking that things or that you are not good enough are related to difficulties you may have at home, on the job, or in relationships. By following along in this first chapter and completing the self-assessment at the end you will determine the degree to which you are a perfectionist and in what ways it is most likely to affect your life. You will find out if you are a more inwardly focused perfectionist like Susan or a more outwardly focused perfectionist like Tom. Because perfectionism can be a very positive trait, you will need to identify the situations or circumstances in which it serves you well in addition to those situations in which it seems to hurt you. Accomplishing this second goal will help focus your attention on learning new ways to cope with times when perfectionism seems to be getting in the way or causing you distress.

The third goal of this book is to teach you to identify times when your perfectionistic beliefs about yourself or others may be inaccurate or distorted in some way and how to straighten out the distortions. If you have a more accurate view of yourself and your world you will be less prone to the emotional upset caused by those distortions. One such belief is the notion that you *have to* be perfect or that others *have to* be perfect.

One of the common problems faced by both kinds of perfectionists is having expectations that are too high or that are difficult to achieve without considerable wear and tear on you and on others. The fourth goal of this book is to help you to determine if your expectations are too high, how close you are to achieving your goals, and what you will need to do to reach a more satisfying level.

Much of the stress that leaves you thinking that you or others are not good enough results from your interactions with other people. It is often difficult to pinpoint the cause of these tensions and to determine what to do about them. Therefore, the fifth and final goal of this book is to help you deal more effectively with other people. Some guidelines are provided on how to manage situations with others that are often difficult, discouraging, or conflictual. Some helpful hints have also been included for the people in your life who want to learn how to interact with you in a way that does not leave you with the sense that you are not good enough.

These methods are based on cognitive-behavior therapy (CBT), a scientifically proven effective treatment for many of the psychological difficulties associated with perfectionism. Starting first with education about perfectionism, then working through the cognitive-behavioral methods for controlling the distress associated with perfection, you will gain a more accurate view of yourself and of others. You will learn what it means to be good enough, see how close you really are to achieving your goals, and reduce the emotional pain associated with seeing yourself and others as not good enough.

THE PERSONAL PAIN OF PERFECTIONISTS

The reach for perfection can be painful because it is often driven by both a desire to do well and a fear of the consequences of not doing well. This is the double-edged sword of perfectionism. On the one hand, it is a good thing to give the best effort, to go the extra mile, and to take pride in one's performance, whether it is keeping a home looking nice, writing a report, repairing a car, or doing brain surgery. It is commendable to attend to details, care about what others will think about your work, and constantly strive to do your best. On the other hand, when despite great efforts you feel as though you keep falling short, never seem to get things just right, never have enough time to do your best, are self-conscious, feel criticized by others, or cannot get others to cooperate in doing the job right the first time, you end up feeling bad.

The difficulty can begin with setting extremely high and sometimes unreasonable goals for yourself or for others. You may not always be aware that you are setting a high goal, you may just have a "gut-level feeling" about how a project or task ought to be done. Unfortunately, in the course of life, perfectionists find that much of the time these standards cannot be met without a great deal of effort and energy, including emotional, psychological, and physical energy. What's wrong with setting high standards and working hard? The problem is not in having high standards or in working hard. Perfectionism becomes a problem when it causes emotional wear and tear or when it keeps you from succeeding or from being happy. Dr. Sidney J. Blatt of Yale University, an expert in this area, has described the destructiveness of perfectionism as an endless striving in which each task is seen as a challenge and no effort is ever good enough, yet the person continues in desperation to avoid mistakes, achieve perfection, and gain approval. The emotional consequences of perfectionism include fear of making mistakes, stress from the pressure to perform, and self-consciousness from feeling both self-confidence and self-doubt. It can also include tension, frustration, disappointment, sadness, anger, or fear of humiliation. These are common experiences for inwardly focused perfectionists. Do any of these sound familiar?

Perfectionism seems to be a psychological vulnerability that stays in the background as you conduct your life. The emotional stress caused by the pursuit of perfection and the failure to achieve this goal can evolve into more severe psychological difficulties. For example, researchers who study perfectionism, including Dr. Paul Hewitt of the University of British Columbia and Dr. Gordon Flett of York University, have found that perfectionists are more vulnerable to depression when stressful events occur, particularly those that leave them feeling as though they are not good enough. In many ways, perfectionistic beliefs set a person up to be disappointed, given that achieving perfection consistently is impossible, or at least hard to come by. Perfectionists who have a family history of depression and may therefore be more biologically vulnerable to developing the psychological and physical symptoms of major depression may be particularly sensitive to events that stimulate their self-doubt and their fear of rejection or humiliation.

The same seems to be true for eating disorders, such as anorexia nervosa and bulimia. Several recent studies have found that even after treatment, where weight was restored in malnourished and underweight women with anorexia, their perfectionistic beliefs persisted and likely contributed to relapse. Their beliefs that they were not good enough were so strong that despite physical evidence that they were too thin or unhealthy, they persisted in pushing themselves to achieve the perfect shape. They say to themselves, "If only I were thin enough I would be OK." Thomas E. Joiner, Jr., and his colleagues at the University of Texas Medical Branch in Galveston found, in their study of nearly a thousand women, that, for women who viewed themselves as overweight, perfectionism was one of the strongest risk factors for developing an eating disorder.

Sometimes the pain of perfectionism is felt in relationships with others. Perfectionists can sometimes put distance between themselves and others unintentionally by demanding perfection, being intolerant of others' mistakes, or by flaunting perfect behavior or accomplishments in front of those who are aware of being merely average. Although they feel justified in their beliefs about what is right and what is wrong, they still suffer the pain of loneliness. Research suggests that people who have more outwardly focused per-

Perfectionism is a problem when:

- it keeps you from succeeding or from being happy;
- no effort is ever good enough;
- you never seem to have enough time to do your best;
- you are self-conscious or feel criticized by others;
- you cannot get others to cooperate in doing the job right the first time;
- your standards cannot be met without a great deal of effort and emotional, psychological, and physical energy;
- it causes emotional wear and tear;
- you become fearful of making mistakes or of being humiliated;
- it leaves you feeling tense, frustrated, disappointed, sad, or angry;
- it distorts your perception of yourself;
- it creates tension in your personal relationships.

fectionism are less likely than inwardly focused perfectionists to suffer from depression or anxiety when they are stressed. However, interpersonal difficulties at home or on the job may be more common.

The good news is that CBT has been proven to be effective for the treatment of depression, eating disorders, anxiety disorders, and relationship difficulties, in many cases even more effective than treatment with medication. Unfortunately, despite CBT's ability to control the symptoms of these disorders, perfectionism seems to be one factor that keeps people from fully recovering or from staying well. The interventions described in this book pick up where standard treatments with CBT leave off, by specifically targeting the underlying beliefs that fuel perfectionism.

HOW DID I GET THIS WAY?

Was I Born this Way?

There has been some controversy over the years about the nature of personality or temperament. Is it something you are born with or is your personality shaped by the experiences of your life? There is considerable scientific evidence that many personality traits are, in fact, inherited genetically. For example, researchers have found that some characteristics, such as sociability, are more similar in identical twins, those that share the same genes, than in fraternal twins who only share half of their genes. Those personality characteristics that you are born with are often referred to as temperament. Psychoanalytic theories of child development, as well as learning or behavioral theories, suggest that children's personalities are slowly shaped through their interactions with their parents and other significant people in their lives. A more integrated view would suggest that both genetics and experience play a role in personality development. Children may be born with certain personality traits, but there is both clinical and scientific evidence that the behavioral responses and their emotional reactions or vulnerabilities can be altered by their experiences with people and with their world, thus shaping their temperament or personality to some extent.

As a student of more behaviorally oriented psychologists, I was uncertain how this all actually worked until I had my first child. He seemed to have a personality right from the start. Clearly we shaped his behaviors by paying more attention or otherwise positively reinforcing the things we thought were cute or smart. And also, we shaped his behavior through correction, by ignoring things we did not want him to repeat, and sometimes by punishing "bad" behavior. Sure enough, it worked, just as my professors had said it would. Many of his actions and his attitudes are like my own and my husband's. I even hear myself in his sense of humor. I know that we have shaped his views of the world by showing him our view of the world. We have also shaped his view of himself by telling him that he is terrific since he was a newborn. As a teenager he has a positive self-image. Surely he was not a completely blank slate at birth for us to write out his life script or his personality. Yet I see myself in him every day. This boy is not a perfectionist. One look at his bedroom and you would instantly know what I mean.

The most fascinating thing happened when my second son was born. He looked like his brother, but he did not act like his brother.

For the most part, we treated him the same way that we treated his older brother, used the same methods to shape his behavior. But this boy was different. My oldest son could sit in his high chair, happily playing with a mound of spaghetti, his face covered with sauce. My second son did not like being covered in goo. Instead, he would wipe his face and hands with a napkin as soon as he was old enough to figure out how to do it. The first time I saw this I was amazed that this kid of mine actually cared about neatness. As he got a little older he kept his room cleaner than his brother. When he learned to write he would erase and rewrite his homework until it was "perfect." This looked a lot like perfectionism to me. Was he born that way? It certainly seemed that he was different from the beginning.

Since I had treated many perfectionists by the time my second child started showing the characteristics of perfectionism, I knew the pros and cons of demanding perfection from yourself. I went out of my way to convince my son that he was "good enough," that his work was "good enough," that he was a terrific person regardless of his performance in school or on the soccer field or in the school band. I think he got the message that he is "good enough" and seems to have very good self-esteem (maybe a little too good at times). At the wise age of twelve he can tell me what projects need a great deal of attention and energy and which do not. I was helping him with his algebra homework a few nights ago. I asked him to rewrite the answer to the problem because I could not read it. I assumed that the teacher would not be able to read it either. The next day my son came home from school and told me that he had talked with his algebra teacher about his homework. He said to me, "Mom, Mrs. Foster said that neatness does not count in her class, so don't worry about it." I guess I had taught my son well. He is no longer overly concerned about neatness in his work. He puts more energy into getting the correct answer than in impressing his teacher with his neatness. So, am I saying that you are born a perfectionist? I think that some people are probably born more perfectionistic than others. However, their environments can influence the direction or shape that their perfectionism takes.

Environmental Influences

It often feels to many of us that we live in a society that demands perfection. Look at the pressure on Olympic athletes to score a perfect 10, for golfers to make the perfect shot, for obstetricians to deliver perfect babies or be sued (my husband's complaint). In raising my three boys I have seen many times where social pressures to be perfect were present. My fourth grader strives to get a perfect score not only on his spelling test, but also on the midweek pretest. That can get him out of taking the final test on Friday and assures that his name will appear on the weekly fourth-grade newsletter announcing him as a "Star Speller." My eleventh grader competes with his peers in band, where the difference between first chair and second or third chairs is a score of 98.5 versus 99 or 100 on a skill test. ("How did you do son?" "I totally messed up. I made one stupid mistake and the other guy did it perfectly. I hate him.") My eighth grader, the most naturally perfectionistic of the three, gets angry when his soccer teammates do not put out the effort to win that he consistently delivers. Coaches want to win. The kids want to win. It is a competitive world out there and my boys are right in the middle of it.

There are other types of societal pressures to be perfect. We hear in the various media that we should have a perfect body, perfect teeth, and perfect breath. There are many cosmetic companies, health programs, and plastic surgeons waiting to make us perfect. The images that we have begun to cherish are the lean, fit, tanned, muscular, shiny-haired beauties. The message we hear is that average is not OK. (I wish we could return to an era when wide hips and rounded tummies were admired. It used to be much easier to be perfect.)

Parental Influences

The evil of conditional praise. Many perfectionists, especially inwardly focused perfectionists, grew up with parents who either directly or indirectly communicated that they were not good enough.

These were often confusing messages, where praise and criticism were given simultaneously. For example, "That was nice (praise), but I bet you could do better (you are not good enough now)." "Wow! (praise), six As and one B on your report card! You need to bring that B up to an A next time (near perfect was not enough)." "Your choir performance was lovely (praise), but that sound system is really poor. We could hardly hear you (it was not good enough)." Many prominent psychologists, such as David Burns, Ph.D., of the University of California, San Francisco, have found that the parents of perfectionists have difficulty rewarding their children's behaviors unconditionally and instead urge them to continue to try to do better. When their children make mistakes or perform below their standards, these parents feel bad and respond by showing disapproval and withdrawing their affection. Many of these children grew up still waiting for the day when they would receive unconditional praise from their parents, such as "nice job!" "the house looks great!" "that was a sensational meal!" or "you look so handsome!" Unconditional praise sends the message that "I approve of you or of what you have done without qualification." If only Mom and Dad thought so, maybe the pressure to be perfect would be off. Unfortunately, with the intention of continuing to motivate their children, these parents kept holding out the emotional carrot: "Just get it right this time and I will approve of you." Some psychological theories suggest that over time the child's need to please her parents becomes internalized, so that she no longer needs to please her parents; she now demands perfection from herself.

When June was a little girl, one of her chores was to sweep the front porch. Tidiness inside the house as well as outside was important to June's mother. June was little and maneuvering that big broom was not easy. Her mother would watch her from the living room window and smile with delight. ("She is so precious. Look at her push that big broom. She is trying so hard.") June's mom thought that it was important for June to help out around the house just like her big sisters. When June finished her chore, her mother would pat her on the head, thank her for doing such a good job, and send her off to play. What she did not know was that as June ran off into the yard she would always look back and see her mother sweeping the porch again, just as June had done. At first, June thought it was peculiar, but later came to realize that her mother was redoing her chore because June had not done a good enough job. The unspoken message was "that was good June, but not good enough for me." June tried harder each time not to miss any of the dirt on the front porch, but no matter how great her effort, Mom would always have to redo her work. June's mother was a perfectionist. For her there was a right way to do a job. She knew that June was doing her best, so she did not openly criticize her for missing spots on the porch. She simply fixed it herself, no harm, no foul.

This might seem like a relatively minor event, but for many people it represents a pattern of interaction between themselves and their parents that sends a mixed message that they were good, but not good enough. Enough direct or subtle messages like this over the years and you will come to believe it.

A tough act to follow. Having a parent who is a superstar in some way also leads children to feel that they will never be good enough. I am not just talking about celebrities who have made it big. I am talking about parents who are either outstanding people or who have done outstanding things in their life. A child who watches her parent excel might try to imagine achieving similar things. From a kid's perspective this looks too hard: "There is no way I could ever be like him." This can also occur when the superstar is an older brother or sister.

Some children of superstar parents grow up thinking that their parents are perfect, which is, of course, a very unrealistic view of adults. They do not see their parents exhausted, fall apart, lose their temper, act like jerks, misbehave, or forget things. Many parents hide their mistakes from their children, so that all they see is the final product. This is especially true of perfectionist parents, who believe that their imperfections or mistakes are unacceptable. The result is that on the surface these parents seem to never make a mistake. They always have the answers, do well, make good choices, take good care of themselves, and so on. The child, on the other hand, sees him- or herself make mistakes all the time. Therefore, the child concludes that she could never be as good as Mom or Dad. So why try?

By watching their perfectionist parents some kids learn to behave in ways that could be considered perfectionistic, which psychologists call learning through modeling. As children they learn to attend to details, keep their environments neat, be well groomed, and follow the rules. They learn that there is a right way and a wrong way to do things, and they learn that persistence is valued. Even though they think they will never be good enough, they have to keep trying. It would not be right to give up. Mom and Dad never gave up.

"I'm just trying to protect you." Terry's mom, Aurora, was an attractive woman. She had a lovely figure, though she had to work very hard to keep it. She had long brown hair that eventually turned to a silvery gray. When she was a young girl she had been criticized for her skinny legs, her pale skin, her straight hair, and her small eyes. This hurt Aurora's feelings a great deal. Assuring her that she was as beautiful as the other girls, Aurora's mother urged her to ignore the pettiness of her peers. However, Aurora thought that her mother did not really take her concerns seriously. "She just says that because she loves me." So Aurora vowed to pay closer attention to her own daughter's appearance so that people would not criticize her. When Terry was born, Aurora was concerned that Terry was too skinny and had little eyes like her own. She was otherwise a wonderful baby and Aurora loved her very much. When Terry entered elementary school, Aurora helped her choose clothing that complimented her figure and coloring. She chose a hairstyle that made Terry's straight hair look stylish. When Terry was a teenager her mother helped her to apply eye makeup in a way that enlarged her eyes. When Terry would come down for breakfast before school her mother would look her over and suggest alternative clothes that would better compliment her figure. Terry had not yet developed womanly curves as had her girlfriends, and Aurora did not want Terry to wear clothes that drew attention to her "underdevelopment." Aurora would tell Terry in her own way that it was OK to not have a perfect body or face as long as you learned ways to compensate for those weaknesses.

Terry appreciated her mother's attention to her appearance on the one hand and resented her on the other. If Terry complained, "I look fine mom," her mother would say, "I'm just trying to protect you." However, the message that consistently came through was "Not only do other people think you are not good enough as you are, I do not think you are good enough either. You are full of imperfections and it is important to hide them from those who would hurt you because of them." Aurora never really explained to Terry why it was important to be accepted by others and why criticism had to be avoided. Over time Terry merged her mother's values and her own doubts about her beauty in adulthood to hide her weaknesses. Although Terry could never meet her mother's expectations of womanly beauty, she had a cute figure and was very pretty. Despite this, Terry continued to look for her own imperfections and hide them from others. During their marriage, her husband, Steve, would make fun of Terry's insistence on looking good before she let anyone see her. He told her that she was beautiful and thought it ridiculous that she had to paint on her face before she would even eat breakfast. She did not believe him. Sadly, Steve's honest admiration could not undo a lifetime of her mother's powerful message that she would never be good enough.

Seeking control over chaos. Some perfectionists tell stories of chaotic childhoods where they never seemed to have control over their lives. Marital breakups, relocations, financial crises, illnesses, and other hardships created an environment of instability. One of the ways in which these people got some sense of order in their otherwise disordered lives was to try to fix things over which they had some control, such as making their immediate home or school environments neat and orderly. This might include keeping their rooms neat and tidy, working exceptionally hard on schoolwork, or attempting to control their younger brothers and sisters. This strategy may have been adaptive in that it helped them to cope with the uncertainty, unpredictability, and chaos in their home lives. As adults, however, when their lives were no longer in flux, they may have continued to work hard to maintain control. This symptom of perfectionism, which was at one point adaptive, later became problematic in various ways.

WHAT KEEPS IT GOING?

So if perfectionism can cause so much trouble, what keeps it going? The simplest answer is that there is considerable reinforcement for doing things perfectly. Reinforcement can come from you or it can come from others. There are two kinds of self-reinforcement. If you are fearful that you will be criticized, ridiculed, humiliated, or otherwise punished for performing less than perfectly, doing the job "just right" lowers your anxiety and keeps those bad things from happening. This is called negative reinforcement.

A second type is positive reinforcement, such as self-approval or a sense of pleasure or personal satisfaction for doing a great job. In fact, it is possible to experience both positive and negative reinforcement at the same time. Usually, perfectionists are more aware of their sense of satisfaction for a job well done than their success at avoiding punishment or rejection.

Positive reinforcement can come from other people as well. Praise is a positive reinforcer that is validating, boosts self-esteem, makes you feel accepted, and confirms that you are a worthwhile individual. We learn early in life that other people seem to value and often will reward perfection. Schoolteachers give gold stars, praise, and provide special rewards to the students who get 100 percent correct on a test. There is considerable scientific and clinical evidence to show that behaviors that are positively reinforced or rewarded are more likely to occur again. Perfect behaviors can be shaped by teachers and parents by rewarding actions that are at first close to perfect (As and Bs on a report card) and later only rewarding behaviors that achieve perfection (straight As). A perfect performance in music earns you the first-chair position in the school band. Coming to school each day earns you the "perfect attendance" certificate. This is a reward that is probably accompanied by praise from parents and teachers. The child who behaves perfectly becomes the "teacher's pet." These reward systems teach children to strive for perfection early in life. Depending on their abilities and personalities, some will come to feel pressured, to be frustrated, or ultimately give up the pursuit. Others will keep trying and many will succeed.

Although positive reinforcement from others feels good, what perfectionists really want is to be accepted by others (especially parents or parental figures) without having to perform at all. Carl Rogers, one of the founders of modern psychotherapy, called this type of acceptance "unconditional positive regard." Most people like it when they receive unconditional positive regard, but are not always aware of how much they need it. Although unconditional acceptance is ultimately what perfectionists want, their belief that perfection will please others, be rewarded, and will help them avoid criticism keeps them striving to do their best. Unfortunately, seeking praise and avoiding criticism from loved ones by doing things perfectly defeats the real goal of gaining acceptance without having to perform at all.

Another behavior modification strategy that shapes perfectionism in some people is punishment. Outwardly focused perfectionists, in particular, tell stories of being punished as children for not doing a job right according to parental standards. The punishment was sometimes verbal, emotional, or physical, and was greatly feared. To find a way to cope, some perfectionists learned to accept their parents' values about work. That is, they learned that there was, in fact, a right and a wrong way to do things and that they had better do things the right way or they would be punished.

Some institutions, for example military training, still utilize this method of shaping behavior. There is an absolute standard of performance, a right way and a wrong way. Getting it partly right or almost perfect is unsatisfactory or "unsat." Unsat performance is punished. Perfection is rewarded. It is simple and clear to all. The beauty in this simplicity is that it allows for consistency in training many different people from different walks of life, in different training facilities, and across time, to all do things the same way. Am I suggesting that shaping people into perfectionists is a good thing? Like most things in life,

---

Take time to think about this.

What the perfectionist really wants is to be accepted by others without having to perform at all. Seeking acceptance from others by doing things perfectly defeats this goal.

it definitely has a place. The trick is to utilize perfectionism without letting it compromise the quality of your life.

FOUR SAMPLES OF PERFECTIONISM

It is usually easier to understand psychological concepts with examples from real people. Therefore, to help teach the concepts of perfectionism I will illustrate how they might work in the lives of four people who struggle with some of the same issues that may have motivated you to read this book—that is, the push and pull of perfectionism. These characteristics are composites of people I have treated over the years. In some cases, I have used stereotypes that make the point easier to illustrate. For the various exercises that are covered in the book, I will show how these four very different people approached the tasks. The first character is June Morgan, a mother and housewife. She is socially conscious, bright, and attractive. She provides us with an example of perfectionism in the home, with her kids, and with her spouse. After two decades of marriage and mothering June isn't having fun anymore. She is exhausted, tense, feels unappreciated, and is worried about her "change of attitude." Lately she has been feeling depressed and is angry with herself for feeling this way.

Our second character is Brent Thompson. He is thirty-two years old, single, and a member of middle management. He is striving for promotion through hard work and good performance, but seems to be stuck on a low rung of the corporate ladder. Brent is looking for Ms. Right but cannot seem to find her. Brent gives us an example of perfectionism in the workplace and how it can affect romantic relationships.

Our third perfectionist is Sergeant Joe Martinez, a retired Marine Corps drill sergeant. Sgt. Joe is precise, neat, and organized. He is very good at his new job as an electrician. He has two sons who are normal adolescent slobs, and they get on his nerves. Joe gives us an example of how perfectionism can negatively affect the relationship between a parent and a child.

Terry Goldman, our fourth and final character, is a thirty-four-year-old, divorced, working mother. She has two bright and adorable

daughters. Terry is a high achiever. She wants to be executive director some day, but sees many obstacles to making it to the top, including being a single mother. Terry can sometimes get hung up on the
details of her work, but does not always see this happening. She provides us with a different example of perfectionism in the workplace
and in interpersonal relationships.

You may be able to identify with elements from each of these four
people, in how they struggle in a complicated world and in how they
come to recognize and learn to control and utilize their perfectionist
tendencies.

ARE YOU A PERFECTIONIST?

Perfectionists share some common characteristics. They are usually
neat in their appearance and are well organized. They seem to push
themselves harder than most other people do. They also seem to push
others as hard as they push themselves. On the outside, perfectionists
usually appear to be very competent and confident individuals. They
are often envied by others because they seem to "have it all together."
Sometimes they seem perfect. On the inside they do not feel perfect,
nor do they feel like they always have control over their own lives.

The question in your mind may be "Am I really a perfectionist?"
Let's look at some of the behaviors of our four characters to help
define the signs and symptoms of perfectionism. When you begin to
compare these characteristics to yourself you may find that you
behave in a perfectionistic manner in some areas of your life, but not
in others. In most cases, perfectionism is not an absolute characteristic. For example, if you saw my wardrobe closet in its usual state of
disarray you would conclude that I am definitely *not* a perfectionist.
But if you watched me work and rework a manuscript that was going
to a professional journal to be critiqued by my peers, you would say
that I am most definitely a perfectionist. Some of my friends would say
that I obsess over the details of my manuscripts to make sure that I do
not make any errors. I probably do, but no one would say that I obsess
over the organization of my closet.

Detail-oriented

Perfectionists are detail-oriented. Sgt. Joe and Terry are both detail-oriented in their work. The biggest difference is that with Joe, his attention to detail makes him an excellent electrician, while in Terry's case it actually interferes with her ability to complete tasks. Some perfectionists cannot help but notice details. They have this special radar that is the envy of nonperfectionists. They can spot crooked pictures, spelling errors, discolorations, and other asymmetries or misalignments. It is not that they are looking for mistakes; they cannot help but notice them. Once a mistake has been identified it cannot be overlooked. That would be unethical as far as Joe is concerned; it would be self-defeating in Terry's way of looking at things.

When Joe rewires someone's home he makes certain that the job is done right. He works quickly and does things right the first time. Checking his work and taking care of any details does not slow his progress. He works alone, so he does not have to oversee the work of others who might not be as careful.

Terry, on the other hand, sometimes gets lost in the details. She is not good with figures, but does not trust her staff enough to use their figures without checking them herself. She gets frustrated with this mundane work and makes mistakes herself. She does not always realize that they are her mistakes and becomes angry with her subordinates for doing poor work. It takes a great deal of time to resolve the inconsistencies between Terry's and her staff's calculations. It slows the process and reports do not get out in time. Terry envies guys like Joe who work alone so quality control is never a problem.

Brent is detail-oriented at work as well. It sometimes slows him down and frustrates his staff when he struggles to work out a detail in scheduling or in a presentation that could be worked out at another time or delegated. ("We could do it Tuesday at 3:00 or Wednesday at 2:00. It will take twenty minutes to set up and twenty minutes for the presentation. Maybe we should be there at 1:30. Oh, but that would conflict with another meeting. Maybe we could . . .") Fortunately, Brent has a wonderful administrative assistant, Sheila, who knows how to move Brent away from details by suggesting that she take care of it or that it be delegated to a subcommittee. Although Sheila can be a perfectionist with some things, she does not seem to get stuck on details. Brent has other bright and hardworking staffmembers whom he can depend on to move things forward even when he gets stuck. Perfectionists can lose the forest for the trees, but they can also learn to navigate more skillfully.

Rules and Structure

Perfectionists can be rigid in their views. For them there is a right way and wrong way to do things. Usually, the right way is synonymous with their way. They can be very stubborn about doing things differently. When Joe takes his boys fishing they have a routine for preparation, for fishing, and for cleanup. It is time-efficient, neat, organized, and consistent. The boys think the "fishing ritual" is overdone and they resent having to comply. They just want to grab their poles, throw them into the back of the truck, grab some worms at the bait shop, and jump into the river. They have tried to argue the point with their father with no success. They comply because he has a fit if they do not.

In June's kitchen there is a right way to bake a cake. If done correctly the cake will be delicious and the kitchen will still be clean. She has special utensils and pans for cake baking, for making the icing, and for decorating the cake. If you are going to take the time to cook in June's kitchen you are going to do things right. The kids are notorious for using salad bowls to mix icing and mixing bowls to make salad. They put her nice knives in the dishwasher and they use the dish sponge on the counter and the counter sponge on the dishes. Her husband is just as bad. He squeezes the toothpaste from the middle of the tube even though he knows it is wrong and it irritates June. He leaves his socks in his shoes and leaves his shoes in the middle of the bedroom. She complains, but her children and husband say that she is too fussy about unimportant things. They do not understand that an organized home is a peaceful home and that taking good care of your belongings will guarantee that they are ready when you need them.

June wonders if her children will ever learn. She imagines their homes in the future and it gives her a sick feeling inside. As for her husband, there is no way he will ever change. He is a good man so she counts her blessings and tolerates his ways.

Some perfectionists have very high moral and ethical standards. They find it hard to bend the rules. While often more accepting of others' behaviors, they have a hard time allowing themselves to behave in ways that could be perceived as unethical. For example, one of my good friends who is a bit of a perfectionist plugs my first book when he gives presentations. His sense of humility and his ethical standards, however, make it uncomfortable for him to plug his own book. When I return the favor by praising his work in front of others he gets a bit embarrassed, but modestly accepts the acknowledgment. According to his rules, self-boasting is not okay; allowing others to boast about him is better, but not great; boasting about others is good friendship.

Expectations Are High

Perfectionists expect a great deal from themselves. They expect themselves to perform perfectly and to rarely make mistakes, especially in the areas of their lives that are most important to them. June's "identity" or "self-esteem" comes from being a loving and caring mother and wife. Keeping her house neat and well-organized is part of that job, so she puts in a lot of time to make sure everything at home is perfect. Joe is similar in that doing his job well makes him feel good about himself. He expects nothing less than perfection from himself. There is no excuse, as far as he is concerned, for doing sloppy work. He acknowledges that sometimes things go wrong on the job, usually things that could not be anticipated or were out of his control. This does not bother him nor does it make him feel like a failure. He simply goes back and fixes the problem until everything works perfectly.

Perfectionists often have high expectations of others as well. Expecting people to do their best is one thing. Expecting perfection from others often means setting unreasonable goals that can be impossible to achieve. For perfectionists, however, there is often no difference in their minds between "doing your best" and doing things perfectly, especially when it pertains to their own performance. It is OK if others cannot always do things perfectly, but they know they can and so they must always do things perfectly themselves. In the Marine Corps, Sgt. Joe's command style included a mix of demanding perfection and expressing belief in his recruits' abilities so that they would come to believe in themselves. He thought that was the essential combination in training young soldiers. With his sons, he can forget to add encouragement to his demands for performance. The kids resent him for expecting too much from them, more than they can handle. The younger son, Sergio, has given up trying to meet his father's expectations.

Brent is an inwardly focused perfectionist when it comes to his work performance, but when it comes to women he has the high expectations of an outwardly focused perfectionist. He has a picture in his mind of Ms. Right. He thinks that when he finds her he will marry her and they will have a perfect life together. He has been looking in earnest since his second year in college. Twelve years later he is still looking, with no potential candidates in sight. He does not have a well-defined set of characteristics in mind. He just has a general impression of an angel, a sexual goddess, a confident, independent, yet thoroughly devoted partner. Blond is preferable, but he's not that picky. Athletic would be great, but shapely is sufficient. He is not a materialistic fellow, but he would not complain if she came from a wealthy family. Brent thinks he wants a competent and beautiful wife, but his low self-confidence makes it difficult for him to tolerate women he thinks are better than him, so he dates women who are less educated than he, less talented, less perfect. While they are nonthreatening and make him feel good about himself, he would prefer a partner who is more his equal. Brent, a lonely man, is stuck between his low self-esteem and his high expectations.

When Terry and her ex-husband, Steve, were married, they often argued over the issue of expectations. Each thought the other expected too much and gave too little. Both were successful individuals who were a little competitive with one another. Steve resented Terry's larger paychecks, trips all over the country, and the social status she seemed to throw in his face. Terry resented his ability to connect with people, especially their daughters. Everyone liked Steve and that secretly annoyed and hurt Terry. They did not give each other any room for being weak, making errors, or feeling vulnerable. These things were not tolerated in themselves or in each other. They both always felt a pressure to perform, to be in control, to be competent in each other's eyes. They could not find a way to be vulnerable, to seek consolation from one another, or to give support when it was needed. Their high expectations for themselves and for each other ended their marriage.

Appearance

Neatness in appearance can also be a sign of perfectionism. Impeccably groomed and dressed individuals are often perfectionists, at least when it comes to hygiene. However, there are plenty of perfectionists for whom personal grooming and physical presentation are not priorities. In other words, they are slobs. Brent's appearance is impeccable. His hair is just the right length, never too long and never with that "just got a haircut" shortness. His car is immaculate as well. Despite the fact that it is not the kind of car that makes a personal statement, it is well maintained and impressive to others. June, Terry, and Joe all have specific standards for their children's appearances as well as their own. They all emphasize that their appearance communicates many things about a person's character. Terry and June's girls understand this and are usually very nicely groomed. Joe's boys don't

---

Take time to think about this.

Perfectionists often have high expectations of others. Expecting people to do their best is one thing. Expecting perfection from others often means setting goals that can be impossible to achieve.

really understand why this is such a big deal. After a lot of arguing with their father, they agree to wear shoes in public, to keep their hair short, and to bathe regularly.

Mistakes Are Avoided

Perfectionists hate to make mistakes. The worst feeling for a perfectionist is when someone sees one of their mistakes before they get a chance to fix it. The humiliation that goes with being caught in an error creates intense psychological pain. Some perfectionists have panic attacks in these situations, while others become furious. Methodical and systematic, Brent and Terry work very hard to not make mistakes at work. They check and recheck their facts before they give a report. Both would say that the worst possible thing that could happen at work would be to have one of their superiors find an error in their work. They would be humiliated beyond belief. Of course, this kind of thing is not likely to happen, because they are extremely careful. If you put Brent on the spot he would recall that there have been times when he has made errors and, although he was embarrassed, there had been no real lasting consequences. He owned up to the error, corrected it, and held his breath for a while, waiting to be fired. Of course, Brent would also say that he had been lucky those times. The next time there could be greater consequences.

Terry can recall times when errors were found in her work. She had been embarrassed at first, but soon grew angry. She knew exactly which of her staffmembers were at fault for the error and vowed never to trust their work again.

Confidence Is Low

Perfectionists can have great difficulty in taking risks, particularly if their personal reputations are on the line. Brent is our best example. He is in a type of job where creativity can be an asset. New ideas from employees, particularly the sales staff, have made the company a lot of money in the past. Coming up with new ideas rather than relying on the tried and true ways of business, however, means making yourself vulnerable to the criticisms of others. If you rely on creative whims rather than facts, you might fail. At least, that is the fear of Brent and other more conservative perfectionists like him. The fear comes, in part, from a lack of self-confidence. ("My ideas are not good enough." "People will laugh at me." "I will look like an idiot." "I could not stand the humiliation.") The risk-takers that Brent hates, and possibly envies or admires, think very highly of themselves and do not care if others hate their ideas. They do not expect themselves to always be right or to always have great ideas. But they know that if they keep trying, soon they will hit upon a winner. If their ideas are rejected, they might get their feelings hurt, but they recover quickly. The consequences of failure for these people do not feel as great as they would to perfectionists.

Being conservative with new ideas is a problem for Brent, because the other people in his company who are taking risks by trying out new ideas are climbing the corporate ladder, leaving Brent behind in their wake. His superiors think of him as a good worker but not having what it takes to make it to the top. Brent does not see this. He is clinging to the idea that his hard work and dedication will advance him.

On the occasions when Brent has had to go out on a limb with a new idea he has been very anxious. He would check out his ideas with co-workers, his assistant, Sheila, his friend Jessica, his mother, and anyone else who would listen. Everyone would think Brent's ideas were fine, but he could not be comforted. Even after the idea was approved and successful, Brent attributed his success to luck and to the mercy of his boss.

Although Brent's perfectionism seems complex and multilayered, it illustrates several aspects of the way that many perfectionists think about themselves. There can be low self-confidence, fear of humiliation and rejection, and an inability to attribute success to their own efforts. Perfectionists like Brent may fend off compliments and maintain their fear of failure even after repeated successes.

Organization and Neatness

June, our housewife, and Brent, our middle manager, both provide excellent examples of perfectionism at home. Perfectionists like Brent and June like things neat and organized and become anxious and sometimes overwhelmed when things are in disarray. Unfortunately, making certain that things are always neat, clean, and well organized takes time and energy that could be spent elsewhere. June worries about what others think of her housekeeping. Her mother was very neat and organized and emphasized to June that your home is a reflection of you, as are your children. She passed the value of perfectionism on to June, so June spends a great deal of time cleaning her house. She cleans up after each family member leaves home and then straightens up at the end of the day after each returns. June is not comfortable going to bed with a messy kitchen. She needs things to be organized before bed or she has difficulty getting everyone off to school and work in the morning.

Early in her marriage, June would follow after her husband, cleaning up as he used dishes, changed clothes, or read the mail. This greatly irritated Bill. When they had their first child, June went through a stressful phase, where she found that she did not have the time and energy to tend to her child and to keep the house the way she liked. She exhausted and frustrated herself trying. June finally had to give in to allowing things to be in some disarray until the end of the day, when the baby was down for the night. She tried to straighten up during the baby's nap time, but did not have the energy until Angela was about six months old.

Brent's mom was very much like June. Unlike his brothers and sisters, Brent appreciated his mother's attention to neatness. As a middle manager, Brent does not have the time to keep his small apartment as neat as he would like. He hired a housekeeper. Actually, he hired several housekeepers until he found one conscientious enough to meet his standards. Of course, there are some things even she is not very good at, and Brent has to redo her work in those areas.

Brent cannot tolerate clutter. It stresses him out. If he needs lots of materials on his desk at one time to complete a project, they are placed in neat piles. He has a small portable filing cabinet about the size of a milk crate that he can put on his desk or on the floor near his desk when many materials are needed. The milk crate has colored hanging folders. He just slips his materials into the color-coded files for ease in identification. Keeping things neat does take extra time and energy, but for Brent it is well worth it, because clutter just slows his thinking and distracts him from his work.

Self-Doubt

Perfectionists can have trouble making decisions. They worry about making a wrong decision, so they toss around in their minds two or three possible options and the consequences if each is wrong. Linda Gorin-Sibner, Ph.D., a clinical psychologist in Los Angeles, California, calls this process "ambivalating." The person feels ambivalent about a choice or decision, thinks it over and over, but fails to reach closure. If the person is lucky, someone else will make the decision for them, thereby assuming responsibility for the outcome. More often the decision is that no decision is made or the decision is made by default. That is, enough time has passed that the decision is made by itself. A simple example is ambivalating over whether to rush to file income tax forms on time or to apply for an extension. If you wait long enough to decide, the only real alternative is to file for an extension. Thus, the decision is made by default. Some perfectionists are comfortable with and even grateful for other people making decisions for them when they are stuck and do not mind when decisions are made by default.

Terry gets stuck in her work when she cannot decide which approach to take on a report or project. When she has two choices of action, each quite different, she tries to compare their advantages and disadvantages. There are usually several pros and cons to each approach and she has trouble deciding how to proceed. Sometimes Terry faces the same dilemma when ordering from a menu or when trying to decide what to wear. She can get overwhelmed by too many choices.

Joe, in comparison, is very decisive and does not seem to be bothered by the idea that he could be making a poor decision. He has
been trained to assess a situation quickly, select a solution, and act—
before someone else's actions interfere with his goals. Making decisions does not bother June either. Like Joe, she knows there is a right
way and a wrong way to do things and she selects the right way—simple enough. With Brent, it depends on the topic. He can be very decisive in managing his staff, or their work, or when executing a project
similar to those he has completed in the past. He gets stuck when the
decision has to do with women and dating. ("Should I call or should I
wait? I don't want to seem pushy or desperate, and I don't want to give
the impression that I'm not interested, just in case she is interested.
What if she doesn't like me? I'll feel like a real jerk. She did give me
her phone number, but what if she was just trying to be polite? She's
probably banking on the fact that I will not call. She'll probably have
an excuse for not being able to go out even if I ask.")

Trusting Others Is Difficult

Perfectionists can appear to others to have a need to be in control. It
may not actually feel like control to them, but they do acknowledge
that they do not trust others to do a job as well as they can. Terry does
not trust the work of her subordinates, so she checks it over, and over,
and over. June does not trust her daughter to handle her own interpersonal problems or to know how to dress herself, so she offers lots
of suggestions and cannot help but intervene when her daughter is
having a problem. At business meetings, Brent will sometimes inter-
rupt one of his underlings during a presentation in front of the "big
boss" to offer clarifications or elaboration. These additions are not
usually helpful. They simply irritate his staff and disrupt the flow of
the presentation. Brent worries that, since his employees are less
experienced than he, they may not be able to make their points as
clearly as he might. These presentations are important, and his staff's
performance will reflect on him and his department.

Joe tries to watch his son patiently as he paints the shutters on the kitchen windows, but he is compelled to show him how to do it right by taking the brush from him often. They both become so frustrated that Joe finishes the job on his own. Relinquishing control can mean that quality may suffer.

In attempting to control outcomes by doing the work themselves or spending time and energy worrying about or checking the work of others, perfectionists waste time and offend others. By checking up on or interfering with other people's actions, perfectionists inadvertently communicate that they do not trust the work of others or do not believe their work is good enough. When those people are your children, these messages of distrust can have unwanted effects on their psychological development.

SELF-ASSESSMENT

To help you begin to define areas in which perfectionism is helping you as well as those that are hurting you, fill out the self-assessment Am I a Perfectionist? If you are willing to take the risk, have someone close to you rate you on these items. Compare answers and ask for feedback whenever there are discrepancies. Sometimes others can more easily see your perfectionism than you can.

Add up your scores on the items with a ✔ next to them. These are items 12, 14–18, and 21–24. This is your score on inwardly focused perfectionism (IFP SCORE). Now add up your scores on the items that have a (◆) next to them. These are items 4–9, 25–27, and 29. This is your score on outwardly focused perfectionism (OFP SCORE). Which score is higher? Are you more of an inwardly focused or outwardly focused perfectionist, or are your scores about even? Remember that perfectionism is usually found in some areas of your life (like my writing), but not in others (like keeping my closet organized), and your perfectionism can be more inwardly focused about some things and more outwardly focused about others. Add all thirty items together to get total score. If your score was less than 30, then you are probably not a perfectionist, although you may have a few of the traits. Scores from 31 to 60 suggest mild perfectionism. When you are stressed your

Am I A Perfectionist?

Below are some ideas that are held by our four perfectionists. Which of these do you see in yourself? To help you decide, rate how strongly you agree with each of the statements below on a scale from 0 to 4.

0	1	2	3	4
I do not agree		I agree somewhat		I agree completely

__ 1.   I have an eye for details that others can miss. (D)

__ 2.   I can get lost in details and forget the real purpose of the task. (D)

__ 3.   I can get overwhelmed by too many details. (D)

__ 4. ◆ It stresses me when people do not want to do things the right way. (R)

__ 5. ◆ There is a right way and a wrong way to do most things. (R)

__ 6. ◆ I do not like my routine to be interrupted. (R)

__ 7. ◆ I expect a great deal from myself. (E)

__ 8. ◆ I expect no less of others than I expect of myself. (E)

__ 9. ◆ People should always do their best. (E)

__ 10.   I am neat in my appearance. (A)

__ 11.   Good grooming is important to me. (A)

__ 12. ✔ I do not like being seen before I have showered and dressed. (A)

__ 13.   I do not like making mistakes. (M)

__ 14. ✔ Receiving criticism is horrible. (M)

__ 15. ✔ It is embarrassing to make mistakes in front of others. (M)

__ 16. ✔ Sharing my new ideas with others makes me anxious. (C)

__ 17. ✔ I worry that my ideas are not good enough. (C)

__ 18. ✔ I do not have a great deal of confidence in myself. (C)

__ 19.   I'm uncomfortable when my environment is untidy or disorganized. (O)

(cont.)

Am I A Perfectionist? *(cont.)*

___ 20.   When things are disorganized it is hard for me to concentrate. (O)

___ 21. ✔ What others think about my home is important to me. (O)

___ 22. ✔ I have trouble making difficult decisions. (S)

___ 23. ✔ I worry that I may make the wrong decision. (S)

___ 24. ✔ Making a bad decision can be disastrous. (S)

___ 25. ◆ I often do not trust others to do the job right. (T)

___ 26. ◆ I check the work of others to make certain it was done correctly. (T)

___ 27. ◆ If I can control the process it will turn out fine. (T)

___ 28.   I am a perfectionist. (G)

___ 29. ◆ I care more about doing a quality job than others do. (G)

___ 30.   It's important to make a good impression. (G)

_____ TOTAL SCORE

_____ IFP SCORE (✔)

_____ OFP SCORE (◆)

D = Detail-oriented   C = Confidence is low
R = Rules and structure   O = Organization and neatness in the environment
E = Expectations are high   S = Self-doubt
A = Appearance   T = Low trust of others
M = Mistakes are avoided   G = General

score may be higher. Scores of 61 to 90 suggest moderate perfectionism. This probably means that perfectionism is causing you trouble in some specific areas (see following), but is not out of control. Scores higher than 91 suggest a level of perfectionism that could cause you serious problems.

The self-assessment items are also grouped in threes, to represent the characteristics of perfectionism previously described, (i.e., attention to details, high expectations). The letter after the statement shows which characteristic the items pertain to. For example, items 1–3 have a (D) following the statement. These items represent the importance of attending to details in one's environment. The letter code and its meaning are at the bottom of the Self-assessment scale. Add up your scores on these subgroupings. Each subgroup will have a score that ranges from 0 to 12. Plot your scores on the grid entitled Your Perfectionism Profile. On which subgroups do you have the highest scores or the lowest scores? Subgroups with the highest scores may be causing you more trouble than subgroups with lower scores. Go back a few pages and reread the section entitled Are You a Perfectionist?, especially those paragraphs that discuss the characteristics of perfectionism that you share with our characters.

When you finish this book and work on the exercises, come back to this self-assessment and check your progress. As you work on controlling your perfectionism, you will find that either the scores will start to decline or that you will still have some perfectionist beliefs, but may choose to respond in new ways that help you avoid problems.

PSYCHOLOGICAL DISORDERS ASSOCIATED WITH PERFECTIONISM

If your overall perfectionism score was high, you may also find that you are experiencing other symptoms or problems associated with perfectionism that could require separate treatment. Perfectionism can be a symptom of some common psychological or psychiatric problems such as obsessive-compulsive disorder, anorexia nervosa, bulimia, and/or depression. You may be wondering if you have any of these disorders, so let's review their definitions. There are specific rules for diagnosing psychiatric disorders that appear in a book called *The Diagnostic and Statistical Manual of Psychiatric Disorders.* It is published by the American Psychiatric Association and can be found in many bookstores. The rules for diagnosis include having

Your Perfectionism Profile

For each of the subscales from the perfectionism test, mark your scores on the grid below. Connect the dots to show where your characteristics of perfectionism are most likely to show.

```
12   •     •     •     •     •     •     •     •     •
11   •     •     •     •     •     •     •     •     •
10   •     •     •     •     •     •     •     •     •
 9   •     •     •     •     •     •     •     •     •
 8   •     •     •     •     •     •     •     •     •
 7   •     •     •     •     •     •     •     •     •
 6   •     •     •     •     •     •     •     •     •
 5   •     •     •     •     •     •     •     •     •
 4   •     •     •     •     •     •     •     •     •
 3   •     •     •     •     •     •     •     •     •
 2   •     •     •     •     •     •     •     •     •
 1   •     •     •     •     •     •     •     •     •
 0   •     •     •     •     •     •     •     •     •
─────────────────────────────────────────────────────
     D     R     E     A     M     C     O     S     T
```

D = Detail-oriented   C = Confidence is low
R = Rules and structure   O = Organization and neatness in the environment
E = Expectations are high   S = Self-doubt
A = Appearance   T = Low trust of others
M = Mistakes are avoided

certain symptoms at the same times and having your ability to function impaired because of these symptoms.

Obsessive-compulsive disorder and obsessive-compulsive personality disorder (OCPD) are two examples. OCPD is what most people associate with perfectionism, because it is characterized by preoccupation with details, neatness, and organization. In addition, some people hoard objects such as newspapers and magazines; others might have high moral standards and rigidity about adhering to rules and structure. It is called a personality disorder because they are present all of the time, though probably more prominent in times of stress. It is considered a disorder when these characteristics are at a level that interferes with the person's life or when it causes significant psychological distress.

Obsessive-compulsive disorder (OCD) is quite different. It is more episodic in nature and is not a personality type. OCD consists of having either obsessions or compulsions that cause marked distress, take a great deal of time, or interfere with a person's ability to function day-to-day. Obsessions are repetitive thoughts that seem foreign to the person and are frightening. One of my patients described it as a mental hiccup. The thought or idea repeats over and over in your head in a way that seems to be beyond your conscious control. The thoughts are sometimes fears that you hurt a person or could hurt a person, did an unlawful act, or that you could engage in a behavior that you would normally find inappropriate. To get rid of these thoughts, people develop rituals or routines that counter the thoughts, like thinking about something else in a systematic way. Usually the person knows that these thoughts and routines are abnormal.

Compulsions are repetitive behaviors, such as counting things or checking repeatedly to make sure doors are locked or stove burners are turned off. The person with OCD thinks that if they do not check, something bad will happen to them or to others. The checking can interfere by making you late for appointments or making it difficult for you to leave the house.

Perfectionism is common in eating disorders as well. In anorexia nervosa, people deny themselves food or use excessive means to lose weight, such as self-induced vomiting, excessive exercise, or laxatives. No matter how thin they get they still see themselves as not good enough. Bulimia is another eating disorder and consists of repetitive binge eating and purging of food or calories. People with bulimia are usually normal weight even though their eating binges are sometimes out of control. With both disorders there is a preoccupation with eating and with weight.

Major depression is another psychiatric condition associated with perfectionism. In major depression, mood and interest drop dramatically from normal levels. There are usually several physical symptoms, such as changes in weight and appetite, as well as changes in sleep patterns, poor concentration, decreased sex drive, and restlessness. There is a negative view that develops, which includes hopelessness about the future, excessive guilt, and feelings of worthlessness. If these symptoms persist for more than two weeks and are severe or interfere with your life, it is diagnosed as major depression. If you think you have any of these disorders, see your doctor to discuss your treatment options.

You may be convinced that you are a perfectionist, but you may have trouble seeing how it causes problems in your world. Throughout this book there will be opportunities for self-assessment, like the one you just completed. These exercises will help you decide where perfectionism is serving you well and where it is getting in the way of having a happy and successful life. Each chapter will cover different topics and will include several exercises for gaining more control over your perfectionism.

2

THE TWO FACES OF

PERFECTIONISM

IS PERFECTIONISM A GOOD THING
OR A BAD THING?

Terry's sister Julie, an assistant professor at the state university, heard about a new opportunity to gain funding for a new research project. The National Institute of Mental Health had a new program for funding new research in childhood disorders and Julie, though relatively new to academics, was very knowledgeable in the field of communication disorders and a real contender for the grant money. She had two months to write a grant proposal and complete dozens of forms. This government agency has lots of rules for completing a grant application, including things such as how large the type can be on the page and how wide the margins can be set. If you make any mistakes they send back your application and you can miss out on your chance at the money. There are a hundred details to attend to and Julie has never been very good with details. She needed help and knew that her sister Terry would be the person to call. Terry quickly agreed, read the fifty pages of instructions, and set to work reviewing Julie's application. Terry found numerous errors that could have cost Julie her chance at winning the grant money. She also found smaller problems, such as spelling and grammatical errors, numbers that did not add up properly, and page-numbering problems. Julie was grateful for Terry's eye for detail and took back all the bad things she had ever said to Terry about being too picky, too rigid, and too much of a perfectionist. In this situation, those characteristics surely paid off.

There have been other times, however, when Terry's perfectionistic tendencies have caused tension in her relationship with Julie. When they shared an apartment during their college years, Julie would complain that Terry's "need for control" drove her crazy. Terry would object that she was not a "control freak," she was just able to concentrate better when their apartment was tidy and when her work space was in order, whereas Julie could study anywhere regardless of how clean the apartment was at the time.

Terry tried to force her sister to keep things neat and organized her way, but Julie resisted. ("You are not my mother, so stop acting like one!") This led to many fights and, ultimately, the decision to live separately. Although her new apartment was clean and organized, Terry was lonely. She missed Julie and Julie's string of friends that seemed to come and go each day. Since she did not have to clean up after her sister anymore, she had more time to study and to think. Cleaning up after Julie had given Terry a way to work off some of her anxieties about school and her limited social life. Although it seemed negative at the time, without that outlet Terry was left with too much time to think about all the aspects of her life that worried her or made her sad. She hadn't realized how much she was giving up in order to have the apartment look the way she wanted. In this scenario, her perfectionism worked against her and her relationship with Julie

When people describe a work of art, a fastball in the last inning of the World Series, or a beautiful woman, as "perfect," it is generally meant as a compliment. In many areas of life, to be perfect is the ultimate achievement. There is nothing that surpasses it, at least until someone else redefines perfection. But when people say "You're such a perfectionist" it is not always intended as a compliment. It is often a criticism that means you are too fussy, too picky, or too compulsive in the things you do. This is confusing. How can it be great for others to achieve perfection, but wrong for you to push for perfection? This is called a "mixed message." Usually, if you achieve perfection on your own or if it is done in the service of others, it is praised and sometimes rewarded (e.g., you get the gold medal). However, if your pursuit of perfection causes others to have to work harder, takes up their time, makes them feel bad, or stalls progress, it is criticized.

In this chapter we will begin to examine the advantages and the disadvantages of perfectionism—its two faces. In studying perfectionism in large groups of women ranging from successful athletes and those suffering from depression or eating disorders, researchers have found clear evidence for both positive and negative aspects of perfectionism. Understanding both sides will allow you to make good decisions about how to make use of it and how to set limits on it when it gets out of control.

First you need to know how perfectionism is influencing your attitude and your actions both positively and negatively. The self-assessments throughout the chapter will help you define areas in which your perfectionism works to your advantage or disadvantage. In most of these areas, the advantages are common to both inwardly and outwardly focused perfectionists. If you completed the self-assessment from Chapter 1 to determine if you are more of an inwardly or outwardly focused perfectionist, you can follow the codes in each of the summary boxes and focus on the topics that might be more applicable to you.

ADVANTAGES OF PERFECTIONISM

Perfectionism can work to your advantage in all areas of your life, with many different people and in various settings. One example is the workplace. As an employer, I have found that perfectionists can make excellent employees if they do not get tripped up by unnecessarily high standards or preoccupation with details. Their drive to perform is internally motivated. Therefore, they do not require a lot of supervision or encouragement to get the job done. They consistently strive to do their best. Some of my employees were motivated to please me and others were eager to avoid my wrath, which they had never actually seen but still anticipated. These employees were better than I was at detailed work, which was important in research where we dealt with thousands of small pieces of data that had to be collected, processed, and entered into the computer accurately. Their work was neater and better organized than mine. They never needed to be pushed; they simply needed direction.

Perfectionism can be important in the home. Neatness and organization make the household run smoothly. It makes everyone happy when they can find things when needed. Everyone appreciates the perfect meal, the perfect piecrust, and the soufflé that doesn't fall. In my house they appreciate when the tortillas come out soft rather than stiff like Frisbees.

Friends and neighbors may value the way that perfectionists keep their homes, their lawns, or their gardens. If you provide a service to others, promptness, neatness, and attention to details are greatly appreciated. Whether it is helping to give a party, mend a neighbor's roof, or put on a school play, a perfectionist's ability to be organized and orderly can make the critical difference in the success of the event.

In our society, perfectionism is not only valued, but is often demanded. Those who provide services to our homes (e.g., painters or wallpaper hangers), to our cars (e.g., mechanics), or to our bodies (e.g., dentists, hairdressers, and surgeons) are expected to do so with great skill and the outcome must be perfect. Sometimes if they fall short or fail, we are willing to take them to court to punish them for their errors.

Having perfectionist standards clearly has a place. Attention to details can improve quality, organization can improve efficiency, and having high expectations for yourself keeps you striving. Having high expectations for others can communicate trust in their abilities and provides encouragement.

To appreciate the advantages of perfectionism, you must take stock of how it works to your advantage in your life. Make a list of the ways that perfectionism helps you to function at home, at work, in your interactions with others in your family and with those outside of your family. Read ahead for some ideas, then use the grid on page 46 to make your list. The self-assessment questions in the boxes after each section will help you think of ways that perfectionism serves you well. Each category in the box has an IFP or OFP after it to indicate that the characteristic or behavior is more common among inwardly focused (IFP) or outwardly focused (OFP) perfectionists. Write in examples of the ways in which perfectionism helps you at home, at work, with yourself, or with others.

At Work

Work is probably the one area where perfectionism is the most useful, most appreciated, and most rewarded. In jobs where details count, the perfectionist is a valuable person on the team. Perfectionists are highly motivated individuals who expect a great deal from themselves. They are self-starters, not requiring a great deal of supervision or nagging to get a job done. In jobs where it is important to follow specific procedures or rules, perfectionists are great at keeping everyone organized and on track. Perfectionists who are conscientious in their work can compensate for others on the job who are less attentive to the smaller details that make a difference between a satisfactory performance and a very good one.

Joe sets his own standards of work as an electrician. He knows how the other guys work, sacrificing quality to save a few dollars or a little time. For Joe, the quality of the work is a reflection on his character as a person. Even if customers cannot see the difference between his quality work and the next guy's, he knows the difference and takes pride in what he does. He is careful not to make mistakes and insists on the best quality materials or he will not do the job. If he is not certain about how a wiring job will work out, he will not take the assignment. ("If I can't personally guarantee the final product, then I don't want to touch it.") You have to admire and respect a person with such high personal standards.

SELF-ASSESSMENT

Advantages of Perfectionism at Work

Eye for Detail: (IFP and OFP)*

Are you good at detailed work? Can others count on you to find errors and fix them? When the job is complete are you confident that you have taken care of all the "loose ends"?

"Do-it-yourselfer": (OFP)

Do you personally oversee all elements of your job to be certain that things are done right? Is it easier, better, or more efficient for you to do a job yourself than to pass it off to someone else?

Forethought: (IFP and OFP)

Do you give a lot of thought to your work before you begin? Do you evaluate your own progress and make changes that improve the quality of your work?

*(IFP) stands for Inwardly Focused Perfectionist; (OFP) stands for Outwardly Focused Perfectionist.

Terry takes personal pride in her work as well. She will take time from her busy schedule to help one of her employees work on smaller elements of a larger project. ("If it is worth doing, it is worth doing right, my Momma always said," exclaimed Terry. "I will not ask my employees to do any task that I am not willing to do myself. It may take extra time, but it is time well spent.") When the team completes a project, Terry can be certain that each part meets her standards.

Being careful in how a job is done is another positive characteristic of the perfectionist. Thinking things through carefully before beginning avoids the errors that are made by impulsively starting a project before thinking about how the final product will look.

At Home

Perfectionism at home can help to create a neat, well-organized, and calm environment. June's home is a well cared for and healthy environment. She puts in a great deal of time cleaning up after her three kids and husband, but does not seem to mind. The end result is well worth it. Things run systematically with minimal disruption or chaos, despite the fact that she and her kids have very busy schedules that keep her carpooling every day. The kids can count on home-cooked meals and clean laundry. June takes care of all the details that make holidays and special events memorable and make a busy family schedule run smoothly.

Joe always seems to know how to get things done around the house, like repairs or special projects. His organizational ability complements his wife's and sons' weaknesses in this area. Whenever someone in the family needs a tool or supplies they can always be found. There is always a new lightbulb, masking tape, or hammer and nail when needed.

These may seem like small things, but if you have ever combed the

---

SELF-ASSESSMENT

Advantages of Perfectionism at Home

Neatness: (IFP and OFP)*

Is your home environment neat and tidy? Are you good at working around others to keep the house the way you like it? Are you proud of the way you are able to stay on top of cleaning chores, even the detailed work? Do you make time to attend to household chores even when you would rather do something more relaxing or more fun?

Organization: (IFP and OFP)

Are things well organized? Can you usually find things when you look for them? Do you keep things organized at home by having a schedule for yourself and for others? Does your schedule help you to stay on top of things at home?

Know-how: (IFP and OFP)

Can others count on you to know how to get a job done? Do you usually know how to proceed, what tools are needed, and what procedure will result in the best outcome?

*(IFP) stands for Inwardly Focused Perfectionist; (OFP) stands for Outwardly Focused Perfectionist.

house for a flashlight when you needed it, you will understand how keeping things in order helps to cope with the smaller and more common stresses of everyday life. In a survey of female executives, Dr. P.S. Fry from the University of Victoria, found that perfectionism, along with a sense of humor and optimism, helped these women to successfully deal with daily hassles in their lives. In fact, perfectionism was associated with effective coping, including strategies that helped to prevent day-to-day problems.

In Relationships With Others

Perfectionist beliefs can influence your interactions with others in positive ways. For example, Joe, Terry, and June have high expectations for their children. They believe that their children are capable of meeting these expectations. When they communicate their expectations to the children they are also expressing their confidence in their children's abilities. This makes the children feel good about themselves. If parents have confidence in their children and communicate this effectively, then children will usually have confidence in themselves. This makes the children feel good about themselves. Confidence can be communicated in many ways. June encourages her daughter to try out for the cheerleading squad because she knows how friendly and cheerful her daughter can be and how her enthusiasm is contagious. Joe pushes his boys to excel in school because he believes they are smart and capable. Terry believes the same about her daughters. They have her intelligence and their father's people skills, something that she lacks. She frequently praises her children for their accomplishments as well as their kind hearts and loving ways.

Brent has high expectations for his employees. He compliments them about their work performance while simultaneously and gently pushing them to do more, making sure they receive proper credit for their work. He helps them to further develop their creative abilities by giving them challenging tasks, assuring them that he has total confidence in their talents.

Another way in which perfectionism can help in relationships with

---

SELF-ASSESSMENT

Advantages of Perfectionism in Relationships

High expectations: (OFP)*

   Do you have high expectations for the people in your life? Do you want to see the important people in your life do their best, excel where they can, and succeed? Do you try to encourage others to try harder?

Motivate others: (OFP)

   Do you try to impress on others the importance of always giving their best? Do you try to motivate the important people in your life? Do you try to set a good example for others to follow?

Cautious: (IFP and OFP)

   Are you cautious about whom you have as friends? Do you take time to get to know about a person before you commit to a friendship?

*(IFP) stands for Inwardly Focused Perfectionist; (OFP) stands for Outwardly Focused Perfectionist.

---

others is in one's choice of friends. Perfectionists are often very sensitive people. They do not impulsively jump into relationships, where they might be hurt or rejected. They take time, attend to details in how people act and think, and make cautious choices about whom to let into their lives. This keeps them from wasting time on relationships that are destined to fail and protects them from possible hurt. While no one can predict with certainty how people will change and how relationships will grow or fail, being cautious reduces the chance of getting hurt.

With Yourself

Perfectionists report that they experience a great deal of personal satisfaction when they accomplish a task perfectly, even if no one is praising their efforts. Unless they were to look carefully, others would not usually notice that great care was taken with a task or project. Not everyone cares that the seams were sewn perfectly straight, or that the colors match perfectly, or that the surface was perfectly smooth, or that the computer program worked without a hitch. The perfectionist knows these things and sometimes that is all that matters. Like having the perfect shine on your car or your shoes or your big brass bed. Getting it "just right" can make you feel good inside.

Another way in which perfectionism can work to your personal advantage is when it gets you what you want. For example, tending to those details in appearance may get you noticed when it is important. Having a flawless performance in music, dance, or athletics can win you top honors. Getting perfect grades can be the key to the future. Giving the perfect dinner party can earn you praise and appreciation from those that you love.

Although perfectionists often complain about their insecurities in their own abilities, there are advantages to this characteristic. Having less confidence in yourself means that you are more careful in what you do or that you try harder, both of which can lead to greater suc-

---

SELF-ASSESSMENT

Advantages of Perfection for Yourself

Personal satisfaction: (IFP and OFP)*

Do you feel a sense of personal satisfaction when you do a job perfectly? Does it feel good even if no one else notices?

Accomplishment: (IFP and OFP)

Do your efforts at looking or acting "just right" get you what you want? Does perfectionism lead to rewards or success?

Careful: (IFP)

Do you think things through thoroughly before you act? Does this save you from making big mistakes? Does it keep you from wasting time or energy?

Strive for success: (IFP and OFP)

Do your high expectations for yourself motivate you to work hard? Do you set higher goals and achieve more than others because you believe in yourself?

*(IFP) stands for Inwardly Focused Perfectionist; (OFP) stands for Outwardly Focused Perfectionist.

The Advantages of Perfectionism

Below is a list of areas in which perfectionism could work to your advantage at home, at work, with yourself, and with others in your world. Fill in the boxes with examples of how each of these characteristics of perfectionism help you succeed. You can refer back to Chapter 1 for a description of each of these characteristics of perfectionism.

Areas of Perfectionism	At Work or School	At Home	With Yourself	With Others
D: Detail-oriented				
R: Rules and structure; have set ways for getting things done				
E: Expectations are high.				
A: Appearance.				
M: Mistakes are avoided by working harder				
C: Confidence is low; you do not take unnecessary risks.				
O: Organization and neatness in the environment				
S: Self-doubt; you think things over carefully to be certain.				
T: Low trust of others; stay personally on top of things				

cess. Having a bit of self-doubt means that you are not likely to act impulsively or make bad decisions in haste.

Perfectionists not only have high expectations of others, they have high expectations of themselves. This can work to your advantage. Having high expectations keeps you striving to succeed, makes you push yourself a little harder rather than settling for just good enough. Good things come from people who set high goals for themselves and work to achieve them. Gordon Flett and his colleagues at York University found that perfectionism in college students was associated with greater commitment to accomplishing their goals. Expecting a great deal from yourself and being careful in how those goals are achieved are paths to successful living. That is, as long as these things are exercised in moderation, so that the striving itself does not begin to work to your disadvantage.

DISADVANTAGES OF PERFECTIONISM

Now that you have taken stock of the ways in which perfectionism helps you to be successful in the world, it is time to examine the ways in which it may cause problems. As with the previous section, the self-assessments in the boxes will help you identify examples of times when your perfectionism works against you. The IFP and OFP designations in the summary boxes are included to remind you of which are more characteristic of inwardly focused (IFP) and outwardly focused (OFP) perfectionists. Use the grid on page 60 to record the disadvantages of perfectionism in your life.

At Work

Just as perfectionism facilitates work, it can also interfere with work. For example, the low confidence that makes you more careful in what you do can keep you from sharing your creative ideas with others. Sharing new ideas means taking the risk that no one else will like your ideas or that they may be critical of you. Not sharing ideas means not having input into how things are done or not voicing that great idea that others may think is terrific and leads to success for you or for your company.

Brent is notorious for not taking risks, which truly is unfortunate, because he has some very creative ideas. They are usually different from those of his peers, so he thinks that others will find his ideas stupid or absurd. He listens while his colleagues give ideas for a new project. He hears them get all excited about someone else's idea that he thinks is boring or lacks originality, but he keeps his criticisms to himself because everyone else seems to be going along with it. If this sounds like you, being too cautious to avoid criticism may keep you from being as successful as you would like.

There are times when perfectionists unwittingly set themselves up to fail. They do not anticipate that their perfectionist standards of performance will slow them down or interfere with completing tasks. They want to give a good impression, so they push very hard and attend to every detail. Unfortunately, perfectionists sometimes underestimate the time it takes to finish a job. Part of the problem is overestimating how much can be done given time constraints. Sometimes those time constraints are self-imposed; that is, they set the deadline themselves. ("I can get it done by the end of the week.") When their self-imposed deadlines approach, they start feeling more and more stressed.

If you consistently set deadlines for yourself that are difficult to meet, you may have unreasonable expectations for yourself. The problem is that these deadlines that you make up in your head feel real rather than something you chose. This is usually because you told someone else about your deadline, and that made it feel like it was carved in stone. You then criticize yourself for not being able to meet the deadline, when in fact the deadline was probably not reasonable from the start. Even worse, when you agree to meet someone else's deadline when it is not reasonable given what you need to do, you disappoint not only yourself, you disappoint other important people in your life. "I should be able to do this" is a common retort.

June agreed to head the garage sale committee for her church. This was not a big task, she was good at organization, and was honored that she was asked. The person who had been in charge had other family commitments and was not able to follow through with the garage sale. June was pleased to be able to do something that someone else could not. The garage sale was in two weeks, the weekend prior to Thanksgiving. June had also agreed to coordinate the poinsettia sale for her son's soccer team, to drive the car pool for her neighbor who had to go out of town, and to help out with the local food drive, which included calling the other mothers of the kids in her daughter's homeroom class and collecting food items for the needy. Each of these was relatively easy to do and should not take a great deal of time. Organization was her strength and people knew they could count on her in a pinch. She also had her usual home responsibilities and she was planning to have her in-laws over for Thanksgiving dinner, an event that always stressed her. The deadline for each activity was nearing. June *was* stressed, unable to sleep well, worrying about not only doing each job, but about adding something special to each so that it had her unique trademark of tending to details that made the event better, more efficient, or more memorable. She told herself "I should be able to do this" and, in fact, she did accomplish each task, but not without losing sleep. In the end, she resented the other parents who did not do their parts, the kids for not helping around the house, her husband for inviting his family to visit, and herself for putting herself in another bind where there was too much to do and not enough time to do it well. June does not have a paid job, but setting unrealistic expectations for oneself, setting unreasonable deadlines, and taking on more than you can handle is a pattern of perfectionistic behavior regardless of whether or not you draw a salary.

Another way in which perfectionists set themselves up to fail is in trying to get things "just right," which can slow them down. Attending to details can keep a person from completing the larger task. For example, getting stuck on this section of this chapter and trying to get it just right can keep me from getting on with the writing of the rest of this book. Usually, wanting to get things just right is a way of trying to avoid making a mistake. For a perfectionist, making a mistake is unacceptable because they believe it makes them look bad in front of others. Public humiliation is a thing to be avoided. Being careful about details is a way to avoid making mistakes.

Terry feels frustrated a great deal of the time. She realizes that she is not advancing at the pace she and others would expect. She knows that she is good at what she does, but there appear to be a number of obstacles in her way. She finds herself getting stuck on tasks, unable to advance or complete them. There always seem to be missing pieces, sections of reports that do not read right, sound awkward, or are confusing. She reworks them until she becomes frustrated and drops them to work on something else. The problem is that she sometimes forgets to return to her original task until the deadline approaches, and it is almost too late to do anything but an imperfect, rushed job.

Organization is another trait of perfectionists that, while helping them, can also slow down the work, particularly when the time used to organize things takes away from the time needed to do the job. Some people have trouble getting started on tasks, so they organize and reorganize until they feel comfortable. In this case, getting organized is a way of avoiding a task. Why avoid it? Terry, for example, is not always certain how to start a project; she may have two or more ideas but is worried about which will be the best. So she puts off having to make the decision by organizing her office, her filing system, her desk, her secretary's duty schedule, or other things until she calms herself, makes a decision, and proceeds. This takes time and time is short.

Some perfectionists are not very good at using the resources of others; they worry about the quality of the job and think it will turn out best if they do the work themselves. They cannot maintain control over the quality of the work of others and are reluctant to trust others to do as good a job as they know they can do themselves. Sometimes perfectionists give overly detailed instructions in attempts to help others complete tasks the way that they would if they did it them-

---

Take time to think about this.

There are times when perfectionists unwittingly set themselves up to fail. They do not anticipate that their perfectionist standards of performance will slow them down or interfere with completing tasks.

SELF-ASSESSMENT

Disadvantages of Perfectionism at Work

Fear of taking risks: (IFP)*

Do you keep quiet rather than offer a suggestion that might be criticized or rejected? Do you get angry when you have to follow someone else's suggestion and it is not as good as your own?

Setting yourself up: (IFP and OFP)

Do you set artificial deadlines for yourself and then get stressed when you are unable to reach them? Do you take on more than you have to? More than others will take on?

"Losing the forest for the trees": (IFP)

Are you more particular about details on the job than most other people? Is it possible that you get stuck on details that could be ignored? Do you frustrate others with your concentration on details while larger elements of projects are put on hold?

Difficulty delegating: (OFP)

Do you have difficulty delegating jobs to other people? Can you delegate without worrying, looking over their shoulders, or double-checking their work? Could you be more efficient if you had someone else do the simpler tasks that did not require your particular skill or abilities?

*(IFP) stands for Inwardly Focused Perfectionist; (OFP) stands for Outwardly Focused Perfectionist.

---

selves. This attempt at giving precise instructions can lead to confusion, as the recipient gets more details than are needed. When the tasks are not completed as instructed, perfectionists draw the conclusion "I was better off doing it myself." Unfortunately, not delegating tasks places more burden on the perfectionist and takes a lot of time. And assuming that if you do the task yourself you can have control over all outcomes is usually a fantasy. We know this all too well when we are in a hurry and the copy machine will not work, people do not show up on time, the computer crashes, or we lose something important. If you have difficulty delegating tasks to others your perfectionism could be keeping you from being consummately effective in what you do. Of course there are co-workers or employees who will not work as hard as you do or will not be able to complete tasks with your level of skill. However, to assume that everyone will fail is often an overgeneralization.

At Home

The organization of a household takes a great deal of time and energy, particularly if you do all the work yourself. Having things "just right" puts pressure on the housekeeper. For example, although June genuinely enjoys all the things in her life, she is driven by an internal pressure. When the job is done and the house is perfect, she feels a sense of inner peace. The rest of the time she is aware of feeling anxious and tired. Recently, she has found herself feeling overwhelmed with her life. And she feels guilty for feeling overwhelmed. ("What do I have to be overwhelmed about? I'm just a housewife.")

Some people are not bothered by the time and energy it takes to keep a household neat and organized because they get "stressed out" when things are in disarray. Clutter in a house or unfinished housework such as dirty laundry or dishes is like a loud irritating noise in the perfectionist's ears. These environmental noises are distracting and irritating. The perfectionist's ability to see details can be a problem at home, especially when there is no time or energy to take care of the house and quiet the noise.

Getting lost in details can slow you down at home just as it can at work. Terry has several home projects that she has not been able to finish. She had been trying to reorganize her home to eliminate all traces of her ex-husband's six-year stay. She wants to reorganize closets her way, but there were so many details. She found old files that needed to be purged, old photographs that needed cataloging, old clothes that needed to be given away, altered, or stored for next season. After two years of trying to reorganize her home, she had not made it out of her bedroom closet.

Perfectionism at home can cause tension among family members.

June makes suggestions for how the kids should organize the desks in their rooms so that it is easier to work. Skippy says OK and lets Mom clean up and organize his desk. Sissy hates the intrusion and rebels, intentionally keeping her room in organized disarray. That is, it's clean but things that could be put away are left on counters, on the bed, or on the floor; the nice white walls with hand-stenciled tulip

---

SELF-ASSESSMENT

Disadvantages of Perfectionism at Home

Exhaustion: (IFP)*

Do you wear yourself out with housework? Would others say that you are overly concerned with neatness and organization?

Intrusions: (IFP and OFP)

Do you make other people at home conform to your way of keeping the house clean? Including how they keep their own personal space? Does this cause tension or arguments?

Getting lost in the closet: (IFP)

Do you have trouble finishing the projects you start? Does getting things "just right" take too much time? Does the level of detail interfere with progress?

Conflict: (OFP)

Do you tell your family that if they are not going to do it right then don't do it at all? Do you have disagreement about how a job should be done? Do you believe that there are only two ways to do a job, a right way and a wrong way?

Noncompliance: (OFP)

Do you get frustrated when your family members do not comply with your wishes? Do you think you are better off doing the work yourself?

Environmental noise: (IFP)

Do you get stressed when the house is in disarray? Is it hard for you to concentrate? When you are trying to work on a project, such as paying bills, are you distracted by household tasks that need attention (e.g., laundry)? Is it hard for you to ignore a mess?

*(IFP) stands for Inwardly Focused Perfectionist; (OFP) stands for Outwardly Focused Perfectionist.

trim that June had painted last Spring are now covered with all manner of wall clutter. It irritates June greatly, but she gave up that fight when Sissy told her how she preferred being at her best friend's house. ("Suzy's mom lets her keep her room however she likes.") After talking to Suzy's mom, June agreed that it was probably OK to allow Sissy this one indulgence. June does fear, though, that this concession might lead Sissy to become a horrible slob in her own home someday, an outcome for which June could not forgive herself. ("No nice young man would want to marry a slob. Only slobs marry slobs.")

Perfectionists sometimes believe that their worlds would be easier to manage if everyone else would either cooperate or leave them alone. The disadvantage of this notion, however, is that the perfectionist gets stuck with a great deal of work. This takes time and leaves the person feeling burdened. When others get used to the idea that this one person will do their chores, they soon forget to say thank you or express gratitude in other ways. Working with others will be covered more thoroughly in Chapter 8, Perfectionism and Getting Along with Others.

In Relationships With Others

Being a perfectionist can color the way you look at other people in your world. Most people, perfectionist or not, assume that other people see things the way that they do. When it doesn't work out that way—and it rarely does—misunderstandings can occur that create bad feelings or damage relationships. June has had this problem with her children. Being a caring parent, June wants every event, every friendship, every aspect of her children's lives to be just perfect. She worries a great deal about her children, mostly Sissy. She wants her daughter to have the best possible experience in high school, and she feels the pain of her daughter's skin problems and crooked teeth. She knows the kids at school make fun of Sissy, although Sissy rarely complains. June is self-conscious of her own appearance and fears criticism. Sissy does not.

June remembers the pain of adolescence and wants to do whatever she can to shelter Sissy from that pain. She assumes that Sissy will get her feelings hurt as easily as June did when she was a teenager. June overlooks that Sissy is a different person with different sensitivities, strengths, and weaknesses. When June assumes that she and Sissy are thinking the same way it usually leads to confusion and some-times conflict.

For example, June tries to counsel Sissy in what to wear to show her strengths and to hide her imperfections, assuming incorrectly that Sissy's imperfections are as bothersome to her daughter as they are to her. In doing so she communicates to her daughter that she thinks Sissy has many noticeable faults. Sissy takes offense and rejects her mother's advice. By incorrectly assuming that Sissy will appreciate this helpful feedback, June inadvertently communicates that she dis-approves of her daughter or does not think that she is capable enough to make her own choices about her appearance. June also tries to help Sissy work out her problems with friends. When it does not seem as if Sissy is taking her advice, June sometimes calls the parents of Sissy's friends just to see if she can help to work things out. Sissy sees these "helpful acts" as embarrassing interferences.

Perfectionism can sometimes interfere with finding a mate. Brent, for example, wants to settle down and have a family. Unfortunately, he has not been able to find Ms. Right. Brent isn't exactly sure what the prob-lem is, but he does know that the girls he has found are not the types you marry. He has perfectionistic standards, girlfriends included.

Brent has tried to reevaluate his last few girlfriends. ("Maybe I was too hasty in cutting off the relationships. Sheila was gorgeous, fairly bright, but she had that annoying little laugh that could make a grown man scream. It was amusing the first few times, then it began to grate on my nerves. Tonya was also beautiful, but more so from a distance. Up close you see how much makeup, mousse, and fake nails it took to pull herself off as a natural beauty. Gloria was nice, fun, witty, bright, upwardly mobile, good family, but those thighs.")

Ann Marie Garrison was the girl of his dreams. They went to high school together and then to junior college. They lost touch after that and only saw each other when home for the holidays. He adored her from afar. They had never dated. He had wanted to since the tenth grade, but never had the nerve to ask. On the cheerleading squad at Hometown High, Ann Marie Garrison was an angel in flight and she had beautiful thighs. She dated all the best athletes and the student body president; of course, she would never want Brent. He fantasized about her throughout college, going as far as thinking about calling her and asking her out during Spring break. But when he finally had the courage, it was too late. She was engaged to be married after graduation. Brent wants perfection and cannot find it. It could be argued that his high personal standards for a girlfriend may not be unreasonable, but it is definitely leading to loneliness.

Another way that perfectionism can interfere with relationships is when the actions of others easily upsets you or lets you down. The majority of people—probably all of us—are quite imperfect. Despite good intentions, people make mistakes at times, hurt one another's feelings, or appear to be thoughtless or inconsiderate. How much of this occurs and how much is tolerable is a question we all ask ourselves. In your relationships, are these weaknesses intolerable? Do

---

SELF-ASSESSMENT

Disadvantages of Perfectionism in Relationships

My thoughts are your thoughts: (IFP and OFP)*

Do you expect the people in your life to behave as you do? Make the choices you would make? See things the way you do?

Distrust: (OFP)

Do you ever feel compelled to act in people's behalf because they do not seem to be handling things correctly on their own? Does this cause tension for you or for others?

Picky-picky: (OFP)

Are you particular about who you date, spend time with, or have as a friend? Is it easy for you to see people's faults and hard for you to ignore them? Are you quick to be critical of people when they make mistakes? Are you unforgiving when people do things to upset you or hurt you?

*(IFP) stands for Inwardly Focused Perfectionist; (OFP) stands for Outwardly Focused Perfectionist.

they outweigh the positive aspects of the relationship? If so, you may be expecting more from people than they can realistically provide.

Sergio, Joe's fifteen-year-old son, seems to be a constant source of disappointment. He has become a moody young man with "an attitude." Joe doesn't care for or trust Sergio's choice of friends. They wear their hair too long or half-shaved, and he even thought he saw one with an earring in his ear. Joe does not trust these kids. ("Ten weeks in boot camp would straighten out that bunch".) Joe seems to have lost touch with his boys. They disappoint him daily and they know it. Although they desperately want his approval, they have all but given up on trying to please him. Joe had always dreamed of retiring and having more time for the kids, but now that he has the time he feels hopeless because he is convinced he has lost them. Not really understanding what went wrong, Joe blames society, the kids, his wife, rock music, his kids' friends, and the lenient public school. But he knows deep down that he has created the great division between them. Lonely and hurt, expecting too much has left him with nothing at all.

With Yourself

In evaluating the disadvantages of perfectionism, you might find that it does not cause problems for other people at home or at work. The consequence may only be to you and how it makes you feel inside. The internal turmoil about making the right decision or worrying about the outcome of your words or actions may be the most painful part. The perfectionists that I have known well have all struggled with making the right decisions. This is not to say they made poor decisions. In fact, much of the time there was no real right or wrong way to do things, but they still feared making a mistake, being ridiculed by others, or not getting the outcome they desired. These are highly competent people, with skills and talents that others envy, including me. I heard their worry or fear. Even when I would give encouragement, express my confidence in their abilities, or remind them of all the things they have done well, it had little effect on their worry or fear. Self-consciousness and self-doubt are common consequences of perfectionism that are difficult for others to see because they are internal and may not affect a person's behavior.

Another characteristic of perfectionism that can cause personal distress is having unreasonably high expectations for yourself. The student who expects As and gets a B in a difficult course is distressed for failing to meet his own goal. "I'm my own worst enemy," one of my patients recently said. "I know I am smart and will do well because I work hard, yet I beat myself up constantly about my grades. I put so much pressure on myself that I get sick." A working mother who expects herself to perform perfectly at work while not missing a beat at home or with her family is another example. While she works hard and may be able to meet all work and home expectations, it is often at great expense to herself. Regardless of the type of job or lifestyle, perfectionists often set goals that are higher than is reasonable to consistently achieve, and then berate themselves for missing the mark, even though the goal they set was arbitrary and there are no real consequences for falling short.

Having unreasonable expectations can even cause you to have difficulty in recovering from illness. For example, Patricia DeBartolo at Smith College and David Barlow at Boston University studied men who suffered from sexual dysfunction. They found that Physicians' ratings of the degree to which psychological factors contribute to this physical problem are strongly associated with perfectionism, suggest-

---

SELF-ASSESSMENT

Disadvantages of Perfection for Self

Internal turmoil: (IFP)*

Do you worry about making the right decisions? Do you worry about the consequences of your words or actions?

Self-criticism: (IFP)

Do you set goals that are higher than is reasonable to achieve? Do you berate yourself for missing the mark even though the goal you set was arbitrary and there are no real consequences?

*(IFP) stands for Inwardly Focused Perfectionist.

ing that the high expectations these men hold for themselves to perform sexually might actually worsen their problem.

Similarly, in the National Institute of Mental Health's Treatment of Depression Collaborative Research Project people who strongly endorsed having perfectionistic beliefs were less likely to recover from major depression regardless of whether they were receiving medication or some form of psychotherapy.

Where Do We Go from Here?

You have examined the advantages and the disadvantages of being a perfectionist. There are a few more pieces of information you need to complete your self-evaluation. Once this has been completed you will be ready to figure out what this all means for you, for your future, and for your relationships with other people. It will help you to set some goals for maintaining the advantages of perfectionism while reducing the disadvantages.

The next task is to list the advantages of not being a perfectionist. This might include being able to relax more, reducing anxiety, or having more self-acceptance. It will also be helpful for you to make a list of the disadvantages of not being a perfectionist. This might include things such as lowering the quality of your work, having a sloppy house, underachieving, or giving up altogether. There will be some overlap between the advantages of perfectionism and the disadvantages of not being a perfectionist. There will also be some overlap between the disadvantages of perfectionism and the advantages of not being a perfectionist.

The next step is to review these lists and place three stars next to those items you believe are most important to you. Place two stars next to those that are very important to you, and place one star next to those that are somewhat important to you. Leave the remaining items without stars.

To complete your self-assessment you need to know whether the advantages and disadvantages you listed are real or are imagined. For example, if you believe that you would eventually earn a promotion and a raise on the job if the work is done perfectly, and there are specific rules in the workplace about promotion that suggest that this is,

The Disadvantages of Perfectionism

Below is a list of areas in which perfectionism can interfere with your performance at home, at work, with yourself, and with others in your world. Fill in the boxes with examples of ways in which perfectionism may keep you from succeeding.

Areas of Perfectionism	At Work or School	At Home	With Yourself	With Others
D: Get stuck on details				
R: Too rigid in following rules and structure				
E: Expectations are unreasonably high				
A: Appearance				
M: Mistakes are feared so job is overworked.				
C: Confidence is low; risks avoided; too conservative.				
O: Organization and neatness takes too much time.				
S: Self-doubt inhibits decisions and action.				
T: Low trust of others; do not delegate; overburdened with work.				

in fact, true, then this advantage of perfectionism could be called "real." If, however, no such rule exists, but you held the belief that you would get ahead by doing things perfectly, then this advantage may not be real, just imagined. The same goes for disadvantages. You might imagine that if you do not stop acting like a perfectionist ("being picky") your children will eventually reject you and you will be alone in your old age. Although your children might get tired of you being picky, they may not ever intend to reject or neglect you, particularly in times of need. Of the advantages marked as important (those with any number of stars), cross out those that are probably imagined and not real. If you are not certain if they are real or not, get more information by asking others what they think.

What you should be left with is an idea of the most important real advantages and disadvantages of perfectionism. Shown is a summary of the self-assessments completed by Joe and Terry. There are some themes in the reasons listed for being and not being a perfectionist. Look at the items that received the most stars. You can begin to see how each struggles with the positive and negative aspects of perfectionism, how it serves them well in their lives and how it seems to be getting them into trouble. Below each table of advantages and disadvantages is a summary of the key issues faced by these individuals. In each case it is difficult to say that perfectionism is a clear problem and should be controlled, because it obviously plays an important role in each of their lives. By the same token, it is difficult to say that perfectionism is clearly advantageous and should be fostered. Each person will have to learn to control or limit perfectionism in order to live life satisfactorily.

What themes do you see in your own self-assessment? Are there clear pluses and minuses to perfectionism on the job, at home, or in your relationships with people? Be careful not to discount or dismiss the advantages of perfectionism in your life just because there are some disadvantages. As mentioned earlier, it is the advantages of perfectionism that keep it going. It is not always a bad thing, but it can get out of control. Look for the patterns in your list of advantages and disadvantages. As we proceed through the chapters, pay particular attention to sections that help you to minimize the problems you associate with perfectionism. Do not give up the advantages all at once. They

Joe

	Being a perfectionist	Not being a perfectionist
Real Advantages	The job is done right the first time.*** Things are orderly.** I set a good example for the boys.** It feels good to do a good job.*** I push myself to keep succeeding rather than giving up like a lot of vets have.***	I could lighten up on the boys.*** My wife would stop nagging me about it.** I could enjoy the boys more and fight with them less.***
Real Disadvantages	My kids hate it.*** My wife hates it.** My son is giving up with life because he can't be like me.*** I get carried away sometimes.*	I might be compelled to give up altogether.*** I would be setting a bad example for my sons.** Sloppiness is intolerable.*** My work might suffer.*

Primary issues for Joe:

1. Having things the ways he likes them versus pushing his boys away
2. Staying in control versus losing control altogether

can serve you well. Going to the extreme of not being a perfectionist can be just as troublesome for your life as being highly perfectionistic.

LET'S SET SOME GOALS

Now that you have completed your self-assessment it is time to set some goals. In general, our program is to reduce or cope with each of

Terry

	Being a perfectionist	Not being a perfectionist
Real Advantages	Others admire the quality of my work.** I avoid criticism that others receive.** It will help me get ahead.*** I am very organized.** My department gets consistently good ratings.**	Life would be a lot easier.** I would not have to check the work of others and would have more time to myself.** I would probably get more done and quantity is as important as quality.*** I could stay focused on tasks.**
Real Disadvantages	I have too much to do.*** I make mistakes when I check everyone's work.** I get stuck on details and can't let go.** This slows my progress.*** I'm not getting the rewards I deserve.***	If I am not careful with the details no one else will be.*** The quality of my department's work reflects on me.*** Mistakes are punished.*** I would be humiliated in front of coworkers.* Disorder stresses me.**

Primary issues for Terry:

1. Seeking rewards versus avoiding punishment
2. Not making mistakes versus not succeeding in business

the real disadvantages of perfectionism. If one of the disadvantages you have identified has to do with getting along with others, then your goal should include improving those relationships. Sometimes the goal will be to eliminate the problem altogether. Sometimes the goal will be to watch yourself more closely to avoid stepping over the line with your perfectionism. When you set goals, you want them to be as specific as possible. They guide your actions and specify what you will do or not do. If the goals you've set are clear, you will be able to identify when and if they have been accomplished. "I want to feel better about myself" is not a specific goal. It is hard to tell what this person will do to feel better about herself. There are no emotional thermometers, so other more specific criteria are needed to determine when a goal has been accomplished. It is very likely that your goals will change as you read further or as you begin to make changes for yourself. Remember that there are no right or wrong answers to goal setting.

Let's review the goals set by Joe and Terry. When you examine Joe's list of advantages and disadvantages of perfection, it seems as if his primary issues include 1) having things the ways he likes them versus pushing his boys away and 2) staying in control versus losing control altogether. These are the items that get the most stars. When Joe thinks about it, he decides that his boys are the most important things in his life. He has just a few more years to establish a relationship with them because soon they will be grown and will move away. If he fails, he may lose them altogether. Although Joe has tried to be a good father, his methods have not given him the results he wants. He must try a new strategy if he wants a stronger relationship with his boys. Joe's first goal is to have more positive interactions with his sons. His second goal is to continue to set a good example for his sons by the way he manages his life and his work. He wants his boys to learn how to take care of themselves but, henceforth, he will try teaching by example rather than by forcing them to be like him.

Looking at Terry's responses on the advantages/disadvantages grid, it seems that her primary issues are 1) seeking rewards versus avoiding punishment and 2) not making mistakes versus not succeeding in business. Terry wants to succeed in her work. She wants and expects to advance, and pleasing her boss seems to be the key. He has told her that she needs to be more productive and more consistent in her work. Terry realizes that one of the places where she gets hung up is in completing projects on time. She knows that she can spend too much time redoing the work of others when it was perfectly fine from

---

Preliminary Goals for Controlling Perfectionism

Review your list of advantages and disadvantages of perfectionism. Pick out the disadvantages that you marked with two or three stars. Your goals might include gaining control over these disadvantages by trying to not let your perfectionism guide your actions. Another goal might be to cope better with these disadvantages so that they do not negatively affect your life or your relationships with others.

The main disadvantages of my perfectionism are:

1. _____

2. _____

My plan for avoiding or coping with these disadvantages include:

1. _____

2. _____

3. _____

4. _____

---

the outset. It would serve her well if she spent more time on creative elements and let her staff do the detail work. One of Terry's goals is to keep herself focused on completing her projects. When she gets stuck, she will get some assistance from her staff or delegate the task altogether. She will also try not to recheck the work of others.

3

SCHEMAS THAT UNDERLIE

PERFECTIONISM

Brent received an employee evaluation with a score of 92 out of 100 and an 8 percent raise in his salary. He went to his office and dwelled on the 8 points short of perfection that he missed, trying to figure out why his supervisor had not given him a perfect score. He felt hurt and angry and thought about quitting. He calmed himself down by reminding himself that he is never going to be good enough and is lucky to have this job. Instead of anger, he felt depressed and rejected. Brent's friend Lily, who has a similar position in another department, received her evaluation with a score of 91 and an 8 percent raise in her salary and wanted to celebrate. "I am so good," she said. She called Brent to brag, but his secretary said he wasn't taking any calls.

The biggest difference between Lily's and Brent's experiences was in how each perceived the scores on their evaluation. Lily does not demand perfection from herself, so for her a score of 91 was high; it meant success and more money. She knew that she was doing a good job and that her supervisor rarely gave anyone a perfect evaluation because he thought it would make his employees stop trying. Although Brent got the raise he needed and expected, he also expected a perfect employee evaluation. ("No matter how hard I try I'm never good enough.") Good enough for Brent meant a score of 100, or maybe 99. The score of 92 was further validation of his faults, how he is unappreciated, and how he is really going nowhere in this job. This nagged at him for several days, until he finally confronted his boss.

Brent's and Lily's perceptions of their evaluations were influenced by their schemas, or what Judith Beck, Ph.D., director at the Beck Institute for Cognitive Therapy and Research, calls "core beliefs." Core beliefs are rules or ideas that people have about themselves, about other people and the world in general, and about the future. When events occur, we interpret the meaning of these events through our schemas or beliefs, like looking at the world through colored glasses. Each schema colors our perceptions in a certain way. These perceptions, in turn, influence the emotions we experience in response to stressful events. Dr. Aaron T. Beck of the University of Pennsylvania calls this process "the cognitive model." In his landmark book, *Cognitive Therapy of Depression,* Dr. Beck and his colleagues described how negative schemas can color your interpretation of events in a way that leads to emotional distress and a choice of actions that can increase rather than decrease problems. The cognitive model is illustrated in the diagram shown. Events occur that are interpreted very quickly through your belief system and lead to automatic thoughts. These interpretations cause emotional reactions as well as behavioral reactions.

Although some schemas are positive or neutral and others are negative, Myrna Weissman, Ph.D., of Columbia University, has found that schemas such as the drive for perfection, needing approval from others, and feelings of inadequacy are associated with depression and other symptoms of psychological distress. Certainly, in Brent's case we can see how events that stimulate his negative schema that

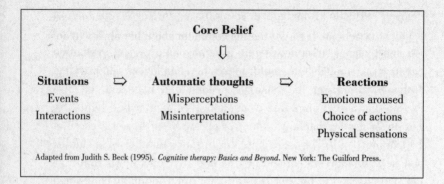

Core Belief

⇩

Situations ⇨	**Automatic thoughts** ⇨	**Reactions**
Events	Misperceptions	Emotions aroused
Interactions	Misinterpretations	Choice of actions
		Physical sensations

Adapted from Judith S. Beck (1995). *Cognitive therapy: Basics and Beyond*. New York: The Guilford Press.

he will never be good enough seem to lead to feelings of sadness and depression.

Lily's schema or core belief about herself is that she is smart and talented, though far from perfect. While she thinks the opinions of others do count, she is never devastated by someone's negative opinion of her. Lily's schema led her to see her employee evaluation as evidence that she is, in fact, a good worker and left her feeling happy and proud. One of Brent's schemas about himself is that he has to be perfect or others will reject him. Brent's schema leads him to view his employee evaluation as a slap in the face by his supervisor and further evidence that no matter how hard he works he will never really be accepted by his boss. This led to feelings of sadness and anger. For both of these individuals, their schemas affected their views of their employee evaluations as well as their emotional reactions.

Schemas can help us to make sense out of the things we see and experience, such as determining how important or significant an event is in our lives. For Lily, her employee evaluation was "not a big deal," because her view is that her boss's opinion of her is not as important as her self-evaluation. In contrast, this was a very important event for Brent, because he cares a great deal about his job performance and how other people view him.

Schemas also help us to make predictions about things in our world. When given a new assignment, Lily predicts that she will do well. Brent's self-schema, on the other hand, leads him to predict that he will have to work extremely hard and that the end result may not be good enough for his supervisor. Schemas can also influence our choices of actions. If Lily is feeling confident about her ability to do a new task, she may wait until after the weekend to start working on it, while Brent's self-view would lead him to panic a little and take work home to get an early start, forgoing a relaxing weekend. In this way, schemas are not only influencing how they view themselves and the emotions they experience, but also their choices of action.

Let's take another example of a schema, one that affects our view of other people. Terry's belief is that people will take advantage of you or hurt you if you let them. Terry's ex-husband Steve's view is that people are generally good-natured and deserve the benefit of the doubt. These are both schemas about other people. When they were still married, if their children's nanny would cancel baby-sitting at the last minute due to illness Terry assumed that she was trying to get out of work now that she was paid a monthly salary, and this made Terry angry. Steve, on the other hand, assumed that the nanny would have been there if she could have and must be quite ill. He does not feel angry, just disappointed about missing an evening out.

"You're such a pushover Steve. I cannot believe you would fall for that. She probably got a date, and as long as we are paying her a monthly salary like you insisted, she can do whatever she pleases."

"You are so suspicious Terry. Not everyone is a superwoman like you, going to work with 102 degree fever."

"At least I take my responsibilities seriously. Why do you always stick up for her? You'll stick up for anyone but me."

"Give me a break. I just can't buy into your negativity. I think people are genuinely good most of the time."

"You are a sucker, Steve. You let people take advantage of you and you know it. If it wasn't for me being cautious we would have been ripped off by the plumber and the electrician as well. Do I need to remind you of that?"

"No. I don't want to hear it again. So much for us having a nice evening together. This is ridiculous."

According to Jesse H. Wright, M.D., Ph.D., Professor of Psychiatry and Behavioral Sciences at the University of Louisville School of Medicine, schemas can be adaptive as well as maladaptive. They

> ### Schemas:
>
> - color your view of yourself and your world
> - help you determine the importance of events in your lives
> - influence your predictions about things in your world
> - help you to understand people
> - guide decision-making
> - prepare you for future events
> - affect your choices of action

help us to make our ways through life, to understand people, to make decisions, and to prepare for future events. In general, negative schemas about ourselves or others can lead to interpretations of events that make us feel sad, angry, or disappointed, while more positive schemas that put a positive twist on events can give us confidence and hope.

Schemas are sometimes correct views of the world or of ourselves and sometimes are inaccurate or distorted. Negative schemas are not always wrong and positive schemas are not always right. For example, Terry's view that people will take advantage of you is not altogether inaccurate. There are, in fact, people in the world who would try to take advantage of or hurt others. Because Terry is cautious, she watches out for these people and keeps them from hurting her or her children. There have been times when Terry's suspiciousness has saved her family a lot of grief, like when she thought the plumber was overcharging her for the work and overestimating the extent of the repairs needed. Terry's negative view of others led her to get another plumbing estimate. In this case, she was right. The first plumber was trying to take advantage of her lack of knowledge about plumbing. What caused conflict for Terry and her husband during their marriage was the number of times that Terry was suspicious about people's intentions. Steve thought her suspiciousness was far greater than was warranted and did not like the way it made her act toward people. She pushed people away with her accusations or looks of disbelief. She embarrassed him a few times in social situations by treating people as if she thought they were lying. When she used her negative schema about others to guide her view of all people, sometimes her guesses about people were wrong.

Steve's positive schema about people got him into trouble as well. He would assume that others would appreciate or reward him for the good things he would do on the job or in the community and often felt disappointed when others failed to even take notice of his work. In contrast, it would make Terry angry with other people because she knew how much effort her husband had put into his projects. It also made her angry with Steve for wasting time on ungrateful people.

Similarly, schemas about yourself are sometimes, but not always, accurate. Perfectionistic schemas are a subset of schemas about yourself, others, the world, and the future. One perfectionistic schema is the belief that perfection is attainable and necessary. Both inwardly and outwardly focused perfectionists hold this belief. In some specific situations this may be correct. However, for most everyday activities, perfection is not necessary and holding to this belief causes people considerable stress and conflict, directly and indirectly. Brent's belief that he must be perfect has the direct effect of making him feel bewildered each time his performance is less than perfect, especially when it is noticed by others.

SCHEMAS ABOUT PERFECTIONISM

There are some schemas about perfectionism that are held by many people. These schemas are usually inaccurate or not applicable to all situations. When they are stimulated by negative life events, they generally stir up negative emotions such as fear, sadness, or anger. Because perfectionistic schemas are often inaccurate or distorted to some degree, they will lead you to misinterpret events. Misperceptions or misinterpretations will lead to choices of actions and emotional reactions that are often inappropriate for the situation. Those reactions can create problems of their own. In this next section we review some common schemas about perfectionism. Pay careful attention and take

---

Take time to think about this.

Perfectionist schemas are those beliefs that suggest that perfection is attainable and necessary. In some specific situations this may be correct. However, for most everyday activities, perfectionist schemas are too extreme, and holding to these beliefs causes people considerable stress and conflict, directly and indirectly.

---

note of the beliefs that may be fueling your perfectionist tendencies. Identifying your underlying beliefs will help you to understand your emotional reactions, your views, and your choice of actions.

"I Must Be Perfect or Else . . ."

Both inwardly and outwardly focused perfectionists subscribe to the commonly held schema that one must be perfect or something bad will happen. The feared outcome for inwardly focused perfectionists is rejection, whereas the feared outcome for outwardly focused perfectionists is more like humiliation. While most people, including perfectionists, understand logically that nothing bad will happen if they make a mistake, the underlying fear can still have a powerful influence on their behavior. They say to themselves, "I know logically that nothing bad will happen, but just in case it is true, I better not mess up." One of my favorite perfectionists used to say something like "I have to get this right, do it the way you want me to, or you are going to be mad at me. I know you never have gotten mad at me, but I don't want to take any chances." Despite reassurances that I would not get angry, this person worked hard to get things perfect. In fact, she always exceeded my standards and I never got mad at her. Ironically, I proved her point that getting it perfect keeps people from getting mad at you.

There are several parts of this schema that are problematic. First, it assumes that there is a "right way" to do something. For inwardly focused perfectionists, the right way is often the way that they think another important person would like it, such as Brent's boss or me in the previous example. This means that the perfectionist not only needs to know exactly what another person expects but also must perform in a way that meets the expectation. Since people do not always verbalize their expectations of others, the pressure is tremendous! Outwardly focused perfectionists have an easier time of it because they define their own standards; the right way is their way. How do they know it is right? "It just feels right."

Another problem with the schema "I must be perfect or someone will be upset with me" is that it assumes that not only do others expect you to be perfect, but that they will, in fact, become upset if the job is not done perfectly. While there are some bosses or supervisors who expect perfection and would get angry if their employees make mistakes, perfectionists, especially inwardly focused perfectionists, expect that all the important people in their lives will react this way. They assume that a potential for anger or even aggression exists in other people. In my case, I was offended by this assumption from my colleague because I had never gotten angry with her or anyone else for not being perfect, nor did I like being viewed as a volcano waiting to erupt. It was contrary to my personal schema that I am an even-tempered person and a good supervisor. For many years my colleague held tightly to her schema that I would be angry if she made a mistake, despite the fact that I had never disapproved of her. "You never know. It could happen next time," she would reply. When she did have the opportunity to see me become angry with someone (who greatly deserved it), it validated her notion of me as a seething volcano. Changing her perfectionistic schema was not easy, because she was sensitive to experiences that reinforced or validated her fears.

Assuming, for the sake of argument, that the belief "I must perform perfectly or you will be angry with me" is true, two other questions come to mind. First, is it reasonable for someone to expect you to be perfect? Is it really appropriate to change your behavior according to an unreasonable standard set by another person? Although they may have high expectations of others, most outwardly focused perfectionists would say that no one has the right to expect them to be perfect. Most inwardly focused perfectionists would reluctantly agree with this sentiment, but find it difficult not to acquiesce to the perceived expectations of others.

If this perfectionistic schema is correct, the second question that comes to mind is, what is so horrible about someone getting angry with you because you made a mistake? As I write this sentence I can hear all the perfectionists who read this screaming out, "What do you mean, what's wrong with someone getting angry with you?!!" I'm not insensitive to this, but I do think it is a question worth asking yourself. For some people, especially inwardly focused perfectionists, anger from others is intolerable at any time because it can hurt your feelings and make you feel sad, and also because anger can be frightening if you think the person might physically harm you in some way. For some perfectionists with the schema "I must be perfect or you might get angry at me," having someone actually angry with them feels like punishment. It hurts, almost like a physical blow. Having said this, would it be so bad if someone does not like your work or does not think it is perfect? Would they really be angry with you, or just not very happy about it? Is there a real consequence other than their displeasure? Do you imagine that it would be worse than it actually is?

Terry, who is more of an outwardly focused perfectionist, exemplifies the perfectionist who does not believe she has to be perfect to keep others from being angry. Terry doesn't hold this particular schema, so when someone gets angry with her because they think her performance is less than perfect, she feels angry, not hurt. Terry submitted a report for the semiannual stockholders' meeting to the Vice President of Marketing, her supervisor's boss. He does not care much for women in business and is not fond of Terry. He saw Terry before the meeting and complained about the organization of the report, which was not structured the way he used to organize these reports when he did them himself. He was having a difficult time finding his way through the numbers and was generally unhappy. He confronted Terry on this fact in front of several of her colleagues. Terry liked the way this report had turned out and had put a great deal of time and energy into it making certain that it was easy to read and accurate. Vice President or not, she was not going to take this kind of abuse from this man.

Standing up and looking him straight in the eyes, she said, in a calm and controlled manner, "You are obviously having a difficult time following the organization of the report, so let me help you. It is different from what you are used to because it contains information that was usually missing from the early formats. As you can see, the top of each page gives a concise title describing the information presented on that page and the bottom of each page has a summary statement or two for those who do not have the time or patience to mull over all the figures. These are statements we thought you would want to present to the stockholders. There is a table of contents that clearly states where you can find each piece of information. The sections are color-coded so that they cannot be mistaken for one another. I had the President of the Board's approval of the format of this report before the final copy was produced. He sent me a letter congratulating me and my department on our exceptional work. Would you like to see it?"

Terry does not like being humiliated, so she is careful with her work. When she has put a lot of energy into something and likes the final product, she has total confidence in her work. She is not intimidated by those who disapprove on the grounds that her style is different than theirs. She hears jealousy in their voices. She is not going to live her life according to the standards of someone she does not know or does not respect and she will not be criticized without reason. Terry may be hard to work with, but you would be grateful to have her on your side.

Terry does not cower when she receives disapproval. She is not uncomfortable with other people expressing anger with her, especially when she knows that she has done a good job. Anger from others does not frighten her because she knows that it is just an expression of emotion and opinion. Besides, she can match anyone's anger with her own fire if needed.

"I Must Be Perfect for Others to Accept Me."

Does this sound familiar? This is another twist on the schema "If I am not perfect no one will like me," a schema shared by all perfection-

---

SELF-ASSESSMENT

"I must be perfect or else . . ."

---

1.   Do you think something bad will happen if you are not perfect (or if what you are doing does not work out properly)?
2.   What is it that you are afraid will happen?
3.   What is the likelihood that this will happen?
4.   Can you do anything to reduce the chance of this happening to you?
5.   If it does happen, how will you cope?

---

ists. Approval from others feels good; it makes us feel accepted, wanted, cared for, and loved. As a child, when you did something good your mother may have told you that you were beautiful, smart, or adorable, and you knew at that moment that she loved you. When you did something wrong she got angry with you, punished you, or withheld affection, even if it was for a short time. It does not take a lot of experiences like these to figure out that approval feels good and disapproval feels bad.

Some people think that criticism means that they are being disapproved of as a person or that other people do not like them. When they perform perfectly and others respond in a positive way, they think that they are gaining approval as a person or receiving affection, rather than just getting a compliment. Once this is learned it sticks with you into your adult life and is reinforced by adult experiences. For example, when someone compliments you on your appearance, it feels good, almost like a verbal hug. A compliment can feel like acceptance. ("He must like me because he said I had a nice smile.") When a compliment is not repeated, this same person might interpret it as "He doesn't really like me." In this example, the perfectionist is making an error of interpretation. She is confusing a compliment for an expression of emotion. "I like what you do or how you look" is not the same as "I like you." This gets confusing for perfectionists because they have had many experiences in life where people who liked them gave them compliments. The important difference between approval (compliments) and affection is that you can have great affection for a person and not necessarily approve of or like the things that she does. For example, a mother can love her child but disapprove of his friends or his choice of music, or a child can love his mother but disapprove of the way she dresses or cooks. Joe is a good example of this. He loves his sons dearly, but does not like many of the things they do. June's husband loves her very much, but is greatly annoyed with her obsession with cleaning. When Joe criticizes his children, or when Bill, June's husband, gets annoyed with her cleaning, they are *not* saying "I don't love you" or "I don't care about you." They are merely disapproving of these actions.

What is most important about the schema, "I must be perfect for others to accept me" is that it assumes that approval or affection from others is based on your performance or your behavior in some way. While it is logical that others will like you if you do good things and will not like you if you do bad things, the perfectionist takes this logic further. The schema is not about doing good things or doing things well, it is about being perfect. Making a good effort or having good intentions are OK for other people, but not for the perfectionist. A perfectionistic schema is that they must be *perfect* for others to accept them or approve of them. When some things do not go perfectly, they wince and wait for rejection. If they do not receive that rejection they might assume it will come later or believe that people think less of them because of their mistake.

Another problem with the schema "I must be perfect for others to accept me" is that it assumes that others will notice perfection. Perfectionists know every error that they make and every imperfection in themselves, so they also know when they have done something perfectly. Most people are not that observant. An acknowledgment or a compliment may not be forthcoming if no one noticed the perfect performance. Failure to notice can feel like a slap in the face when you have worked very hard to get things "just right." It is an indirect criticism for some. ("It must not have been good enough for her or she would have said something.") Does that sound familiar? If so, you may hold this perfectionist schema.

Another related problem is that, just as beauty is in the eyes of the beholder, so is perfection. What is perfect to one person is not perfect

---

Schema Reality Check

1. Do you really believe that if you are perfect people will give you approval or affection? Is there any other way to gain affection?
2. When things do not go perfectly do you hold your breath and wait for rejection? How often does rejection actually occur?
3. Do others notice when you do things perfectly? How often do they reward your efforts?
4. Do others define perfection the same way you do? Are your standards higher than those of other people you know?
5. Is pushing yourself to be perfect worth the effort?

---

to someone else. So if you have to perform perfectly in order to be accepted, you must also be pretty good at guessing how each person defines perfection, and then change yourself to match that definition. Worrying about this takes a lot of energy.

Perfectionists, being very sensitive people, often know for whom they must perform perfectly. They know that their bosses and their spouses will expect nothing less than perfection, whereas their dogs and their best friends do not care about such things. Emotionally safe relationships are those in which perfectionists feel comfortable and accepted no matter how they look or act.

"If I Do It Perfectly Then . . ."—Fantasized Outcomes

Under every perfectionist schema is a hidden fantasy. The fantasy is that some really good thing will come from being perfect. ("I will finally be accepted." " I can finally stop worrying." "I will get what I have been working toward." "I can finally relax.") What is your fantasized outcome? Often these fantasized outcomes start with an underlying belief that if you do things perfectly, important people will notice it. The reactions of others are important to inwardly focused perfectionists. Usually these people are important because they are in a position to reward the perfectionist in some way, to give them love, a promotion, more money, the gold medal, or fame. We discussed previously the problems associated with trying to be noticed or gain acceptance from others. It is more complicated than it might initially seem.

Of course, sometimes the fantasized rewards are something intrinsic, such as a sense of personal satisfaction, inner peace, enlightenment, or a place in heaven. Outwardly focused perfectionists tend to be driven by the hope of internal rewards and are less concerned about acknowledgment from others. However, digging a little deeper one might still find an advantage of perfectionism that has to do with getting positive reactions from other important people (e.g., God, Mom, spouse, someone who rejected you).

A second assumption underlying the schema "if I do it perfectly then something good will happen" is that when the perfection is noticed it will lead to a reward. This is problematic, whether the reward is something you receive from others or something you give to yourself. The first problem is one of timing. How much perfection is needed before you get the reward? In some areas, for example job performance, there are actual rules about how much work needs to be done before a reward is given (e.g., a paycheck, a bonus, a promotion, a vacation with pay). For most things in life there are no such rules. How long do you have to push yourself before it is reasonable to

---

SELF-ASSESSMENT

Fill in the blanks below to define your fantasies about being perfect.

"If I am perfect then…"

I will _____

others will _____

life will _____

"If I do things perfectly then…"

This will happen: _____

This will not happen: _____

Take time to think about this.

How perfect do you have to be before you get the reward? How long do you
have to push yourself before it is reasonable to expect that reward?

---

expect that reward? I have known perfectionists who push themselves
for a lifetime, usually because they do not really know why they are
pushing themselves so hard or, if they do know, what they are working toward cannot be achieved, at least not by being perfect.

The second problem with assuming that perfection will lead to a
reward has to do with the availability of the reward. Perhaps what you
are shooting for is not really possible. Let's take the case of intrinsic
rewards first. If what you are aiming for is a type of inner peace or
sense of personal satisfaction, the fact that you are a perfectionist
may make this reward unattainable. ("When I finally do things well
enough, I will feel better about myself.") Achieving inner peace
comes from a self-schema of "I am good enough." The perfectionist
holds the self-schema "I am not good enough," which may be the
motivation to keep pushing. You would have to change schemas in
order to achieve inner peace, and if you did that you would no longer
be a perfectionist. To state it more simply, the perfectionist thinks
that the path to inner peace is from striving to be perfect, but this is
not true. The path to inner peace is from having a better self-view, and
you cannot get to a better self-view by continually trying to be perfect.
This is what I mean when I say that the reward that is sought by the
perfectionist may not be available.

If you look at the situation in which the fantasized reward comes
from another person, the problem may be the same: The reward may
not be available. Let's take the example of gaining acceptance from
an important person, such as a parent. ("If I am perfect then my father
will finally approve of me.") If you asked Brent how he would know if
his father approved of him, he would say that his father would praise
his work, say he loves him, and give him a hug or, at least, a pat on
the back, or finally stop treating him like a child. The reason this
reward may not be attainable is not because Brent can never be good
enough, but because his father is not capable of providing these

rewards. It may not be in his father's nature to be affectionate. He may not have the communication skills needed to communicate approval. In this case, not receiving approval has nothing to do with Brent's abilities. It has to do with his father's abilities.

Another problem with the assumption that perfection will be rewarded is that you may be the only person who knows this. If someone does not know that you expect a reward for your actions, they may not provide one. How could they not know? They may be working under a different set of assumptions or a different schema. They may think that you push yourself so hard because you want to, not because you seek acceptance or rewards from others. If their schema is that you work hard because it is the right thing to do whether rewarded or not, then they will not look for opportunities to reward you for your good work. If your spouse does not know that you spend extra time to look nice because you want praise and approval, then he may not be inclined to provide it. This does not mean that your efforts go unnoticed. They just do not realize that they are supposed to let you know that they notice and appreciate the effort.

"If I do things right I will finally be accepted." Inwardly focused perfectionists may openly acknowledge this fantasy. Outwardly focused perfectionists need acceptance too, but may be less likely to openly admit to this schema. For each type of perfectionist, acceptance can mean something different. Usually acceptance brings to mind a warm feeling between two people. In Chapter 1 we discussed that an ultimate goal for perfectionists might be unconditional acceptance. That means that they would be accepted for who they are and not for what they do or how they look. Unconditional acceptance is given no matter how well you perform at something or how many prizes you win. It is acceptance with no strings attached. You can make mistakes, look bad, forget to do things, and whomever you seek acceptance from loves you all the same, because their feelings for you have nothing to do with how perfectly you can perform.

There are several glitches in seeking acceptance. The first is in how you define acceptance. How would you know if you were being accepted? "I would just know" is a usual retort. There is nothing magical about acceptance. It is something real that can be seen in the way people act, in the things they say or do not say, in the expressions on their faces, and in the tones of their voices. If you are seeking acceptance, you must define more specifically what you are looking for so you will know when you have found it. For some people, acceptance is a demonstration of affection that might be complicated (e.g., proposal of marriage, giving financial control, allowing you to make your own choices). For others, gaining acceptance means that an important person will understand important things about you, such as how you view the world or what you want to accomplish in life. This understanding is demonstrated in words or actions. When you look closely at your fantasy, you might find that it is not really acceptance you seek, but rather some other outcome that is equally important. You may have mislabeled it as acceptance from others. For example, maybe what you want is affection. Maybe you want someone to agree with you or see things the way you do. It is important to be clear about what you want or expect from others so you can pursue it more directly. Trying to be perfect may not be the most direct path.

A second difficulty in seeking acceptance is that when it happens, perfectionists cannot always see it or believe it. Take the case of my favorite perfectionist that I mentioned earlier. I felt unconditional acceptance of her. There were no strings attached. It did not matter how well she performed because my acceptance was of her and not of her actions. I tried to communicate this directly with words and through my actions in demonstrating my confidence in her abilities and my understanding of her view on things, even when it differed from my view. Despite my attempts at communicating acceptance of her, she never really felt accepted. She was not accepted by her mother in the way she needed and could not shake the idea that I was the same. In her thinking, it was not that I had accepted her, it was that I had not yet rejected her. In her mind, as long as she pushed herself and performed as perfectly as possible, my rejection of her could be delayed or avoided.

Take time to think about this.

How would you know if others accepted you?

Wanting acceptance from others is a very reasonable goal. Being able to recognize it when it is there is critical. That is why it is important to define acceptance very carefully, so you know what you are looking for and you are not relying solely on instincts or "gut-level" feelings. Once you have defined what you mean by acceptance, you can make observations of your interactions with the people from whom you wish acceptance to determine if the behaviors you defined as acceptance have actually occurred. Giving people the benefit of the doubt that they do accept you until you can prove otherwise is another important step. In later sections, we will discuss how to decide whether or not your views of others are correct or incorrect.

There is another glitch in the notion that if you do well you will be accepted. If you cannot accept yourself as you are, imperfections and all, it is very hard to receive acceptance from others. When you do not accept yourself you believe that everyone else can see your flaws, especially when you do not cover them up well. You also assume that since those flaws are unacceptable to you, they will be unacceptable to others. This is where the logic breaks down. Not everyone expects perfection from you.

"If I do things perfectly everything will work out just right." This fantasy is in the back of most outwardly focused perfectionists' minds and causes them great frustration when it proves to be false. This fantasized outcome shares the complexities described above. It suggests that rewards are expected in exchange for doing things perfectly. It also implies that other people will cooperate to make things work out just right if you do things perfectly. For example, "If I get this job, everything will work out in my marriage." This fantasized outcome oversimplifies things in life. It assumes that you can have control over

---

Take time to think about this.

When you do not accept yourself you believe that everyone else can see your flaws. You also assume that since those flaws are unacceptable to you, they will be unacceptable to others. This is where the logic breaks down. Not everyone expects perfection from you.

things in your world when you have control over yourself. Unfortunately, the reality is that we seldom have control over other people or other things in our world, and just because we do things right does not mean that others will do the right thing in response. Usually, to make things work out "just right" more effort is needed than simply doing things perfectly. Some of the things that help to make everything work out perfectly occur by chance. For example, when the rain stops in time for an outdoor wedding, when the delivery gets there in time to meet your deadline, or when someone else's delay keeps you from appearing to be late.

"If I Make a Mistake, Then . . ."—Fear of Bad Outcomes

This schema is the flip side of the perfectionistic schema "if I am perfect then it will be rewarded." It suggests that when a mistake is made it will undoubtedly lead to a catastrophic outcome. The more a person thinks about that outcome, the scarier it gets. This kind of thinking is more typical of inwardly focused than outwardly focused perfectionists. For example, June was worried about a mistake she made in her calculation of the money raised at a recent garage sale for the church. She made a hundred-dollar error somewhere to the church's expense. ("Oh my, I have a hundred dollars less than I told the church secretary. I don't know where I made the mistake. Maybe I lost the money. Maybe I added wrong. They are going to think I kept the money for myself. They are going to put the numbers in the treasury report and everyone will see it. They will never trust me with another project again. They must think I am a complete idiot. I'll never be able to show my face again. I'll have to put in my own money to cover the difference. Bill will be so mad. I'll have to find a way to get the money without him knowing. Look at me, I'm even thinking like a thief.")

The more June thought about the mistake, the worse it got. One logical response would have been to tell the church secretary that she made a mistake in her calculations and to correct the figure in the report. She decided to confide in her husband, and he convinced her to do this. She feared humiliation and rejection, but confessed her

error and prepared herself to take the consequences. No overt consequences followed, but June was convinced that she would never be
trusted again. She withdrew from others in the church, stopped going
to committee meetings, and felt depressed. She was not going to wait
around to be rejected. She, in fact, fulfilled her own fantasy that making an error would lead to exclusion from church activities.

This kind of thinking is called "catastrophizing." Thinking about
all the possible bad outcomes made a small event seem like a catastrophe. Sometimes the outcome that is feared is very real. The majority of the time, however, the feared outcome has a very small chance
of occurring and can usually be prevented.

"If I make a mistake, then I am a failure." Some people
give themselves very little room for making mistakes. If they get
things just right they feel good; if they make mistakes, they see themselves as total failures. ("I can't believe I missed that. I totally
screwed up." "I should have known the answer." "I shouldn't have
said that. I'm so stupid.") Perfectionists feel downhearted when they
make mistakes. This is because for them mistakes are not just mistakes, they are indicators that they are flawed. Being flawed is fine for
other people, but it is definitely not OK with perfectionists. Even
worse is being flawed and other people knowing about it, because
that's where making mistakes carries a double penalty. It makes perfectionists feel like a failure and humiliates them in front of others. It
is not the event itself that makes them feel bad; rather, it is the meaning of the event that makes them feel bad.

If your sense of self-worth or self-esteem has to do with how well
you perform on the job, at home, with others, or on the sporting field,
then making mistakes can make you feel worthless. You value perfection. Imperfection has no value or, worse yet, it is despised. This is
one way that perfectionists beat themselves up emotionally. They put
an unreasonable amount of pressure on themselves to never make
mistakes in a world where making mistakes is inevitable. It is too
hard to always be perfect because it takes a great deal of time, energy,
and emotion. Though exhausted by the process, perfectionists continue the pursuit for perfection. "I'm not good enough, I must keep

trying" is the motto. And so they continue to work hard. When they have setbacks, make mistakes, and feel like failures, their motto changes to "I will never be good enough." This is when hopelessness sets in and depression begins.

"There Is a Right Way and a Wrong Way To Do Things"

All the perfectionists that I have met have this schema. Usually the right way is their way of doing things. Sometimes the right way is the way taught to them by parents, teachers, bosses, spouses, or mentors of some type. In talking with couples about this it is not unusual to hear one say that their spouse insists that some things be done a certain way, the right way. Sometimes this is a source of conflict, but the path of least resistance is usually taken to avoid an argument ("OK. We'll do it your

---

POINT–COUNTER POINT

For every negative schema there is another view that is more accurate. The Point–Counter Point exercise will help you examine these alternate views. Practice restating your perfectionist schemas in a way that is less absolute, less emotional, and less unforgiving. If this is too difficult, pretend that you are advising another perfectionist. Some examples are shown.

Point	Counterpoint
Mistakes are indicators that I am flawed.	Mistakes are behaviors, not personality characteristics.
Being flawed is not OK .	Being flawed or making mistakes is normal for all human beings.
It is OK for others to make mistakes, but it is not OK for me to make mistakes.	There is no reason that I should be held to a higher standard than everyone else.
It is horrible for other people to know that I have made a mistake or have a weakness.	If they cannot handle watching me make a mistake, then they have a real problem.

Take time to think about this.

The "right way" is simply a matter of opinion. It would be more accurate to say that it is your "preferred" way to do things, rather than the "right" way to do things.

---

way.") Interestingly, if you sit ten perfectionists in a room and ask them how to do a certain task, clean a garage as an example, you will hear ten different explanations of how to do it right. If you believe there is a right way and a wrong way to do things, how can it be that there are ten right ways? The simple answer is that the "right way" is simply a matter of opinion. It would probably be more accurate to say that it is your "preferred" way to do things, rather than the "right" way to do things.

Perfectionists incorrectly assume that other people in their world know "the right way" to do things. When people do things the wrong way, some perfectionists get upset not only because of the error, but because they believe the other person *intentionally* did it the wrong way. When this issue comes up in marital therapy, the spouse who believes that he has been wronged usually assumes that his wife was trying to hurt him or make him angry. Worse yet, these errors are assumed to be a sign that his wife does not really care. In fact, when perfectionists see people doing things incorrectly they often believe that those individuals are capable of doings things right, but simply do not care enough to do so. It is more likely, however, that either the other person is not aware that there is an expected way to do things or has his own idea of what it means to do things "right."

SELF-ASSESSMENT

Schemas can help you make sense out of things, make predictions, and prepare for events. They can also distort your perceptions of reality and make you feel bad.

What are the advantages and the disadvantages of holding the schema *"There is a right way and a wrong way to do things"*?

Do the advantages of holding this view outweigh the disadvantages? Is there another way to keep the advantages and eliminate the disadvantages in your life?

"Perfection Can Be Attained"

Another schema held by most perfectionists is that perfection can, in fact, be attained. Some believe that you reach perfection through hard work. Others believe it is attained by chance or by the grace of God. Perfection does occur from time to time. And it is awesome and wonderful when it does. I remember watching with amazement when Mary Lou Retton received a perfect score of 10 on the vault in the 1984 Olympics. Although it has been equally as long ago, I can clearly remember my son's perfect little face the first time I laid eyes on him. I've had blue jeans fit perfectly. I've seen Troy Aikman's perfect passes caught by the intended receiver to win the Super Bowl. My wallpaper was even hung perfectly, though not by me. It happens. Perfectionists often do things perfectly. Each time they achieve perfection their schemas about perfectionism are reinforced. ("See, it can be done if you just put your mind to it.") If perfection were never achieved, even perfectionists would eventually give up the pursuit and learn to be satisfied with just good enough.

HOW DO SCHEMAS OR BELIEFS AFFECT YOUR LIFE?

As mentioned earlier in this chapter, we are talking about schemas because they are the beliefs that underlie the pursuit of perfection as well as the notion that you are never good enough. These schemas are beliefs or attitudes that affect the way you interpret experiences in your life. These interpretations or views strongly influence your emotional reactions. For example, when most people think something is threatening, they will feel frightened. If they think an action is wrong and they do it anyway, they will feel guilty. If they think they must succeed—but cannot—they will feel sad or frustrated. If they think they must have something in order to be happy, they will feel sad without it. How you view situations affects your emotional reactions.

Schemas can also have influence on your choice of actions. For example, if you think you have hurt someone's feelings your choice of action might be to apologize. If you think it is usually best to be assertive and speak your mind, then you might choose to speak up. If you think it is important to not make mistakes, then you will be careful in your work. If you think door-to-door salesmen cannot be trusted, then you will turn them away.

Like other types of schemas, perfectionistic schemas also influence views, emotions, and choices of actions. For example, Joe believes strongly that there is a right way and a wrong way to do things (his schema), including how to dress, organize space, and catch a fish. His boys do things differently than Joe expects. That is to say, they do it the wrong way by their father's standards, and this makes Joe angry. In this way, his schema has affected his interpretation of his sons' actions ("They are wrong.") and his feelings (anger).

One of Brent's schemas is that if he does things right he will finally be accepted. At work, when he and Lily were returning from a break, Brent said hello to the big boss as they passed in the hall. The big boss completely ignored Brent. Not only did he feel rejected, Brent assumed that he must have done something wrong, since doing things right would have led to a greeting from the boss, which Brent defines as acceptance. Viewing his interaction with the big boss in a self-blaming way, Brent will go back to his office to ruminate over what he did and how to fix it so the next time he'll get the acceptance he needs. Lily, on the other hand, said, "What a big jerk. He wants us to work late, but he doesn't have the decency to be courteous to his employees." She does not share Brent's schema about acceptance. Indeed, her choice of action is to refuse to work late that night.

Some schemas may be more believable than others. Shown are schemas about perfectionism. How strongly do you believe each one? When you are through, put a circle around the three schemas you rated the highest. In the next chapter we will begin to look more closely at their accuracy. Our goal will be to evaluate each schema and decide if it is true at all, if it is only true for specific situations, or if it should be rejected altogether.

Remember that inaccurate schemas leave you emotionally distraught and affect your choice of actions adversely. The next step in our program is to adjust, correct, or eliminate schemas that are inac-

SELF-ASSESSMENT

Do I have perfectionistic schemas?

Rate the intensity with which you believe each of these statements, with 100 percent indicating complete agreement and 0 percent indicating that you do not believe it at all.

_____ I must be perfect or I will be rejected.

_____ If I make a mistake it will be horrible.

_____ If I do it perfectly then I will be accepted.

_____ I must be perfect or I will be embarrassed

_____ If I make a mistake I will be humiliated.

_____ When I get it right I will finally accept myself.

_____ When I achieve perfection I will find inner peace.

_____ If I do it perfectly then it will be rewarded.

_____ If others do not approve of me then I am not OK.

_____ If I make a mistake then I am worthless.

_____ I'm not good enough. I must keep trying.

_____ I must be perfect or others will disapprove of me.

_____ If I do it perfectly then everything will work out right.

_____ I'll never be good enough.

_____ If others approve of me then I must be OK.

_____ If I do it perfectly then everyone will notice.

_____ I must be perfect or I will fail.

_____ Things should be done the right way.

_____ There is a right way and a wrong way to do things.

_____ It is possible to do things perfectly.

curate. Having a more accurate view of yourself, your future, others, and the world in general will allow you to make choices that are better for you and reduce the intensity of negative emotions stirred up by perfectionistic schemas.

4

CHALLENGING

YOUR BELIEFS

June's schema is "If I do it perfectly then everything will work out just right." One summer day, June hosted a baby shower for her niece. Twenty women were expected at 2:00 P.M. on a Saturday for a catered luncheon in the garden. June made the cake and decorated for the party. By 1:00 P.M. the sky began to look a little cloudy. June and her daughters quickly moved the tables under the patio, and the rain began to fall by 1:30. June optimistically thought to herself, "These summer showers never last long and it will leave the air feeling moist and fresh." Her anxiety was at a minimum. But by 1:40, when the sprinkle turned into a real rain shower and the caterer had not yet arrived, June was in an absolute panic. She called the caterer and found that he was on his way, delayed by the storm.

In the middle of the commotion, the guests arrived. The first was her niece's mother-in-law, a woman both June and her niece had dreaded seeing. The doorbell rang just as June was looking through her cupboard for something she could make into a quick lunch in case the caterer never came. When she opened the door, June saw the caterer over the mother-in-law's shoulders. The rain slowed, but had not stopped. The mother-in-law was quite peeved that June and her niece had not made better arrangements with Mother Nature. Besides, she felt that this baby shower should have been closer to town so she could avoid the forty-five-minute drive and, by the way, it really should have been scheduled sooner. "My son was a preemie, don't you know," she said. "She can't possibly go to full-term with that child." June's anxiety turned to discouragement and then to despair. Noticing June's changed demeanor, her niece stepped up and quickly engaged her mother-in-law in conversation about the baby. ("Oh, look, Mother Butler, the baby is kicking up a storm. Come feel her. I hope she has beautiful eyes like yours.")

Before June realized, the rain stopped, the caterer set up the lunch, and the party was in full swing. He had even returned the tables in the garden to their original arrangement. June spent the rest of the afternoon waiting for the next disaster. The mother-in-law threw a few curves, but otherwise the shower was a success and June's niece was radiantly happy. June still felt bad about how things started and apologized profusely to her niece. It did not matter how many times her niece reassured her and thanked her, June could not be comforted: "I should have made the lunch myself. I should have known better than to believe the weatherman's report. Your mother-in-law must think your family is not good enough for her son."

"Don't worry," the niece retorted. "I'll never be worthy of her son as far as she is concerned. She doesn't realize just how lucky her son is to be part of a loving family like ours."

June was caught off guard by the problems at the shower. She had done everything right and had expected everything else to fall in line. Remember that her schema is "if I do it perfectly then everything will work out just right." Because everything did not work out "just right" from June's perspective, despite the fact that her niece was pleased and thought the shower was a great success, June blamed herself.

Take time to think about this.

Perfectionist schemas can lead you to make mistakes in your interpretation of events. These misperceptions will influence your choice of actions. If your perceptions are inaccurate, your choice of actions may also be wrong.

That is, she concluded that she must *not* have done everything just right. This is an error in logic.

In the last chapter you began to identify the schemas or beliefs that underlie your perfectionism. In this chapter you will learn some ways to examine them more closely. Whether you hold beliefs that are more typical of inwardly focused or outwardly focused perfectionists, you must decide whether or not your beliefs are valid or true. Perhaps you will find that they are true in some areas of your life but not in others. Perhaps they are true with some of the people in your life, but not with others. Perhaps you will find that some of your beliefs are not true at all. We will discuss several ways to evaluate your beliefs.

Before we proceed, let's review the reasons why you would want to evaluate or challenge your schemas. First of all, schemas are the underlying beliefs or ideas that guide your perceptions of the world, of yourself, and of your future. Schemas that are negative, distorted, or unrealistic will lead you to make mistakes in your interpretation of events. That is, you may see things differently than they really are. Perfectionist schemas are the kinds of ideas that can lead to misperceptions of yourself, of situations, and of other people. These misperceptions will influence your choice of actions. If your perceptions are inaccurate, your choice of actions may also be wrong. Your core beliefs or schemas are in the background all of the time, even if you are not thinking about them, stimulated by situations or events that lead to automatic thoughts. Negative automatic thoughts are those misperceptions or misinterpretations of events that quickly pop into your head in response to a stressful situation. These negative thoughts lead to emotional reactions, behavioral responses, and, sometimes, physiological events, such as having your heart race or your stomach ache.

HOW SCHEMAS INFLUENCE EVENTS

Although Terry is an outwardly focused perfectionist in most situations, she does hold the belief that if she makes a mistake it will be horrible. As she is sitting at her desk signing a letter that was typed by her secretary, she notices an error in the wording. Terry feels the anger and anxiety well up in her. She feels as though she is about to explode. Her immediate thoughts are, "Oh, my God! If this had been sent like this I would have looked like a real idiot. It would have caused me so much embarrassment I would have lost all of the credibility I have worked so hard to gain. They would have thought me incompetent and careless and certainly would not have wanted to trust me with their accounts. I can't believe my secretary did this to me again. I'm going to let her have it. But first I have to check the rest of this letter. I wonder what else has been sent out of here with mistakes. I trusted her on the last few letters without reading them over. I am so stupid. Doesn't she realize my reputation is on the line!"

Terry's actions followed from her perception of the potential consequences of what had happened. Terry called her staff into the office for an emergency meeting. With an angry edge in her voice she described the error in the letter and its implications. She embarrassed her secretary in front of the others: "If I fail, you fail. I pay your salary. Do your job right or you will not have a job. Am I understood?" Terry's secretary left for the ladies' room in silent tears. Terry followed her in and told her to pull herself together. In a more controlled tone, "I have to protect you and all the others. You have to help me by doing your part. Your work is like a mirror held to me. It not only conveys information, it is a reflection of who I am. If it has mistakes in it, I look incompetent. I'm trying to protect all of us. I'm sorry if I came on too strong."

Although there have been some suggestions in the popular psychology literature that you should "let it out" when you are angry or stressed, this free expression of emotions can carry severe consequences if it offends others. Sometimes when we are angry we say things that we do not mean, we say them too loudly or too strongly, or we use words to fight back at someone who has hurt us. The emotion is intense because the stressful event is fresh in our minds and because it is influenced by our immediate take on the situation.

This whole incident was caused by two of Terry's perfectionistic schemas: "If I make a mistake it will be horrible" and "No one cares about doing a good job except me." It was these schemas that influenced Terry's perception of the seriousness of the error in the letter and who was to blame. It led her to view it as a terrible event with potential major consequences for her future. It led her to view her secretary very negatively, and it led to feelings of both anxiety and anger. Terry's choice of action was also influenced by her schema. It made her think that she had to do something about the problem right away, so she lectured her staff and scolded her secretary. Although she tried to put a caring twist on things when she realized that she may have overreacted, she cannot keep her staff from feeling fearful of her—as well as angry and disgusted with her. If making a mistake were not so important to Terry, this incident would not have evolved in this way.

A person with the schema "Mistakes happen, but they are not the end of the world" would have dealt with the incident quite differently. She may have informed the secretary of the error and asked her to be more careful, but probably would have dropped the issue after that. There would not have been the intensity of anger or anxiety experienced by Terry.

Schemas influence your perceptions of things. These perceptions or thoughts pop into your mind quickly and automatically, and are usually accompanied by a burst of emotions. In the next chapter we will learn ways to catch the automatic thoughts that run through your mind when you are troubled. This chapter focuses on the underlying beliefs that influence your automatic thoughts.

CHALLENGING AND CHANGING SCHEMAS

Schemas are hard to change because you have had them for most of your life and are comfortable with them. You may not even be aware of your schemas because they are such a natural part of your perception of things. You change your schemas by taking notice of the experiences you have that are inconsistent with, contrary to, or otherwise do not fit with them. When you are ready to conclude that it is not completely accurate, you change it to make it more accurate. June started attending a women's group at the church and is beginning to learn, with the help of their leader, that some of her schemas are not very accurate. For example, her schema "If I do it perfectly I will be rewarded," which she believed with 90 percent certainty, has turned out to be not true in many cases. She does a number of things perfectly that others do not even notice. June would tell herself that there would be a reward from her husband or her children for taking the extra time to iron their clothes perfectly. "Thanks, Mom" was all she got from her daughter. Her son did not even realize his shirts had been ironed. When Mother's Day came she got the usual candy and flowers. No special treats or special recognition for her extra efforts. It was the same at the kids' schools. She did a lot of work for them, and the reward was a brief compliment and then a request for her to do more work, because she was "sooo good at it."

When June begins to notice the inaccuracy of her schema about there being a reward for perfection, she begins to think twice before volunteering to do extra tasks for the school. She even begins to reevaluate how she spends her time at home. If there is no real reward for going the extra mile, then why do it? She decides that if it makes her feel good, then she will do it. If it is just extra work that no one will notice, then she may skip it. She is certain that there are some things that she does, such as iron the bedsheets, which no one sees or really cares about. As a matter of fact, June does not really care if her sheets are ironed. However, she does like the feel of a freshly ironed pillow cover, so she will continue that chore. With the time that June

---

Take time to think about this.

Ultimately, schemas change when you begin to notice that the experiences you have are inconsistent with, contrary to, or otherwise do not fit with your old views.

is saving, she plans to have some fun. She will reward herself with playtime in exchange for all the hard work she does.

Evaluating Your Schemas

If June can make changes like this, so can you. Here is how you get started. Begin by choosing one of the schemas you rated highest in the exercise "Do I Have Perfectionist Schemas?" from Chapter 3. These are the schemas that you believe most strongly. If your schema is something similar to "Being perfect will lead to something good" or "Not being perfect will lead to something bad," then do Schema Exercise Number 1. If you chose another type of schema, read ahead and follow the exercise that best fits your schema.

In Schema Exercise Number 1 you will have to think about the experiences in your life that have proven that the schema is true. Here June's list is shown.

For the schema you have chosen to evaluate, make a list of the experiences that you have had that could be considered evidence that your schema is true. Write these down in the section of the accompanying box that is labeled "Experiences that Support my Schema." For example, if you chose the schema "I must be perfect or I will be

---

June's Schema Exercise Number 1

Part 1

A. This is my schema:

   "If I do it perfectly then I will be rewarded."

B. Experiences that support my schema:

   1. In 1992, I received a certification of recognition from my daughter's school as "Volunteer of the Year."
   2. Two years ago, my garden was selected to be part of our local Women's Club's "Kaleidoscope of Gardens Spring Tour."
   3. My daughter was chosen prom queen wearing the dress that I made by hand.
   4. Other small recognitions.

embarrassed," make a list of all the times you were less than perfect and you were embarrassed in some way. The embarrassment would probably come from someone recognizing your flaws or from you openly admitting your flaws. If your schema was "If I make a mistake I will be humiliated," make a list of the times you were humiliated in front of others because of your mistakes. Do you get the idea? You might find that for some of the schemas it is not easy to identify times when the schema was true because the circumstances have not happened yet. For example, if your schema is "If I do it perfectly then I will be accepted" you may not have had any experiences where you felt truly accepted. Your conclusion may be that this is because you have not achieved perfection yet. We will address this type of schema in another exercise.

SELF-ASSESSMENT

Schema Exercise Number 1

Part 1

From the schemas you rated at the end of Chapter 3, choose the one you rated the highest, the one you believe the most strongly. Write it in the space (A) below. Make a list of the experiences you have had in your life that you would consider to be evidence that your schema is true. See June's examples to help you get started.

A. This is my schema:

B. Experiences that support my schema:

1. _____

2. _____

3. _____

4. _____

5. _____

The next part of Schema Exercise 1 is a little more difficult. In the box shown, make a list of the experiences you can recall when your schema turned out to be wrong. In June's example, she recalled all of the times when she did things perfectly and she was not rewarded. Some of these were mentioned above. If the schema you chose to evaluate was "I must be perfect or I will be embarrassed" or "If I make a mistake I will be humiliated," make a list of the times you were not perfect, that is, you made a mistake and you were not embarrassed or humiliated. Perhaps you were not embarrassed because no one noticed the error, because no one cared that you had made an error, or you covered for the error so that it was not noticeable to others. *Almost* humiliated does not count.

This is usually a difficult task, because most of these kinds of experiences in life are relatively minor. It is easy to remember the big humiliating events. It is more difficult to remember all the small events that contradict your schema. For example, I experienced a fairly humiliating event last Spring that could be considered evidence in support of the schema "If you make a mistake, especially one that hurts other people, it would be horrible!" I made the rather big mistake of forgetting to pick up my friend from his hotel to take him with me to an important meeting at the convention center. I did not realize that I had forgotten him until he was about ten minutes late for the meeting. When I did realize, I felt frantic at first, so I tried to reach him by phone with no success. When I finally met up with him he could not believe that I had forgotten him. He blamed himself for the mix-up, because he thought me incapable of screwing up so royally. This made me feel guilty, embarrassed, and sad, so I apologized profusely and repeatedly. My automatic thoughts were "I let down a friend, inconvenienced him, put him in a very uncomfortable position, hurt him. He probably thinks that I do not care about him or that I am irresponsible." Because I hold the belief that inconveniencing other people is bad, these particular automatic thoughts were stimulated. This was an experience that I will not soon forget, and my friend has decided not to let me forget it just yet either. (He doesn't expect perfection in me or in others, but he is relishing the opportunity to torture me just a little.)

During this same convention I made a number of other smaller mistakes, but they did not produce the same intense feelings of embarrassment or guilt. I made reservations for lunch with two friends so that we could eat and work on a new book that we are writing. I chose a restaurant that I had not been to in nine years, but I was confident that I could find my way without looking at a map. Of course, I got us so lost that we nearly ran out of time for lunch. My friends were good-natured about it and we enjoyed an impromptu tour of the beach area. We talked while we drove and eventually found a place to eat before our next meeting. No great harm was done. This event would be evidence against my schema that mistakes that affect other people are bad. I made several other small mistakes during that week. I forgot some materials in my hotel room that I needed for a course I was teaching, so my students had to make do without. And I did not recognize my colleague's wife, whom I had met two years prior, so I reintroduced myself to her as if she were a perfect stranger. That was a little embarrassing, but she was as happy to see me as I was to see her, so it turned out to be a fun evening. Knowing myself, I am certain that I made other errors that I was unaware of or do not recall. All other smaller events would be considered evidence against my schema. They were smaller than leaving my friend stranded so they would be easier to overlook.

To sum it up, I had one big experience that could be considered evidence that would support the schema "If I make a mistake that hurts or inconveniences other people, it would be horrible." I also had several experiences that were contrary to the schema. That is, I was not perfect and nothing really bad happened. Those experiences would go into the accompanying box in the section "Experiences that DO NOT support my schema." Do you get the idea?

If you have been able to find any experiences to put in the section of events that DO NOT support your schema, then this means that your schema is probably not 100 percent true. If the evidence does not strongly support your schema, then perhaps it needs to be modified. For example, instead of "I must be perfect or I will be embarrassed," a more accurate schema might be "I worry about what others

SELF-ASSESSMENT

Schema Exercise Number 1

Part 2

Make a list of the experiences you have had in your life that you would consider to be evidence that your schema is not true. See my examples in the text to help you get started.

A. This is my schema:

B. Experiences that DO NOT support my schema:

1. _____

2. _____

3. _____

4. _____

5. _____

think of me or that others will not like me" or "When I make a mistake I worry that others will overlook the good things that I have done and focus only on my errors." Another possibility is that your schema is accurate, but only in certain situations or with certain people. For example, if you have to perform for people who are very likely to be outwardly critical of you, then your assumption that an error will lead to humiliation is probably accurate. I worked in an environment like that at one time. I found myself becoming more self-conscious, as I spent more and more of my time checking my work or watching my because the supervisor's favorite disciplinary style was public humiliation. It was very unpleasant for everyone. Some people learned to be perfect; some learned to lie to cover their errors; and some, like myself, moved on to other work environments.

If your schema is not 100 percent accurate, change it to make it sound more accurate or specify the conditions under which it is accurate. Fill in Part 3 of "Schema Exercise 1" in the box shown with these changes.

If you modified your original schema you are off to a good start. To change your schema altogether you will have to continue to gather evidence that your old schema is inaccurate and that your new schema is more accurate, by making mental notes of your new experiences. If your new schema is working, it will produce less stress than the old one when problems occur. Before you are able to change your schema permanently, you will probably feel a tendency to revert back to your old schema when bad things happen. ("See I was right. You do get embarrassed if you are not perfect.") When you have an emotional shift, ask yourself if you are viewing the situation through your old schema or your new schema. If both your old and new schemas are troublesome, you will need to do some more work to evaluate their accuracy and restate your schema in a way that better fits your experiences. Do not give up on this too quickly. It took many years to develop your old schema, so you should expect that it will take some time to develop a new one.

SELF-ASSESSMENT

Schema Exercise Number 1

Part 3

A. This was my original schema:

B. This schema is only true under the following circumstances:

C. This is a more accurate way to state my original schema:

IN PURSUIT OF PEACE

If the outcome of being perfect that you are searching for is something more existential, then "Schema Exercise 1" probably did not apply. This is because you may not yet have achieved the goal you are pursuing, like self-acceptance, fulfillment, or inner peace, or perhaps you have been lucky enough to experience these things, but only for short periods of time. Perhaps you were so stressed out and exhausted with trying to achieve perfection that when fulfillment came you could not enjoy it. To evaluate these schemas you have to try to understand the logic behind them.

Let's start with the schemas "When I get it right I will finally accept myself" and "When I achieve perfection I will feel better about myself." The big question you need to ask yourself is "Why do I think this way?" The answer is probably something similar to "I don't know. I just do." "Why" questions are hard to answer, so let's go down a different path, starting with the obvious. If you believe that getting things just right in your life will lead to acceptance, then you must not be feeling accepted right now.

Brent feels as though something is missing in his life. He can't exactly put his finger on it, but he thinks it is more of a subjective feeling of being at peace than something material such as a bigger car or a promotion. He wants to feel comfortable with himself. June shares this desire. She wants to stop feeling anxious and being so hard on herself and feel "free" instead. Both June and Brent admire people who seem unburdened by worry or self-consciousness. Their freedom of thought and action is evident in the way they carry themselves, in the looks on their faces, and in the way they do not panic in the face of adversity. That's what June, Brent, and other perfectionists really want, but they think in order to achieve that level of comfort they must be perfect. When they take time to think about it, June and Brent both realize that the people they admire are far from perfect, but they are still reluctant to give up the idea that perfection will lead to a subjective feeling of acceptance. Maybe they don't know how else to achieve that feeling. Perhaps one way to feel self-acceptance is to change the things about you that you do not like.

If you do not feel that you accept yourself, what is it about yourself that you do not like? Is there something that you are doing that causes you a problem? Is there something that you would like to do or that you should be doing? Is there something missing from your life? If you can figure out what is missing, perhaps you can focus on adding these things to your life. If there is something about yourself that you feel the need to change, then maybe you can focus your attention on trying to make that change. Sometimes, if you can accomplish something specific and concrete, it makes you feel better about yourself. This leads us to Schema Exercise 2. List some of the things you would like to change about yourself. Try to be as specific as possible. What things could you do differently that would make you feel better about who you are? These can be new things, such as learning a skill or changing your weight. These can be old things, such as changing a habit, such as smoking, or restarting something you had neglected, such as reading for pleasure or playing golf.

Some perfectionists have accomplished their goals and still do not feel acceptance. They have tested out their schema that perfection will lead to feeling good and have found it to be inaccurate, yet they continue to strive for perfection. While there is nothing wrong with the pursuit, it is troublesome if the pursuit feels like a marathon that never ends.

Acceptance is a subjective feeling, not unlike an emotion. As we have already demonstrated, emotions are influenced by your views. Rather than changing your life or your actions, perhaps peace will be found in a different, less absolute, point of view. Instead of "I must have perfection first, before I can have peace of mind," change it to something less demanding. Perhaps an alternative view is something

---

SELF-ASSESSMENT

Schema Exercise Number 2

If you do not think that you are accepting yourself right now, what would make you feel better about yourself? What are some of the things you would like to stop doing? What things do you need to add to your life?

like "I need to give myself credit for what I do well, even if it is not perfect." Take inventory of your accomplishments or assets. Perhaps you are not giving yourself credit where it is deserved. Perhaps you are withholding approval from yourself.

APPROVAL FROM OTHERS

If the schemas you rated most highly in the exercise "Do I Have Perfectionistic Schemas?" (Chapter 3) have to do with other people's opinions of you as a mirror of your self-worth, then a different strategy is needed for examining them. These include "If other people do not approve of me then I am not OK" or "If other people approve of me then I must be OK." They are more typical of inwardly focused perfectionists, but even outwardly focused perfectionists are not immune to the evaluations of others. Schemas about approval or acceptance are slightly different from the ones discussed previously, because they involve the actions of two people. One is you, a person trying to do his or her best, and the second is the observer or evaluator. This makes it twice as difficult to evaluate, because gaining acceptance depends upon both sides doing their parts. You have to perform well and the other person has to notice, evaluate, and approve of your performance. Remember how distressed Brent felt when he received a less than perfect evaluation from his boss and was then ignored by the big boss as they passed in the hall. Brent took these events very personally. In Brent's mind, these demonstrations seemed like disapproval from others and meant that he was not good enough.

Schema Exercise 3 may help you to determine how accurate these schemas really are, by focusing on the logic behind them. Step 1, do you know when you have done something well? Do you know the difference between a good performance and a poor performance? I know you expect a great deal from yourself, so this is a difficult question to answer. You probably know that most people perform below a level you would consider acceptable, and that average work for you is really good work for someone else. However, if you take time to think about it, I bet you can look at your own work and decide how well you did. If you are capable of evaluating your own performance and making judgments for yourself, you do not need other people to tell you that you did well. You know when you have performed well and when you have not. In fact, you know that the judgments of others are not always correct. Other people may be quick to praise work that you think is substandard or that is not your best. Despite this, the schemas you hold suggest that you only think you have value if other people approve of you. Do you see how the logic breaks down? Step 2 is to question your logic.

Usually what keeps schemas such as "If other people approve of me then I must be OK" alive and well is that these other people are in control of something you want or need, such as a job. Their approval is important, because it means that you might get a raise, keep your job during downsizing, get a bonus or promotion, or it might keep them off of your back. Their approval does not mean that you are OK as a person. Their approval means that you get to keep your job. Keeping your job is important, but it is only one element of your life. Needing approval in order to get the goodies in life that you want, such as a good job, can easily be confused with needing approval in order to feel like you are a worthwhile person. If you do not get the job, you can find another (although you might not want to), but if you do not get approval, you still have yourself and all the other things about you that give you value.

Let's look at another example. Perhaps it is not a job you want to keep, but a relationship. Approval from a significant other can mean that he stays in the relationship with you; disapproval or rejection can mean that he is out the door. The schema "If other people approve of me

---

Take time to think about this.

Do you know when you have done something well? If you are capable of evaluating your own performance, you do not really need approval from others to feel like you have done well.

then I must be OK" can become more significant in romantic relationships, for example, "If he loves me then I have value." In other words, to maintain your sense of self-esteem, the other person must love you. If you are worried and you want a relationship really badly, you may start to think that you have to do everything just right so that the other person will love you. If the target of your affection does not show enough interest, you blame yourself. ("Something is wrong with me. I must not be OK. I must not have value.") Does this sound familiar?

Here are two examples to illustrate the many problems with this line of reasoning. In the last month, two women, Dolores and Kim, came to see me separately for help with depression. Although their circumstances were very different, both had recently been rejected by important men in their lives and felt devalued by their experiences. They both thought that there must be something inherently wrong with them or these men would not have rejected them. Both reasoned that if they had been perfect these men would not have cheated on them, lied to them, stolen from them, or left them. They believed that acceptance by these men determined their worth as human beings. In their minds, rejection by these men meant that they were worthless. Both women were extremely depressed and had even contemplated suicide. Interestingly, in both cases, the men had serious emotional and interpersonal problems, had been through numerous failed relationships, and were having difficulty with their work as well as their personal lives. Dolores and Kim's friends and relatives tried to convince them that these men were not worth keeping. They had caused these women repeated emotional stress, there had been a great deal of conflict, and the future of each looked bleak.

Objectively, each woman could see the errors in her logic. Emotionally, however, each still felt distressed because she believed that "If other people approve of me then I must be OK." To cope with their distress and depression, they had to look more closely at their underlying schema, that if they had only been better partners (i.e., perfect partners), then they would not have been rejected by these men. When each came to my office, she viewed herself as worthless, flawed, weak, and unlovable. Because each held the schema that led to an interpretation of their breakup as being their fault, because they were not perfect, neither of them considered that there were other possible explanations for their relationship problems.

People use their schemas or beliefs to help them make sense of the events in their lives. If an experience seems to fit your schema, you do not challenge your interpretations. If your belief is negative or distorted in some way, you will draw the wrong conclusion, just as Kim and Dolores in the previous example. When they concluded that the relationship problems were their faults, they were left with tremendous sadness and guilt. Those emotions were intense and persistent and interfered with other areas of their lives. To get a handle on their emotional distress they needed a more accurate view of the situation. To accomplish this they needed to generate other possible explanations for their relationships ending and choose a view that made the most sense, one that could be supported by available evidence. This is Step 3. Shown are some examples of their alternative explanations for the breakups.

After they completed their lists, each woman concluded that she had only looked at her half of the problem and had ignored her partner's contribution. They also concluded that allowing their self-esteem to be determined by the evaluations of other people was not a good plan for them. What if that other person is wrong or has dysfunctional or distorted beliefs of his own? Their schema "If other peo-

Kim	Dolores
• Maybe he was seeing someone else.	• Maybe we just weren't meant to be.
• He couldn't handle the fact that I made more money than him.	• Maybe I pushed him away.
• I'm not pretty enough. He wanted someone else.	• He had a bad temper.
• He's just been through a divorce and isn't ready to settle down yet.	• My weight bothered him.
• We are not a good combination. I felt uncomfortable with the relationship.	• He has been cheating on me for years.
	• He cares about himself, not me.
	• He doesn't realize what he's losing.
	• There is something wrong with him.

Take time to think about this.

Your schema helps you interpret events. However, perfectionist schemas may lead you to draw the wrong conclusion. Unfortunately, when your interpretations of events seem to fit with your underlying schema you stop there and do not consider alternative explanations. To help yourself out of this loop, you must consider alternative explanations or interpretations for events.

---

ple approve of me then I must be OK" could be more accurately stated as "What I think of myself is more important than what other people think of me." I would probably add to this something like "Approval from others feels good, but without it I still like myself."

In general, you must treat your perfectionistic schemas as hypotheses rather than facts. Maybe you are right or maybe you are wrong. Perhaps they apply in some situations but not in others (e.g., at work, but not at home) or with some people, such as your uptight boss, but not with others, such as your new boyfriend. Rather than stating your schema as a fact, restate it as a suggestion. For example, "It seems to me that I have to be perfect in order to be accepted" or "Perhaps if I can get everything just right, I will feel better about myself and my life." Consider the possibility that these assumptions are incorrect or oversimplify what you really need to do to feel OK about yourself or to have a good life. Gather evidence from your experiences in the past, from your observations from others, or by talking to other people to determine if your schemas are accurate. Do things always happen in a way that your schemas would predict? If not, it is time to try on a new schema. This is Step 4.

In the next chapter we will begin to address your immediate emotional reactions to events that seem to be stimulated by perfectionist schemas. If you can closely examine and modify your schemas about being perfect your immediate reactions to stressful events will become less intense. While this chapter started with changing your basic beliefs, you can also work toward gaining better control over your perfectionism by getting a handle on the spontaneous and immediate thoughts that fuel your emotions and strengthen your negative perfectionistic schemas.

5

AUTOMATIC THOUGHTS

AND THINKING ERRORS

Brent had invited his date, Susan, to come up to his apartment for a drink before going out to dinner. Susan had arrived and was sitting on the couch while Brent poured the wine. As he walked toward her with the glasses he tripped and dropped and broke one of the glasses of wine against the coffee table, spilling wine on his new shirt. He immediately felt both embarrassment and fear. His automatic thoughts were at first self-critical. ("I am such an idiot. I can't believe I did that.") They quickly changed to negative predictions. ("She must think I am a total loser. She probably wants to get out of here as quickly as she can. She is going to tell everyone at work about this. I will be humiliated even more than I am now. I should never have dated a woman from the office.") His anxiety turned to panic and he thought, "This is the only bottle of wine I chilled, what am I going to do? My shirt is ruined and I don't have anything else decent to wear. This is not going to work. The evening is ruined." He had not even reached down to pick up the pieces of glass before he had run through all of these thoughts and many more. That is the nature of automatic thoughts. They flood your thinking in response to stressful events.

Susan had some automatic thoughts of her own. She thought, "Oh my God! Poor guy. Is he OK? That's something I would have done. I'm so glad it was him and not me. He is probably freaking out right now. He gets so nervous about things. He probably thinks I'll hate him. I'll help him clean up." Her feelings were empathy and amusement. They cleaned up and had a nice evening. Brent has hardwood floors in his living room, so the wine did not stain anything. His date helped him with the choice of shirts by telling him he looked great in blue. So he switched to a blue shirt that he thought she would like. His predictions about her were not accurate and he was able to calm himself, while she shared some of her most embarrassing dating experiences with him. They both laughed, and he stopped thinking of himself as such a loser.

If you read the earlier chapters you already know that the way you think about things and your emotions are strongly connected to one another. Intense emotions that make you feel bad are usually accompanied by negative automatic thoughts. Positive or neutral automatic thoughts usually accompany positive or neutral emotions. Automatic thoughts, the ideas that just pop into your head quickly, without effort, and with little or no awareness, happen thousands of times each day. When you are upset by something, automatic thoughts run through your head telling you how to view the situation.

When you get upset, you may not be aware of your automatic thoughts, but you can usually feel the emotions that go along with them. For some people, the emotion produces some kind of physical reaction, such as stomach discomfort, tears in the eyes, tightness in the shoulders or neck, or nail biting. When you recognize these feelings you know that something upsetting is going on.

Most important, negative automatic thoughts are often inaccurate in some way or altogether wrong. They may "feel right" at some instinctual level, even if you have no proof that they are right. Some people call these gut-level feelings. Remember that negative automatic thoughts are usually accompanied by intense negative emotions such as sadness, anger, or panic. Therefore, if your thinking is inaccurate your emotional reaction may also be distorted. Negative automatic thoughts are shaped by your underlying schemas, such as the ones discussed in Chapter 3. Brent's schema of "I must be perfect or I will be rejected" is what stimulated his negative predictions that his date would reject him in some way because he spilled the wine.

Although everyone is susceptible to having negative automatic thoughts in response to stressful events, scholars such as Steve Hollon, Ph.D., at Vanderbilt University have found that negative automatic thoughts are more common among people who are experiencing depression than in nondepressed individuals. In fact, A. John Rush, M.D., and G. Gregory Eaves at the University of Texas Southwestern Medical Center at Dallas have found that the more depressed an individual feels, the more she is likely to report having negative automatic thoughts.

While you are working on challenging and changing your perfectionist schemas you will still have emotional or negative automatic thoughts that cause you to be upset. The exercises in this chapter will help you to recognize negative automatic thoughts when they occur and change them so that they are more accurate or logical. This will help to reduce your intense emotional reactions that go along with these negative thoughts. These methods for controlling negative automatic thoughts, which are based on Dr. Beck's Cognitive Therapy methods, have been proven in numerous clinical studies to greatly improve symptoms of depression. Although you may get distressed and not clinically depressed, these methods will help

---

Automatic Thoughts

- Automatic thoughts are the ideas that just pop into your head without effort. They happen thousands of times each day.
- Negative automatic thoughts are accompanied by lots of emotion.
- Negative automatic thoughts are often inaccurate in some way or altogether wrong.

you control the negative emotional experiences that are stimulated by your negative automatic thoughts.

THINKING ERRORS

There are some common negative automatic thoughts that people have that are usually incorrect. These patterns are called "thinking errors" because they result from mistakes or errors in processing information. David Burns, in his book *Feeling Good: The New Mood Therapy,* has described more than a dozen types of thinking errors that fall into roughly three groups. The first group of thinking errors involves misperceptions of events. The second group, clairvoyant thinking, involves making guesses about other people or events. The third group is called tunnel vision and occurs when you have a narrow view of things and miss additional important information. The thinking error most common among perfectionists, oversimplification, is a type of tunnel vision where conclusions are drawn that overlook important details and lead to an oversimplified view of situations. In this chapter we will briefly explore these groups of thinking errors, and look more closely at oversimplification. The next chapter deals specifically with learning techniques for correcting oversimplification.

Misperceptions

Magnification. Brent got a call from the budget office telling him that his department was running out of money. His projected expenditures for the next quarter exceeded his budget. Brent had always been very careful in managing his department's budget so that this kind of thing never happened. He would rather give back money at the end of the year than be in the hole. Brent, true to character, took this news hard. He felt angry with himself, humiliated in front of the budget director, and he was fearful for his department. What if he couldn't cover salaries? He would have to go to his boss and admit that he had made a mistake in his calculation and "borrow" money from the company until he could recoup his losses. How embarrassing!

One of the most common types of misperceptions is called magnification. In magnification, a person sees a problem as being larger or more unmanageable than it really is. Sometimes this is called "blowing it out of proportion." As the problem grows in size, the emotion grows in intensity. As the emotion escalates, the scariness of the thought is magnified.

As it turns out, the budgeting error was caused by some expenses in a new project that he had not anticipated. Brent took care of the problem and no one went without a paycheck. The humiliation really set him back, however. He withdrew from his colleagues who knew about his budget, checked and rechecked figures the next time, and began to question his own judgment. His superiors, however, hardly noticed the event. They know that departments in his company go over budget all of the time. Budgets are just good guesses, because department heads cannot always anticipate every expense. No one thought this was a big deal except for Brent. The event had been magnified in his head and left him feeling distressed.

One of the most effective and quickest ways to fix misperceptions is to get feedback from other people. Friends, relatives, or co-workers can see your situation from a different angle. Brent could have called his friend Lily to ask if she had ever been over budget and what the consequences had been. Lily would have told him that it is common for departments to have temporary money problems and that no one expects him to always be perfectly on budget. Besides, the amount of his overage was only about 1 percent of his annual budget. She would have said, "Calm down. So you make mistakes like the rest of us. This is not a big deal."

Another way to try to correct your misperceptions is to do the exercise from Chapter 4 where you examined the evidence that supports your view and the evidence against your view. In Brent's case, he could have made a list of the things that made him think that the budget problem was a big deal. Then he could have made a list of things that suggested that this was not a big deal. Brent's evidence for the idea would have included the fact that he needed more money and that he had made an error in calculations. He would have also included that he had heard stories about his predecessor, who had been poor at managing money and had been fired for repeatedly going over his budget. He would instinctually want to add to the list that his boss thought he was an idiot, but this would be just his guess. His boss had never been directly or indirectly critical on this issue, so it would have been more of an assumption than a fact. On the list of evidence against the idea that this was a big problem Brent probably would have written that there was a procedure for adding money to your budget when needed, therefore this must not be an unusual occurrence. His friend on the fifth floor had gone over budget last quarter and had no real problems. Brent did not think badly of him; neither did anyone else. He might have also included on this side that when the budget director called him to inform him of the problem, he did not act as though it was a problem. He told Brent how to fix it. Besides, unlike his predecessor, Brent has always been very good at managing money and at completing tasks very close to budget. If Brent had done this exercise instead of torturing himself, he would have calmed down when he realized that there was no problem with the budget that could not be fixed easily and that no one really thought twice about it except for him.

Minimization. Another type of misperception is called "minimization." This thinking error leads people to make less of positive things. A common example is when a person is feeling low and something good happens. There may be a tendency to dismiss the good event as not important given all the negative aspects of his life. In this case, the person perceived the event as being smaller or less signifi-

---

Combating Magnification

1. Become aware of your tendency to magnify the negative or minimize the positive.
2. Get feedback from other people.
3. Examine the evidence that supports your view and the evidence against your view.

Take time to think about this.

If you are looking for big events or big changes, small accomplishments mean less. The problem is that life is generally made up of a lot of small positive events and relatively few big positive events. If you ignore the small ones and wait for the big ones you are going to feel unfulfilled or unhappy much of the time.

---

cant than it was. Another way to minimize is to say to yourself that the good event, for example a compliment from someone or a small task completed, does not really count, because there is so much more to do, so far to go. In this way, the positive events seem too small to count given the larger amount of work needing to be accomplished. Another way to minimize is to say, "If it is easy to accomplish, then it really doesn't count." If you are looking for big events or big changes, small accomplishments mean less. The problem is that life is generally made up of lot of a small positive events and relatively few big positive events. If you ignore or disregard the small ones and wait for the big ones you are going to feel unfulfilled or unhappy much of the time.

As with all thinking errors, part of the process of reducing error is to become aware of your tendency to misperceive events. If you think you have a tendency to magnify the negative and minimize the positive, watch for it. If it happens, it will usually be in response to an event and will be accompanied by a noticeable shift in emotions.

To address minimizing, it is helpful to take time at the end of each day to think about all the small positive events that occurred during the day. These can be events that made you feel good or that gave you a sense of accomplishment. Keep a running list. See how the small accomplishments add up to larger gains. If you are accustomed to looking at events as either good or bad, you may have trouble with this exercise. Minimization of the positive will lead you to conclude that all but the really great events do not count. Rather than limiting yourself to two choices, good events and those that do not count, think about positive events on more of a continuum. For example, imagine that good events range on a continuum from not at all good (0 percent good) to fabulous (100 percent good). Most events are not at either

0–25% Good	25–50% Good	50–75% Good	75–100% Good
The doughnuts were not stale. No bills came in the mail today.	Found a good parking space when I was in a hurry. I had a good workout at the gym.	Donna in accounting smiled at me when I walked by her desk. My computer did not have any problems today.	The budget problem was solved. I did not get fired.

extreme, but fall somewhere in the middle: "Not bad, but not great." Divide your continuum into four parts: 0% to 25% good, 25% to 50% good, 50% to 75% good, and 75% to 100% good. When you sit back and take stock of your day, categorize the good events into one of the four categories. Shown is an example from Brent's day.

Brent is training himself to stop minimizing the positive and maximizing the negative. He knows that he has a tendency to dwell on negative experiences and overlook positive experiences. Part of his program is that he makes himself take stock of his day, particularly when he is feeling stressed or upset. This forces him to acknowledge when things go right, even if they are not big events. He is becoming more skilled at paying attention to small positive events as they occur throughout the day. This gives him a more balanced perspective on his day, rather than having his internal radar tuned only to bad experiences.

Clairvoyant Thinking

There appear to be some people in the world with the gift of being able to read the thoughts of others or to foresee future events. I have never met anyone with these gifts, but I have heard enough tales and read enough stories to believe that they exist. These are fairly unique gifts, not found or not readily accessible in the average person. Unfortunately, most people believe that they are able to read the minds of others, predict everyday events, or "know" what has happened without sufficient information. They usually make educated guesses about what people might be thinking based on their experiences and their personal feelings and, occasionally, they are correct. Because they guess correctly some of the time, their false belief in their ability to read minds is reinforced. When people try to guess about events or predict the future, these guesses are often based on their fears rather than on facts. But sometimes their predictions are correct, so it gives them confidence to continue making guesses and predictions. "Mind reading," "fortune-telling," and "jumping to conclusions" are three types of clairvoyant thinking. They are generally incorrect predictions that people make about others, about events, or about the future and are often negative.

Mind reading. Almost everyday in my clinical practice I hear someone say that they know what their friend, or boss, or child, or spouse is thinking. It is not unusual for people to say that they know what I am thinking. What is fascinating to me is how often they are wrong. Their incorrect guesses come from misinterpretations of facial expressions or other body language as well as from their belief in their own ability to read minds. Mind reading leads to trouble when it is incorrect, when it makes you feel bad about others, and when it leads to the wrong choice of actions. It is very unfair to others because it does not give them the opportunity to convey their own thoughts. I try to train married couples out of mind reading. I encourage them to ask questions rather than make assumptions. That way they will know what is really going on and they will make fewer mistakes. The way to verify your guesses about people is to ask. You can first tell them your guess ("You look like you are mad at me") and then ask for verification ("Are you?"). This is much better than "I know you are mad at me, so don't deny it."

Take time to think about this.

Mind reading leads to trouble when it is incorrect, when it makes you feel bad about others, and when it leads to the wrong choice of actions. Ask questions rather than make assumptions.

Fortune-telling. Fortune-telling is often inaccurate because the predictions are influenced by emotion rather than by logic. Negative predictions are usually accompanied by fear. Sometimes this is called catastrophizing, because the more the person thinks about what could happen the worse it gets, until it seems as if she is headed for a catastrophe. For example, June got a letter from her mother-in-law indicating that she planned to visit at the end of the month. June knows that her mother-in-law is not in great health and can be very demanding at times. In June's imagination she saw herself being a slave to this woman. She imagined that her mother-in-law would have another stroke while she was in town and would become further disabled and unable to return home. June would be stuck with this woman forever, because none of her sisters-in-laws would tolerate this woman in their homes. June's anxiety was sky-high until her mother-in-law finished her visit and left her house in good health.

Fortune-telling errors will alter your course of action in the wrong direction. This is not to say that you will always be wrong when you make guesses. Those guesses that are based on information, including past experiences and other relevant events, are not necessarily fortune-telling. If you predict that a bad thing is going to happen and cannot explain why, or if your only reason is "I just think it will happen" or "I can feel it," then you are very likely making a fortune-telling error.

The best way to tell fact from fortune-telling is to look at the evidence you have to support your prediction and the evidence you have against your prediction. If you cannot tell the difference between fact and fantasy, then you probably need more information. Ask others what they think. If your prediction is correct and the event you anticipate is a bad one, think about how you can prevent the bad event from occurring. Also take some time to plan what you will do if the bad event does occur.

Sorting Fact from Fiction

The best way to tell a fact from a fortune-telling error is to look at the evidence you have to support your prediction and the evidence you have against your prediction.

Jumping to Conclusions. Jumping to conclusions is probably the most common form of clairvoyant thinking. It involves making assumptions about an event before you have enough information. This is different from fortune-telling because the event has already occurred and you are making assumptions about what has happened. Jumping to a conclusion can be a problem if you draw a negative conclusion about something and your conclusion is wrong. For example, you get a voice-mail message from your boss that he wants to see you and his tone of voice sounds funny. You could jump to the conclusion that you are in trouble. These thoughts are usually accompanied by a great deal of anxiety. If you act on your fears, you would probably make the wrong choice of actions. Jumping to conclusions usually leads to trouble, because you are making guesses rather than getting more information and reacting to facts.

The conclusion you draw may be the first one that pops into your head. Because it came to you quickly you might assume that it is accurate. To keep yourself from jumping to inaccurate conclusions you have to make yourself slow down and think of other possible explanations or interpretations. In the prior example, a call from the boss led to a quick conclusion that you were in trouble. If you take a minute to consider other explanations for the funny tone you heard in your boss's voice, you might conclude that you imagined a negative tone that was not there. Perhaps he had a negative tone, but it had nothing to do with you, or perhaps his negative tone had something to do with you, but it is not a problem that you could not handle. This type of exercise is called generating alternative explanations. When you do this exercise, let yourself generate all kinds of alternative explanations, not just the most obvious ones. As you are making the list, do not stop to consider the likelihood that each is true. Just let yourself be creative and make the list. If it were my boss, I would probably have wondered if that tone in his voice was a result of sinus congestion, a fight this morning with his wife, his use of a speakerphone, wrinkling his nose to push his glasses up, constipation, a sip of old coffee, some other worker who irritated him just before the phone call, bad news from his stockbroker, or bad news from his teenage son. After you have made the list you can look it over and

> ### Generate Alternative Explanations
>
> Jumping to conclusions usually leads to trouble because you are making guesses rather than getting more information and reacting to facts. Slow down and consider other possible conclusions. Here are the steps:
>
> 1. Generate all kinds of alternative explanations, not just the most obvious ones.
> 2. Do not stop to evaluate each idea.
> 3. Look over the list and cross out any explanations that are not at all likely.
> 4. Of the remaining explanations, try to choose one that is the most likely explanation.
> 5. If you are still uncertain, gather more information.

cross out any explanations that are not at all likely. It is easier to do this on a piece of paper than in your head. Of the remaining explanations, try to choose one that is the most likely explanation. If, after the exercise, you are still uncertain, you will need to gather more information by talking with your boss before drawing your conclusion. In the meantime, rather than spending your time and energy imagining the worst-case scenario, take a moment to calm yourself with some deep breaths or by walking away for a few minutes. This way your words or actions will not be driven by your fears. If you cannot help but worry, you can either distract yourself from the problem until you can deal with it directly or you can use some of the mental energy to develop a plan for how to cope with the worst-case scenario.

Tunnel Vision

The third group of thinking errors involves having "tunnel vision." In tunnel vision you are focused too narrowly and miss important information that is outside the tunnel. This leads to distortions, inaccuracies, or an incomplete view of situations. Self-blame is an example of tunnel vision. Self-blame focuses narrowly on how you may have done something wrong, without looking at the bigger picture of what is happening around you. You ignore additional information that is outside of the tunnel and focus only on the pieces you see initially. People who habitually blame themselves do it automatically, without a great deal of thought. Self-blame is often accompanied by feelings of guilt. The guiltier you may feel, the easier it is to blame yourself and to ignore facts that lead to a different conclusion. Self-blame, like other thinking errors, is driven by emotion and not likely to be entirely accurate. When this happens you need to make the logical part of you work to counter the negativity coming from the emotional part of you. Most people, when they are upset, know in the back of their minds that they are being too hard on themselves. Logically they know that they are not entirely to blame. Despite knowing this, when they are upset they ignore what the rational part of their thinking is saying and tune in to the emotional messages only. For example, "I know there is a good reason why I didn't get that job, but I feel so stupid. I'm a failure. I can't do anything right." The way out of self-blame is to make yourself listen to the rational voice in your head. If this is too difficult, try putting yourself in the position of adviser to someone with the same problem. For example, what would you tell your best friend or your partner if he was feeling bad over the same kind of situation that you are in. What if it was your sister who did not get the job? Would you tell her that she is stupid, that she is a failure, or that she cannot do anything right? Probably not! Instead, you would offer some alternative ways of looking at the problem. Pretend that you are giving the advice to others and listen to your voice of logic. Believe me, it is much easier to give advice to others than to yourself.

Oversimplification. Perfectionists frequently make the error of

---

Ways to Cope

While you are trying to work through a thinking error, take a moment to calm yourself. This way your words or actions will not be driven by your emotions. Instead, control your emotions so that you have better control over your actions. If you cannot help but worry either distract yourself from the problem until you can deal with it directly or you can use some of the mental energy to develop a plan for how to cope with the worst case scenario.

oversimplification, a type of tunnel vision. With oversimplification, things are inaccurately viewed as belonging to only one of two simple categories such as right or wrong, good or bad, perfect or not. When conclusions about people or events are oversimplified, it is because additional information that does not neatly fit into either category is overlooked, ignored, or disregarded. Because errors of oversimplification lead to absolute or black or white conclusions about things, it has also been referred to by cognitive therapists as absolute, dichotomous, all-or-nothing, and black-and-white thinking, because the perfectionist cannot always see the shades of gray between the extremes. Because perfectionists hold the belief that perfect is the way things ought to be, anything else can only fit into the category of less than perfect, thus a two-category system emerges.

There are several ways in which oversimplification causes trouble for perfectionists. To begin with, it can leave you feeling overwhelmed and stuck. Imagine that you have not had time to keep up with things at your office or in your home. Each time you walk into the room you see a hundred different things that need to be done. You experience the work as one big mess and you know that you will never have enough time or energy to start, let alone finish, it all. Thinking about it arouses a mix of feelings, leaving you feeling overwhelmed. When you are overwhelmed, you have even less energy, less interest in doing the work, and very little motivation. You are stuck. It is too much to handle right now, so you do nothing. The work piles up and you continue to feel overwhelmed when you think about being behind. To cope, it is often easier to turn your back to it and do something else that is more interesting or gratifying. Some people read to escape, watch television, or leave the problem behind and go elsewhere. Some people get busy with other chores that are more tolerable and ignore the mess. Oversimplification leaves you with only two options: do it all or do nothing. Joseph R. Ferrari and William T. Mautz of De Paul University in Chicago found that in older college students, perfectionism was associated with what they called "attitudinal inflexibility," such as seeing things in black and white or oversimplified terms. This was particularly true for those with more inwardly oriented perfectionism.

Take time to think about this.

When you see chores to be done as one big mess, you oversimplify the problem. You may even say to yourself something like "I can't get it all done" or "I can't stand to look at it," or you may just feel overwhelmed and walk away. You cannot get started because you cannot imagine getting it all done.

In contrast, those who do not oversimplify can see each individual task when they look at a big mess. Let's take housekeeping as an example. Oversimplification makes you see the housework as one big problem that you cannot even begin to fix. If you do not oversimplify, but are able to look at one chore at a time, you start to see things differently. You see that clothes need to be put away or washed. You see that some carpet areas need to be vacuumed and some floors need to be swept. You might see that things need to be put away or that shelves need to be dusted. If you can see individual tasks then you can try to do one thing at a time rather than taking on the whole cleaning job at one time. Use the skills of a perfectionist. Be detail-oriented. Look at smaller details apart from the whole task. Take on one piece at a time. You will begin to make progress and feel a sense of accomplishment. This will, in turn, improve your motivation and your mood.

Another place that oversimplification can cause you trouble is when you are unable to accomplish a goal that you have set for yourself. Joe's younger brother, John, was out of work after hurting his

---

Getting Unstuck

For a task or problem that feels overwhelming, make a list of its smaller steps or parts. Arrange the list of steps or parts in order, if there is one, so that number one is the first thing to be accomplished. Make a plan for accomplishing the first step. When you have made progress, go on to the next step. Sometimes it is easier to complete the smaller or simpler steps first. Set goals for when you would like to complete each step. Give yourself credit for completing each step.

back on the job. He is a hardworking man and had not taken well to being out of work or disabled. His doctor had cleared him to return to work, but he would have to do a job that was easier on his back until he was stronger. This meant desk work. John thought it would be humiliating to be stuck at a low-level job. He was used to working with his crew and being in charge. The thought of not being able to work at his usual level made him feel worse. He got more depressed, his back pain worsened, and he had to delay returning to work. The psychological burden of not being able to reach his employment goal left him feeling like a total failure. In fact, he would say that if he could not go back to his old job he would rather not work at all. He wanted it all or nothing.

Terry's best friend, Joann, had a bout of depression last Fall. By early spring she was feeling more like her old self, though not 100 percent quite yet. She had been in therapy and had learned several ways to control her depressed moods and her negative thoughts. With effort, she was able to return to her usual household and work routines. One Saturday morning she awoke feeling rotten. She had not felt this way for a month and had thought it was all behind her. Joann became very distressed about the fact that she felt sad. She also felt angry and criticized herself for being weak. Her mood seemed to worsen. The hours passed until she realized that she had stayed in bed and read books or watched television for the entire weekend. When she saw her therapist on Monday, she reported how she "had failed." She thought that she had recovered from the depression, but this weekend had been proof that she was back where she had started. The therapist helped Joann understand how this was another example of oversimplification. From Joann's point of view, if she was not 100 percent well then she must be sick. Since she had been fine the previous week, Joann thought she had lost all of her therapeutic gains. In fact, she was significantly better than she had been in the Fall. Her troubles over the weekend started with an unexplainable shift in her mood, but got much worse because of the way she had handled it, with self-criticism, inactivity, and isolation. Getting over a depression is not simple. It does not turn on and then turn off. Going back to work is not that simple. It is not usually the case that you are unemployed at one moment and in the job of your dreams the next (unless you are very lucky). Going from one place to the other generally takes time, and setbacks are likely to occur. Persistence helps you to achieve your goal.

When things go wrong, oversimplification will stop you in your tracks. If you oversimplify and see your efforts as either successes or failures, anything short of complete success will make you feel like a failure. Here is another way to think about it. Picture yourself sitting back in your chair and wadding up a piece of paper to throw it in the wastebasket across the room. You throw the paper and sometimes it makes it in the basket and sometimes it does not. Every wad of paper that lands in the basket is a success (like a slam dunk or a three-pointer). Every piece of paper that does not make it into the basket falls onto the floor. Those missed shots represent failures (like a missed free throw). With oversimplification, any attempt that you make that is not a success feels like a failure, no matter how close you got to the basket. Almost is not good enough. You either made it or you didn't. Because getting it just right is difficult to achieve and occurs only a small portion of the time, the rest of the time you are left feeling like a failure, no matter how close you were to actually achieving your goal. You never feel good enough.

This kind of thinking is rough on perfectionists who are feeling down because they are out of work, injured, having family troubles, or experiencing other kinds of hardships. At these times in life it is difficult to make everything go just right. Getting problems straightened out or getting back on your feet usually takes time. Sometimes you have to work at achieving your goals one small step at a time. A leap to the kind of success you might want is not always possible. This is very frustrating for perfectionists.

John and Joann think like inwardly focused perfectionists. Outwardly focused perfectionists oversimplify in a different way. Going back to our basketball analogy, outwardly focused perfectionists are like fans on the sideline watching the player try to make the basket. When the player (usually an employee, a student, a child, or a spouse) throws the ball and misses the basket, the perfectionist "fan" criticizes him as a loser or a failure. Labels such as these are simple ways to size up a situation ("He's stupid, lazy, a jerk, or a loser"), but they are usually oversimplifications of what is really going on.

For outwardly focused perfectionists, getting close or almost making it does not really count, for three reasons. First, the person did not make the basket (did not succeed). Second, you could have made the basket if you had done it yourself. Third, you are expected by others to always make the basket. What is expected of you, you expect of others. This is only fair, and many people believe that life should be fair—and get upset when it is not. When an outwardly focused perfectionist oversimplifies things it causes problems for both him and for the target of his criticism. In contrast to the inwardly focused perfectionist, whose oversimplification leads to feelings of sadness or anxiety, the outwardly focused perfectionist feels anger and frustration. For some, oversimplification only occurs when they are already in an angry or irritable mood and are viewing things negatively. Disappointments (missing the basket) only confirm the negative mind-set that things will never be good enough.

Most people make mistakes and will not perform perfectly all of the time. If the outwardly focused perfectionist expects others to always do things right, he is going to be disappointed and frustrated a great deal of the time. For example, I sometimes drive in a car pool with a perfectionist who expects other drivers on the road to drive as well as she does. Inevitably, she gets angry with the drivers who are going too slow, too fast, cut in front of her, or take too long to move after the light turns green. She oversimplifies when she gets angry because she views the other drivers' performances as "wrong." It is very simple for her because she has a clear picture of the right and wrong way to drive. Unfortunately, the other drivers follow a different set of rules and could care less what my friend thinks.

A patient of mine who is more of an outwardly focused perfectionist feels angry when other people make errors, forget things, misplace objects that he needs, respond too slowly, or give him incorrect information. These kinds of things would probably bother most people, but for some perfectionists these errors feel personal. It can seem as if others are intentionally doing these things just to irritate you. In most cases, these situations are not that simple. They do not involve just the perpetrator (the one who made the mistake) trying to do harm to the victim (the perfectionist). There are usually many other circumstances that influence the situation. For example, the person giving misinformation may be new on the job, may have been misinformed by her boss, may be correct under different circumstances, or may have misunderstood the question. When you oversimplify, none of these "excuses" matter because you are focused only on the wrongdoing and your upset feelings.

Oversimplification can cause problems with other people and sooner or later the perfectionist must pay the consequences for overreacting. When Joe locked himself out of his car he called his wife, Maria, to bring him another set of keys, but she was not home. Joe paged Maria on her beeper, but thirty minutes passed and she did not respond. Joe was furious. He was behind schedule and was not sure how he was going to get out of this predicament. Forty-five minutes after he paged his wife she finally called him back. She had been out for her morning walk and had not carried her beeper. She got Joe's message on the answering machine, called him back, and took him his keys. Joe was fuming by the time Maria got to him. He lashed out at her for keeping him waiting, for not carrying her beeper, and for letting him down when he needed her. Maria had suspected that Joe would probably be in a bad mood when she got there. As she was driving to meet him she told herself to not take it personally when he turned on her. She tried to keep her mouth shut, but Joe's anger had ruined her lovely morning. Maria did not mind taking him his keys, but she did mind his anger. She tried to show compassion for his frustration. She tried to explain that when she exercised she did not carry a beeper. When his anger continued and he refused to accept her "excuses" she defended herself by counterattacking.

In the back of Joe's mind he knew that he was angry and that it could make him say things he really didn't mean. Before Maria arrived he tried to tell himself not to get angry with her. But in Joe's mind, the matter was really quite simple; Maria had not been there when he needed her. In addition to locking himself out of his car and missing appointments, Joe now had a marital problem on his hands.

Maria does not bounce back quickly from these kinds of arguments. She would still be angry with him at the end of the day.

Oversimplified criticisms of strangers will not create problems if they cannot hear your criticism ("You moron!"). However, when the target of the oversimplification is someone you have to get along with or someone who will counterattack, problems can quickly develop. For example, if you misinterpret someone's mistake as being a personal offense ("She wasn't there when I needed her"), you will feel bad about them and about the relationship and it will show in your behavior. Another way that oversimplification causes relationship problems is that it makes people feel bad about you if you are critical or if you do not give them the opportunity to defend themselves.

Oversimplification can also cause relationship problems when your partner tries to talk you out of your oversimplification. This is particularly true when you are angry with someone else and your partner tries to intervene. If she tries to explain that you are oversimplifying the situation and that really it is much more complicated, it can lead to conflict. Although your partner may be trying to be helpful, it usually feels like she is taking sides against you. I made this mistake with my husband several times before I realized what I was doing. My husband would come home from work in the emergency room with complaints about the nurses that work there. I would listen and then try to reason with him. I would explain the psychology of ER work and the role of nurses and doctors. I thought that I was being perfectly logical and reasonable. I believed that if my husband could see it from my point of view he would have a better understanding of ER dynamics and would calm down. But all my husband could hear was that I was siding with the nurses against him. I was either with him or against him, simple as that. It took a while before I figured out that what seemed like a logical and reasonable approach was leading to conflict. Once I figured it out, I was able to look at the situation from my husband's point of view. For him it was a simple matter of taking sides. Once I recognized how he saw things, I was able to respond to his needs more effectively. After that, when he would come home and complain about the nurses, I would listen to his complaints and then say something such as "I'm sorry you had a bad day. Is there anything I can do for you right now?" Once he could get it all out, he would calm down on his own. He did not need my psychological insights. He just needed comfort after a hard day.

WHY NOT KEEP IT SIMPLE?

There is usually a good side and a bad side to most ways of thinking. Before you try to change your way of thinking altogether it is usually a good idea to know what you will lose by changing your view. For perfectionists, oversimplification is the thinking error that causes them the most grief. We've explored the disadvantages, so what are the advantages of oversimplification? First of all, it simplifies life. If you have only two categories to choose from it is easier to sort things out as good or bad. You have one set of rules that applies to everyone. Everyone either follows or breaks your rules. Second, if you are trying to figure things out for yourself or if you are trying to judge others, you can categorize situations or people more easily if you only have two choices, good and bad, right and wrong, success or failure.

It may seem a lot easier to raise children when you oversimplify. You tell them what is right and wrong, good or bad, and they know what to do. As long as they experience people and situations that fall into one of those two groups, they can understand their world. Unfortunately, it does not take long for your children to realize that some bad things are actually good ideas and some good things are hurtful to others. Some bad people do good things and some good people do bad things. Your children will make mistakes, fail, act stupid, forget their manners, or tell a lie. Sometimes they will do these things to protect themselves, defend themselves, make others feel good, or just because they are feeling playful. How do you apply the rigid rules of right and wrong in these situations? It is not so simple, is it? To more fully understand the world and the people in your lives, you have to expand your view.

There are three big disadvantages of oversimplification. The first is that oversimplification causes considerable emotional distress. If you have oversimplified definitions of success and failure, where success is perfection or getting things "just right," you will feel like a failure every time you do not meet that standard. Perfection is rarely achieved. "Close" and "almost" do not count for you. Therefore, you have to live life feeling like a failure—and hoping that no one else finds out the truth.

The second big disadvantage of oversimplification is that it leads to practical consequences. Trying to be perfect means that too much time and energy is spent getting things "just right." That time and energy could be committed to other aspects of life that are more enjoyable. If you have oversimplified definitions of what is good and what is not, you will waste a lot of good stuff (ideas, work, products) because they did not seem good enough.

The third big disadvantage of oversimplification is that it can cause a lot of problems in your relationships with others. If you find yourself judging people, feeling irritated with their actions, or being tough on them in some other way, you both lose out. You lose the support and help that you might need from the relationship and the other person feels hurt or rejected. If this pattern is common in your relationship, those who are judged or criticized in an oversimplified manner will turn away from you.

How do you stop oversimplifying? The way to do this is to move from a two-category system, where things are oversimplified as good

---

Advantages of Oversimplification

1. It simplifies life.
2. You can categorize situations or people more easily if you only have two choices, good and bad.
3. It is a lot easier to raise children when you oversimplify. You tell them what is right and wrong, good or bad, and they know what to do.

Disadvantages of Oversimplification

1. It causes considerable emotional distress.
2. Too much time and energy is spent getting things "just right."
3. It can cause problems in your relationships with others.

or bad, and move to a system where you can see all the shades of gray in between. The next chapter focuses on ways to avoid or reduce over-simplification by developing a "cognitive continuum" that helps you expand your way of viewing yourself and others. Before you can apply this new way of thinking you have to catch yourself oversimplifying. That is the hard part. You have to listen to yourself for words that are critical (e.g., stupid, crazy, loser) and words that suggest extreme or black and white thinking (e.g., always, never, every, all). It may be easier to notice changes in your mood, such as anger, irritation, or frustration, particularly with other people. These may be clues that you are oversimplifying a situation in a troublesome way.

6

BEATING

OVERSIMPLIFICATION

Before he took his recent job, Brent tried to start a small business. He and his cousin Mike pulled some money together and opened a computer store. Both men loved to tinker with computers and seemed to have a knack for understanding the latest technologies. They made some great deals and sold computers for small business and home office use. They sidelined in computer installation, which helped to keep cash flowing in the lean months. For the first year the business seemed like a dream come true. Brent was good with people. He contacted hardware and software manufacturers, made the deals, bought equipment, and set it up in the store. Mike handled the day-to-day business operations, including deposits, accounts payable, taxes, store promotions, and supervision of part-time personnel. Suddenly, one day the dream ended. Brent came into the store one Saturday morning to find that the electricity and the phones had been disconnected. He went through Mike's desk and found overdue notices from the utility companies and several angry letters from vendors who had not yet been paid. Brent tried not to panic. He was certain that there was a good explanation for all of this. Mike was family, after all, and he would not knowingly jeopardize their business. Brent drove over to Mike's apartment. As he had secretly feared, Mike had mismanaged their money and had put them in debt and ruined their credit. The money in the till was too tempting for Mike. When Brent was away making deals, Mike was having fun. He borrowed on his future paychecks at first, but when he met a girl in Newport Beach he lost control. In the end he lost the business and the girl. Brent tried to show compassion for his cousin. He knew that wanting a woman can make you crazy. He ultimately blamed himself for the failure of their business.

"I should have paid more attention to the day-to-day work. I knew that this was too much fun to be a real business. Who am I to think that I could be a businessman? I'm a joke, a failure. Now I'm broke. I will have to borrow from my dad. How humiliating! He tried to talk me out of going into business with Mike. He said I couldn't handle it and he was right. Now he will know that I am a failure. I am twenty-seven years old, no work, no wife, and no home of my own. I'm a failure."

Brent knew he was becoming increasingly depressed over the situation, so he went to see his old therapist and told his story: "My life was going great and now it's over. Now what am I going to do?"

"What about your cousin Mike?" the therapist inquired.

"Mike is the kind of guy who always manages to land on his feet. His mom will take care of him as best she can. I should have helped him more. Mike is no businessman. I knew that. He is a nice guy. He seemed to be doing OK, and he was having so much fun. I thought that if he felt good about himself he would gain the confidence to make it on his own. The money put too much pressure on him. His family never had any money when he was growing up. My grandfather would give help only after he gave my aunt, Mike's mom, a lecture and made her feel bad. She is a failure in the family's eyes. So is Mike. I guess I am too now."

"Brent, you keep saying that you are a failure. Is it really that simple? Success or failure? It seems to me that in the past, when you have gotten upset, you tended to see things in black and white terms. How did you put it just now? 'My life was going great and now it's over.' It's all or it's nothing?"

"You're right. I should have remembered that. See, I can't even do therapy right. I'm such an idiot."

"Well, Brent, I bet you came here because you wanted some sort of help. What do you think you need?"

"I feel so bad. I just need some help in sorting this all out. I need to make some sense of what happened and I need to quickly make some plans for the future. I don't want to make the same mistakes again. Deep down inside I'm afraid that I'm destined to fail."

"OK. Tell me how seeing yourself as a failure makes you feel inside."

"I feel sad and desperate. It's hard to breathe. My chest is heavy and my shoulders burn. It makes me feel totally hopeless about the future and completely worthless."

"Let's start with your oversimplification of the problem. I'm talking about those big statements about being a failure. You are obviously seeing your computer store experience as one big failure and it is making you feel sad, guilty, and angry. Let's take a closer look at the business. Are you sure that your experience with this was a total failure? Were there some elements of the business that went well? You said some things were actually fun."

"It was fun. I enjoyed making the deals to purchase hardware. I talked with various vendors, negotiated purchases, and arranged for the inventory to be shipped to the store. I put together the store displays and talked to customers about their small business or home office needs. I helped people choose the systems that best suited them. I helped with some installation. It really isn't all that difficult, but new computer owners are afraid of their machines at first. They just want someone to set it up, install the software, and tell them how to turn it on. If people were willing to pay for my time, I was willing to help."

"Brent, this all sounds great. You clearly had some fun with it. But where is the failure part? I don't hear it."

"OK, you're right. I guess it isn't all failure. I was having a good time until the floor fell out from under me. The failure part was that I was so wrapped up in my part of the business, I ignored the day-to-day operations. That is what ultimately hurt us. I know that my cousin Mike screwed up, but I was responsible for Mike. I knew that he might not be totally responsible, but I read somewhere that if you give someone responsibility they will act responsibly. I was trying to help him to grow up a little. He really is a good person. He just got his priorities out of order and did not have the maturity to tell me or to stop himself. If I had been more involved, I would have seen it coming and probably could have stopped it before it got out of hand. I share the blame with Mike fifty-fifty. I don't think that is an exaggeration."

"So how does all of this fit with the idea that you are a failure and that your life was great and now it is over?"

"Well, Doc, you got me there. I was seeing it in black and white terms. If I wasn't totally successful, then I failed. OK, let me restate it. My business failed partly because my cousin Mike mismanaged the money and partly because I did not keep a better eye on him despite my concerns. Is that better?"

"That's better. When you think about it that way how does it make you feel?"

"I'm disappointed in Mike and angry with myself. I still feel bad about it."

"How is this different from seeing yourself as a failure? What does it do to your despair, hopelessness, and sense of worthlessness?"

"Seeing myself as a failure left me with nowhere to go. Looking at it more closely, I don't feel so hopeless. I know that I did well in a lot of ways. I'm still disappointed with Mike, but I'm not as angry with myself. I guess it is not the end of the world."

"It sounds like you found out that you are quite good at some aspects of business. That business degree seems to be paying off. What now?"

"Now I get a job and get back on my feet. I may have to borrow some money, probably from my dad, to pay off the vendors we owe if I can't sell the stock. I think it would be good to make Mike pay some of the debt too. He can sell a few of the items he bought with our money, like his new stereo system. He doesn't want me to be mad at him, so I know he will try."

"Boy, that was easy. You just rattled off a great plan. Is this something you have been thinking about?"

"Well, sort of, but not really. I've been mostly thinking about how bad I feel."

"Do you see a connection between feeling bad and not knowing what to do?'

"When I feel bad, I don't think very clearly about solutions. I get stuck on how much the problem hurts."

"Why do you suppose it hurts so much to have a problem like this?"

"It's not supposed to happen."

"What's not supposed to happen?"

"I'm not supposed to fail."

"That sounds familiar. Didn't we talk about that schema once before?"

"Yes, we did. And we decided that it was wrong, but when I get upset I start seeing things in these black and white ways all over again."

"You're right. What do you think you need to do about it?"

"I need to remind myself that this is what I do when I get emotional. I oversimplify the situation as either a success or a failure. I inevitably think it is a failure, and I instantly fall into this deep dark hole of despair where I wallow in my own misery."

"Sounds painful."

"It's no picnic. Luckily, these slumps don't last very long. I can usually talk myself out of it. And if I can't I call for help. Right now I need to work on solving the problem, not just beating myself up about it."

"Sounds like you have it figured out."

Brent coped with feeling overwhelmed with failure by addressing the cognitive error of oversimplification, a thinking error he had made many times in the past. It is not easy to stop making thinking errors, but you can start by trying to recognize when it is happening. Brent coped with oversimplification by looking more closely at his business experience, and in doing so he could see that there had been many successes. His therapist did not try to talk him out of the idea that he was a failure. She simply helped him to identify the nature of the problem more accurately. Once the problem was defined he knew what had gone wrong and what he had to watch out for in the future. Brent moved from a two-category system where problems are seen in black or white terms (success or failure) to a system in which he was able to see his experience in shades of gray, the areas of strength and the areas of weakness.

June also tends to oversimplify things when she feels down or overwhelmed. She sees herself as a bad mother and a terrible wife and cannot be talked out of it by her husband or her children. June periodically suffers from depression. When she has a spell, she has difficulty getting things done. She loses interest in her usual household chores, her community activities, and her family. During these times she is aware that her attitude has changed and she feels extremely guilty about it. ("I'm letting everyone down. I have a nice family, a good husband, and loving children. I should be taking better care of them. I wish I could just disappear. They would all be better off without me.")

June has had little energy for the past month, since her depression began. She tries to do her chores, but her motivation is gone and she runs out of steam too easily. She finds herself sitting on the couch staring at the television. She waits until 2:00 P.M., when the kids are about to come home, and she hustles. She puts everything she has into cleaning, organizing, and cooking. When the kids come home they get lost in their activities and they never know that she has spent the morning crying or staring out into space. After dinner June preoccupies herself in the kitchen washing dishes and doing a load of laundry. The kids are occupied with homework. Her husband is reading the paper, and June thinks she has made it through another day. She does not realize that her husband notices her sleeplessness, how little she eats at mealtime, her lack of enthusiasm about sex, and the circles under her eyes. In fact, her daughter Sissy also notices that something is wrong, but doesn't say a word. She just tries to help out and not put any undue pressure on her mother. It will pass. Sissy has seen it before. It always seems to pass.

One morning after the kids were off to school and Bill had gone to work, June found herself contemplating suicide. She didn't even realize that she was thinking about it at first. When she caught herself looking through her medicine chest for pills to take she got scared. ("Oh, my God. What am I thinking? I must be crazy like that lady in the newspaper. I need help and I need it now.") June called her family doctor to make an appointment, but he was out of town. June called her church and talked with Sister Theresa. Sister Theresa called the parish counselor and made arrangements for June to be seen that very afternoon.

June and Mrs. McBride, the parish counselor, determined that June did not really want to kill herself. She wanted to feel better and the thoughts about suicide were more like fleeting ideas that now seemed foreign to her. Mrs. McBride explained to June that she was depressed and that it was not likely brought about because she could not keep up with housework but, rather, the other way around. She explained to June that sometimes depression made people see themselves and other people in their lives, and their future, in a negative light. In June's case, the depression made her feel like a bad mother. It also caused some physical symptoms such as low energy and insomnia that made it difficult for June to keep up with her usual activities. These changes in behavior made June feel worse. She blamed herself for not keeping up with the family and the house the way she should when, in fact, the real problem was depression, something that June could not have necessarily prevented. June was astounded by how well Mrs. McBride seemed to understand her problem. "Unfortunately," Mrs. McBride continued, "these changes in view or attitude make you feel worse rather than better. This is something I can help you with." Mrs. McBride explained that June's depression could be treated with either medication, psychotherapy, or both, and suggested she talk with her doctor when he gets back in town. To help relieve some of June's distress, Mrs. McBride helped her work through one of her depressing thoughts, that she was a bad wife and mother. After listening to June criticize herself for all that she was unable to do, Mrs. McBride determined that June was greatly oversimplifying her problem when she saw herself as a bad mother.

She was lumping together all that she had done in the past and what she had been unable to do currently into one big label of "bad mother."

Mrs. McBride explained that when June saw herself as a bad wife and mother, she was oversimplifying the issue. Given the kind of woman that June appeared to be and how much she cared for her family, Mrs. McBride found it hard to believe that June had the ability to be a bad mother or wife. She explained to June that depression can make you see things in black and white terms and that perhaps the issue was a bit more complex than her simply being a bad mother. June listened as Mrs. McBride explained: "You see, my dear, when you are feeling bad you take everything you do and everything you are and lump it into one big pile and call it failure or being a bad mother, in your case. It is really not that simple. There may be some things that you are not doing as well as you used to, but I bet in the past and even now, there are many things you do well for your family."

"You are probably right," June replied, "but I don't see them right now."

"Exactly," added Mrs. McBride. "You only see the things you have not done, not the many things that you accomplish."

Mrs. McBride explained that, in life, most things we do are only partially successful. We do better some times more than other times. Few things in life are really black or white. Seeing things as simply successes or failures makes you feel bad when you are not well enough to do everything right.

June did not really understand what Mrs. McBride was trying to say.

"You look puzzled, June. Let me see if I can give you an example to help explain what I mean. You oversimplify your problem by saying you are a bad mother or a bad wife. That is too general. There are really many things that go into being a mother and a wife. I bet you can think of at least ten things you do as a mother."

"Well, that's probably true."

"Let's write down some of the things that constitute your role or your responsibility as a mother. Where do you want to start?"

June sat quietly for a minute and then took the marker and began to list on the board the things she did as a wife and mother. June's list follows. By doing this exercise, the therapist was beginning to help June construct a different system for evaluating herself and her performance. She wanted June to get away from oversimplifying the matter as one big failure and instead look more closely at the various aspects of her life that constitute her roles of wife and mother. This is the first step in developing a cognitive continuum, which is a way of evaluating each area of performance on a scale from 0 percent success to 100 percent success rather than using the two-basket system. If June could look at her performance at home more accurately, she would see that there were many things that she managed to do well despite the fact that she was not feeling well. It was very important to June that she take good care of her family. Being a good mother was an important element of her self-esteem. June's perception that she was a failure in this area was worsening her depression.

After June listed her areas of responsibility as a wife and mother, her therapist had her rate each as either satisfactory (SAT) or unsatisfactory (UNSAT). (We'll borrow Sergeant Joe's military terminology for a while.) Although this is just another two-category system, it was a step toward getting June to see things more accurately. June needed to be able to sort out her areas of difficulty. She recognized some of her areas of performance as being satisfactory for the moment. These were taken off her list of worries so that more energy could be focused on the problems that were bothering her the most. Let's review June's list and her ratings. The items in the left column are those listed by June. Mrs. McBride pushed June to break each area down into its separate components. These appear on the right.

Before she began to look more closely at her areas of performance at home and with the family, it was easy for June to give global ratings of UNSAT to each area (the left column). When the therapist got June to examine the various components of each of her responsibilities at home she was able to see that she was actually satisfied with various aspects of her appearance, her housekeeping, and her role as mother. This made the oversimplified statement of "I'm not a good mother" seem not altogether correct.

"June," Mrs. McBride inquired, "how do all these satisfactory ratings fit with the idea that you are not a good mother?"

		June's List of Home Responsibilities	
SAT	UNSAT	SAT	UNSAT
( )	(X) *Home care:*	(X)	( ) tidiness
		( )	(X) cleanliness
		(X)	( ) decor
		(X)	( ) closets, shelves, drawers
		(X)	( ) organization
		( )	(X) meal preparation
		( )	(X) laundry
		( )	(X) ironing
		(X)	( ) bill paying
		(X)	( ) car cleanliness
		(X)	( ) garage organization
		(X)	( ) yard—lawn care
		(X)	( ) yard—garden care
		(X)	( ) pet care
( )	(X) *Care for children:*	(X)	( ) cleanliness
		( )	(X) room tidiness
		(X)	( ) manners
		(X)	( ) appearance
		(X)	( ) performance in school
		(X)	( ) performance in sports
		(X)	( ) performance in other activities
		(X)	( ) peer relations
		(X)	( ) homework
		( )	(X) affection toward them
		( )	(X) enjoying them
		( )	(X) playing with them
( )	(X) *Looking nice:*	( )	(X) hair
		(X)	( ) skin
		( )	(X) makeup
		(X)	( ) weight
		(X)	( ) health

SAT = Satisfactory; UNSAT = Unsatisfactory

"I don't know," June commented at first. "I guess I'm not that bad, but I'm not taking care of things the way I would like. Most important, I don't really feel like being around my family or taking care of myself or the house. That makes me feel like a bad person. What kind of mother doesn't want to play with her kids?"

"Do you understand that when a person is depressed they lose interest in things for a while? Sometimes they do not want to play with their kids because it takes too much energy and they are feeling tired. Sometimes it is because they cannot concentrate and some games or even some conversations take a lot of mental energy. In your case, I wonder if, when you are with your family, you spend a great deal of mental energy criticizing yourself for not having the energy or motivation to take care of things the way you would like."

"That sounds like me," June answered.

"The way you view things will greatly affect your emotions and even your actions. If you see yourself as a bad mother, how does it make you feel inside?"

"I feel angry with myself, and guilty."

"When you have these feelings, what happens to your energy, your motivation, and your ability to think clearly?" Mrs. McBride inquired.

"They get worse. All I can think about is how I must be disappointing my family."

"When we look at the list that we have made and all the things you have rated as satisfactory, how does that make you feel?"

June could see where she was heading. "You're right. I'm not all that bad, but I think I am sick. I haven't told anyone in the family what is happening, but I think they know that something is wrong."

"Do you think it would help if they understood?" Mrs. McBride inquired.

"I guess so. But what am I going to do about the house?" June asked nervously.

"Well, June, it seems to me that you have had pretty strict standards about how to take care of your home and your family. When you have been feeling bad you have not been able to meet your own standards. And even though your family is not complaining, it still bothers you. You have been oversimplifying the problem. Getting most, but not all, things accomplished has been OK for your family, but it has been eating you up inside. You see things in an all or nothing way. You cannot do it all, so you see yourself as a bad mother. Am I getting it right so far?"

June acknowledged that Mrs. McBride had described her dilemma perfectly. But how was she going to get out of this: "I know I'm a perfectionist. I won't try to deny it. It is just the way I am."

"I bet that most of the time your perfectionism helps you to do a good job, but right now it is making your depression worse. Let's find a way out of it. Let's look at your performance as a mother in a slightly different way than just as a good mother or a bad mother. Let's take the areas in which you are unsatisfied with yourself. For each one we are going to expand your view from each being either satisfactory or unsatisfactory and move it to a continuum. For example, if we were to look at laundry on a continuum we would think of a range of performance from one hundred percent successful at laundry, where everything is clean, ironed, and put away, to zero percent success, where everything you had was dirty. We can draw a continuum (as shown)."

"Where would you mark your success in taking care of your laundry? Mark it on the line."

June took a pencil and marked the line at about 60 percent. She had been able to keep up with the majority of the laundry. No one would go without clothes this week. The sheets could be changed in a few days.

"Seeing yourself as sixty percent successful at getting your laundry done is very different from seeing yourself as a bad mother. When you think of it this new way, what happens to your feelings of guilt and anger?"

June had to take a minute to think this over. "I guess I don't feel

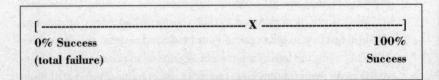

nearly as bad. I am doing a lot, when I think about it. No one has complained. I guess I could ask my husband if he thinks I'm doing OK at home."

June's therapist helped her to look at each of her areas of dissatisfaction on a continuum. There was room for improvement, particularly in her interactions with the children. She realized that she spent more time avoiding interactions than she liked. Her children were a source of joy and avoiding them deprived her of a source of pleasure that she sorely needed during this time.

DEVELOPING A COGNITIVE CONTINUUM

Defining the Problem

To move yourself from a two-category or two-basket way of looking at things to a broader view with various shades of gray, you can construct a cognitive continuum like June's. The first step is to pick an area of performance that is bothering you and that you might be viewing in an oversimplified way, like an area that makes you feel like a failure. A clue might be that you use words such as never, always, every time, every one, completely, totally, or absolutely to describe this problem area. Perhaps you are seeing yourself either at home or at work in a negative way, or perhaps you are upset with another person in your life and are seeing them in black and white terms. If you completed Schema Exercise 2 in Chapter 4, you may have already defined areas you want to improve upon.

June was calling herself a *bad* mother. In the last chapter Brent was calling himself a *failure* in business. Joe said his wife *wasn't there* when he needed her. Joann saw herself as *sick* after a bad weekend. John thought that since he could not do his old job, he could not do *anything*. These are all oversimplifications, or absolute statements. In each case, these automatic thoughts were accompanied by intense emotions, and none led the person toward a reasonable solution to the problem. This is usually the case with oversimplification. In fact, when things are seen in black and white terms, the solutions that are

---

COGNITIVE CONTINUUM EXERCISE NUMBER 1

Defining the Problem

1. Choose an area of your life with which you are most dissatisfied.
2. In your inner thoughts, do you see your performance in a black or white way, failure or success, good or bad?
3. List those thoughts.
4. When you think about it, how does it make you feel inside?
5. List those feelings.

---

generated often have the same quality. They sound absolute or extreme. For example, Joe contemplated leaving his wife, Joann did nothing but stay in bed, Brent saw nowhere to turn, John could not work, and June thought it would be best to die and leave her family in better hands. These extreme solutions are full of emotion as well. Decisions made in highly emotional states may feel right at the time, but are usually ineffective, address the wrong problem, or make things worse. Joe was angry with his wife for not being available when he needed her, and anger was what led him to think about leaving her for good. Guilt fueled June's extreme view of herself as a bad mother and guilt led her to conclude that she should just die and leave them in better hands.

What are your oversimplifications? When you think about them, how do they make you feel inside? Write down these thoughts and these feelings. After you do the exercise following you will want to refer back to these thoughts and these feelings.

Emotions are not usually all or nothing phenomena. In other words, it is not usually the case that you are angry or not, depressed or not, disgusted or not. Emotions occur at different degrees of intensity. You can be a little upset or very upset. Try to gauge the intensity of the emotions you feel when you think about the oversimplification you have identified. Use a simple scale to rate the intensity of your emotion. Let 100 percent mean the most intense that feeling can be. Let 0 percent mean that you do not have the feeling at all. For example, June felt 100 percent guilty when she thought of herself as a bad

---

Cognitive Continuum Exercise Number 1

Joe's evaluation of his wife:

Oversimplification: "She was not there when I needed her." (70% Belief)
Emotion: Anger (95% intensity)

Cognitive Continuum Exercise Number 1

Brent's self-evaluation about his business:

Oversimplification: "I'm a failure" (100% Belief)
Emotion: Sadness (80% Intensity)
        Guilt (85% Intensity)

Cognitive Continuum Exercise Number 1

John's self-evaluation about returning to work after an injury:

Oversimplification: "I can't do menial work" (100% Belief)
Emotion: Disgust (80% Intensity)
        Anger (70% Intensity)

---

mother. John felt 80 percent disgusted when he thought he could not return to work. Joe felt 95 percent angry with his wife when she did not show up to bring him his keys. It may also be helpful for you to rate the intensity with which you believe the oversimplified thought. Use the same 0 percent to 100 percent scale. For example, Brent believed with 100 percent certainty that he had failed.

Defining Your Expectations

Once you have defined the area or situation that is upsetting you or causing you trouble you can move toward looking at the problem more closely. In Exercise Number 2 you will start to define the problem more closely by listing your responsibilities in the area of difficulty that you have identified. If you are having trouble with home responsibilities, your list might be similar to June's list. If you are a student, you might have a list of responsibilities that include studying or going to class. If you are a real estate agent, your list might include checking listings or pleasing your customers. If you are feeling OK about yourself, but are angry, frustrated, or disgusted with others, your list might include your expectations of other people, such as tasks your employees or your children are supposed to complete.

Once you have made your list of expectations or responsibilities for yourself or others, try to evaluate each area as satisfactory (SAT) or unsatisfactory (UNSAT). Remember how June's therapist made her be specific about the areas she was rating. Within housework there were several subtasks, just as there were under caring for her children. On the next page are some examples from our characters in the last chapter.

Looking for Shades of Gray

Oversimplification or two-basket thinking gives you only two types of performance. In the previous examples the choices were satisfactory or unsatisfactory. Sometimes the choices are good or bad, right or wrong, or even OK and not OK. To combat the emotional pain of this all-or-nothing view of things you have to build a new system for evaluating yourself and others.

Let us start with a simple example of moving from a categorical system to a continuum. Imagine the last three movies you saw on television or at the theater. Did you like them? Were they good? If you answered yes or no you were looking at each movie in an all or nothing way. This is an example of oversimplifying your view of the movies. Now try to rate each movie on a scale from 1 to 5, with 5 meaning cinematic perfection and a rating of 1 meaning a total flop and a waste of your time. Ratings of 2, 3, or 4 on this scale are shades of gray. In the two-basket system, the 5s would have been good movies and those with ratings of 1 to 4 would have been considered bad or movies that

COGNITIVE CONTINUUM EXERCISE NUMBER 2

Joe's areas of expectation for his wife

SAT   **UNSAT**

( )   (X)   Help him.

(X)   ( )   Care for the children.

( )   (X)   Be able to be contacted when needed for emergencies.

( )   (X)   Wear her beeper.

(X)   ( )   Keep the house in order and cook dinner.

(X)   ( )   Be faithful to him.

COGNITIVE CONTINUUM EXERCISE NUMBER 2

Brent's areas of expectation

SAT   **UNSAT**

( )   (X)   Watch over Mike.

(X)   ( )   Purchase stock.

( )   (X)   Help with daily operations.

( )   (X)   Check with vendors to be sure they were paid.

(X)   ( )   Have up-to-date information on computer technology.

(X)   ( )   Install computers for customers.

COGNITIVE CONTINUUM EXERCISE NUMBER 2

John's areas of expectation

SAT   **UNSAT**

( )   (X)   Go back to work.

( )   (X)   Bring home a paycheck.

(X)   ( )   Contribute to the family.

(X)   ( )   Be a good father.

( )   (X)   Protect the family.

(X)   ( )   Work hard at overcoming my disability.

Cognitive Continuum

[--]
0% success   100%
(total failure)   success

you did not like. If you gave the movies ratings of 2, 3, or 4 you are using a continuum rather than just two categories. You may already be using a continuum most of the time, except for situations that make you feel bad or that stimulate some particular sensitivity in you. Exercise Number 3 is to build a cognitive continuum where 100 percent success is at one end of the scale and 0 percent success (or total failure) is at the other end. Between are varying shades of perfection.

The ends of the continuum are anchor points. To use the scale, we have to attach meaning to the points along the scale. Let's take one of June's examples. She rated her ability to keep up with the laundry as unsatisfactory. If we try to get her to use a continuum such as the one above we have to know how she defines perfection in laundry. How would she know or how would other people know that she has reached perfection in this area? Essentially we are asking, "What does perfection look like?" June defined laundry perfection and

Laundry

[--]
0% success   100%
(total failure)   success

All laundry is clean, folded, and put away. Ironing is caught up. Draperies and bed linens are clean. At the end of each day these tasks are completed.

placed it under the 100 percent success mark on the continuum shown.

Joe would have defined 100 percent success as his wife being available in emergencies and immediately responding when paged. John would have rated 100 percent success in returning to work as being able to go back to his original position for a full day without feeling pain from his injuries, or if pain was present that would not slow him down or interfere with his work. Terry would have defined a 100 percent successful day as one in which she was able to be successful at work, get the attention of the boss, or successfully negotiate for something she wanted, have fun with the kids, eat a nutritious meal, exercise before bedtime, and still have some time to read a good book. Perhaps she would even have time for a personal phone call or to paint her toenails. Choose an area of your own preference or of someone else's performance that you consider to be unsatisfactory and construct a continuum similar to June's.

To flesh out the rest of the continuum we must know what absolute failure (or 0 percent success) looks like. How would you know if you were a total failure? Shown is what June described as total failure, or 0 percent success in laundry.

For Joe, total failure of his wife to help in emergencies would be that she either never returned the call or if she did return the call she said, "Tough luck buddy, you solve your own problems." John rated

---

Laundry

[---]
0% Success   **100%**
(total failure)   **Success**

All clothes are dirty. They are strewn all over the house. Hampers smell. Kids wear dirty socks to school.	All laundry is clean, folded, and put away. Ironing is caught up. Draperies, bed linens are clean. At the end of the day tasks are completed.

Laundry

[---]

0% Success	50%	100%
(total failure)		**Success**
All clothes are dirty. They are strewn all over the house. Hampers smell. Kids wear dirty socks to school.	Kids have clean clothes to wear. There are enough towels for showers. Sheets are not bad.	All laundry is clean, folded, and put away. Ironing is caught up. Draperies, bed linens are clean. At the end of the day tasks are completed.

total failure as never being able to go back to work or getting better physically but losing his job and being unable to find anything else. The family ends up homeless. Terry defined 0 percent success in her day as sleeping through the alarm clock and missing an important meeting, her children having a tantrum about going to school and about missing their daddy, being publicly reprimanded by her boss, and finding out at the end of the day that she had gained five pounds. Fill in your cognitive continuum with a description of zero percent success. Remember that this means *total* failure in the area of performance you are evaluating.

The next logical step in constructing the continuum is to fill in the midpoint. What does the halfway point look like? How would you know if you were 50 percent successful? You can try to define additional points on the continuum, such as the 25 percent mark, if it would be helpful. June's response is shown.

Self-Evaluation

Your next task in building a new system is to evaluate your performance for each of the areas you rated as unsatisfactory (UNSAT) in the earlier exercise. This means that instead of seeing things in an all

---

Cognitive Continuum Exercise Number 3

Building a cognitive continuum

1. Draw a line that represents your performance in an area you marked as UNSAT in exercise number 2. Mark the right end of the line as 100% success and the left end as 0% success.
2. Define what 0%, 50%, and 100% success would look like in each area.

---

or nothing way, you either succeeded or failed, define how much success you have actually achieved. For each of the continuums you have constructed, mark your current level of functioning with an X. June rated her success at keeping up with the laundry at 60 percent. Shown is how she rated her progress in each of the other areas she marked as UNSAT.

The goal of this intervention is to move from an oversimplified, two-category system of looking at things to a more continuous system,

---

June's List of Home Responsibilities

UNSAT	% SUCCESS
Home care:	
(X) cleanliness	75%
(X) meal preparation	50%
(X) laundry	60%
(X) ironing	30%
Care for children:	
(X) room tidiness	50%
(X) affection toward them	70%
(X) enjoying them	20%
(X) playing with them	10%
Looking nice:	
(X) hair	25%
(X) makeup	25%

where you can see things in shades of gray. That means that success can no longer be defined as absolute perfection. Instead, your performance is somewhere on a continuum. To help you rate yourself on a continuum of performance you need a few more anchor points to help you judge your progress. You have already figured out where you stand in the important areas of your life. If you were rating someone else you have figured out where they stand in your mind, as in Joe's case. His ratings on his wife are listed.

The next task is to rate the level of success you *prefer* in each area. To help you with these ratings, refer back to your own definition of 100 percent success in each area. Is 100 percent success necessary? In earlier chapters you examined the advantages and disadvantages of being perfect. You probably found that achieving perfection is not without costs. The goal, as mentioned in Chapter 2, is to minimize the disadvantages and maximize the advantages in your pursuit of perfection. Given that, what level of success would you prefer in each of the areas you are rating? Some examples are shown.

You can mark these preferred levels on the continuum you drew with the letter P. You may see some distance between where you are and where you would prefer to be in each of the areas you rated. If you have carefully defined the points on the continuum this should give you an idea of what you need to do to move your performance from its current level to the level you prefer.

If you have a busy life with lots of responsibilities you might find that, while your preferred levels of performance are what you would ideally like to accomplish, in reality you may not have the time or

---

Joe's Evaluation of His Wife

Areas of expectation for his wife:

UNSAT	% SUCCESS
(X) Help him.	80%
(X) Be able to be contacted when needed for emergencies.	95%
(X) Wear her beeper.	60%

Joe's Evaluation of His Wife

Areas of expectation for his wife:

UNSAT	% SUCCESS	PREFERRED
(X) Help him.	80%	90%
(X) Be able to be contacted when needed for emergencies.	95%	100%
(X) Wear her beeper.	60%	95%

June's List of Home Responsibilities

UNSAT	% SUCCESS	PREFERRED
Home Care:		
(X) cleanliness	75%	95%
(X) meal preparation	50%	98%
(X) laundry	60%	90%
(X) ironing	30%	50%
Care for children:		
(X) room tidiness	50%	80%
(X) affection toward them	70%	90%
(X) enjoying them	20%	90%
(X) playing with them	10%	85%
Looking nice:		
(X) hair	25%	75%
(X) makeup	25%	75%

energy to do so. It may be possible to reach your preferred level of performance on things that are especially important to you, but most people find it hard to be all things and do all things perfectly. That is probably what led you to read this book. Given that this is the case, you need another mark on each continuum indicating the percentage of success you would find acceptable for now. Mark that point on the line as "OK." You might find that the OK point is somewhere between your actual and your preferred level of performance. If the OK level

---

Cognitive Continuum Exercise Number 4

For each area of performance, rate your current level of functioning by marking the line with an X. Indicate your preferred level of functioning by marking
the line with a P. Mark a level that you would find satisfactory for now by marking the line OK.

---

is lower than your current performance level, then you are probably
working too hard. This is an easier problem to deal with, because the
intervention is to do less rather than more. The goal is to relax a bit
and move your energy to other areas of your life (such as having fun).
If your actual, preferred, and OK markings are all pretty close to each
other then you are fine. There is probably no need for change in these
areas. If your actual level is lower than what is OK with you, then you
have some work to do.

MAKING CHANGES

Mrs. McBride, June's therapist, helped June to pick out the items that
bothered her most or that made her feel like she was a bad mother.
After examining the list carefully, June concluded that her personal
appearance, although rated pretty low, did not really bother her that
much; neither did the ironing. The kids and her husband think she
irons things unnecessarily and could care less if there are a few wrin-
kles in things. What bothered her the most was how she behaved with
the children. She avoided interaction by keeping busy with small projects, and she did not stop what she was doing to make time to play
with them or visit with them. They enjoyed those times as much as
June. They had not complained because they knew something was
wrong with June and stayed out of her way to help reduce her stress.
Sissy had seen to that. Meal preparation was usually a time when
everyone was in the kitchen talking. Sometimes the kids helped,
sometimes they just watched and told June about their day. June had
been relying on fast-food dinners several nights each week or had
thrown together something that required little preparation time. The

kids loved to order pizza or Chinese takeout, so these changes did not bother them, but they bothered June. Since meal preparation was family time, she was also missing out on her time with the kids. If she had to change one thing, it would probably be to interact with her kids at dinnertime and at breakfast in the morning. She was not always hungry in the morning, but she could sit with them and have a cup of coffee. Their beautiful faces really did brighten her morning.

John's self-evaluation showed that he was most dissatisfied with his inability to go back to work. His success in this area was rated 0 percent because he was home and not back on the job. He was bringing home money to his family through workmen's compensation, so he was actually contributing even though he was home. And the amount he received was very close to his regular salary without overtime hours, so he rated this at 85 percent. It bothered him that he was physically disabled and could not physically protect his family in the event of an emergency. John knew that his sons were bigger than him and probably just as strong, so they did not really need his protection. His wife kept telling him that she could take care of herself, but in John's mind, she was little and too trusting. His wife had never felt physically threatened and was generally very cautious. Even though there was no immediate need to physically protect his family, John still felt vulnerable, so he rated his success in this area at 30 percent. He could watch over them, make sure the security system on the house worked properly, and give his usual instructions about being careful before they left the house. He was still too weak and too slow,

---

John's Self-evaluation About Returning to Work After an Injury

Areas of expectation:

UNSAT	% SUCCESS
(X) Go back to work.	0%
(X) Bring home a paycheck.	85%
(X) Protect the family.	30%

but he was doing everything he could to recover and regain his strength.

What bothered John more than anything was that he was capable of working to some degree, and instead he was sitting at home watching *Oprah* and *The Price Is Right.* This is not how a workingman spends his time. He hated the idea of doing a desk job that, in his mind, was menial work. He was accustomed to being in charge, not sitting behind a desk. But, finally, he decided that it was better to work than to not work, even if the job was "beneath him." He was a man, and a real man does what he has to do for his family. He knew he would heal and be able to spend more time out on a work site as he got stronger. He thought about his position with the company and how he had always been well-respected. No one would dare make fun of him. If they did, he would take care of it in his own way and it would never happen again.

If you completed Exercise Number 4, you have a pretty clear description of what your OK levels look like. This is your guide for change. You must get yourself from where you are to that point in some systematic way. The choices are (1) to make no changes now, but have a plan for when you will make time to work on improvements; (2) you can tackle the problem all at once. Since that would be more of an all or nothing approach, it is not what I would recommend; (3) the intermediate-level strategy would be to slowly work toward achieving your preferred levels of performance. Do a little at a time. Perhaps this is not your style; you will have to find a way that fits with your energy, time, and interest. June, for example, is not pleased with her ironing performance, but does not really care a lot about it. The kids are more important, so she will address that area first. Because she is depressed she may have trouble getting started or accomplishing a lot at one time. June thought about which area of her performance as a mother made her feel like a bad mom and started there. John thought about what bothered him most about not being at work and made that his goal.

The key to what needs to be addressed first is to examine the oversimplification that set you on the path to this intervention in the first place. Review your responses to Exercise Number 1. For Brent, it was feeling like a failure. The issues that seemed to bother him the most had to do with the financial troubles he now faced. He was also concerned about his future and his cousin's well-being. His first priority was to pay his debt and avoid damage to his credit. He was concerned about his father's disappointment in him, but that would have to wait for another day. Other things were more pressing and Dad would probably take a lot of time and energy.

Remember that the model we are working from is that the way you think about things (yourself, your future, and others in your world) influences your emotions and your choice of actions. When you do this cognitive continuum exercise and look at what needs to be done to

---

June's Self-evaluation

Initial oversimplification: "I'm a bad mother." (90% Belief)

Initial emotion: Sadness (100% Intensity)
                    Anger (50% Intensity)
                    Guilt (99% Intensity)

Restatement: "I'm still a good mother, but I am depressed and need help. I would feel better if I gave my children more attention." (100%)

Changes in emotion: Sadness (40% Intensity)
                       Anger (0% Intensity)
                       Guilt (25% Intensity)

Sergeant Joe's Evaluation of His Wife

Initial oversimplification: "She was not there when I needed her." (85% Belief)

Initial emotion: Anger (90% Intensity)

Restatement: "Maria is a good wife. It's not her fault that I locked my keys in my car, but I do wish she carried her beeper more often." (100% Belief)

Changes in emotion: Anger (10% Intensity)

improve in the areas that bother you, you have changed your thinking from oversimplification to a more detailed view that allows you to see the shades of gray in your life. If you have done all of these steps, go back and rate the intensity of the emotions you listed in Exercise Number 1 and rate how strongly you believe the oversimplified idea you stated there. The final step is to restate the oversimplified idea in a way that is more accurate. Shown is how our characters changed their views and the shift in their emotions that subsequently occurred.

The oversimplified belief was replaced with a more accurate view. The emotions were not eliminated, but were reduced in intensity,

---

Brent's Self-evaluation About His Business

Initial oversimplification: "I'm a failure." (90% Belief)
Initial emotion: Sadness (80% Intensity)
              Guilt (85% Intensity)

Restatement: "This business failed, but it doesn't mean that it was all my fault. I will learn from this and do better next time. Mike and I share the responsibility fifty-fifty." (90%)

Changes in emotion: Sadness (30% Intensity)
              Guilt (30% Intensity)

John's Self-evaluation About Returning to Work After an Injury

Initial oversimplification: "I can't do a menial job." (100% Belief)

Initial emotion: Disgust (80% Intensity)
              Anger (70% Intensity)

Restatement: "I'm tired of being stuck at home. I would rather work even though I hate doing work that is lower in status. I will get stronger." (90%)

Changes in emotion: Frustration (20% Intensity)
              Anger (10% Intensity)

making it easier to think more clearly and creatively about a problem. Solutions can be more easily generated when you are no longer overwhelmed and stuck. John is still bothered about his injury, so his anger and frustration are still present, but they are not as intense. He thinks that he will get stronger and be able to return to his old job, but the doctors say that there are no guarantees that he will return to his preinjury levels. That is why he only believes his restatement with only 90 percent certainty. He is hopeful, but he is also a realist. Joe is still a little angry (10 percent) after his restatement. He is upset with himself for losing his cool and he is a little upset with Maria. During their fight she said some pretty hurtful things. Even though he thinks he may have deserved them, he is still a little upset with her.

Try constructing a cognitive continuum for the important areas of your life. Your levels of preferred performance and your actual levels of functioning will change over time as the demands of your life change. When you start to "beat yourself up" over difficulties you are having, pay attention to your own words. Listen for big, global, critical, or condemning statements. Remember that these are the signs that you may be oversimplifying the situation. Look more closely and you may find your way out of the problem.

7

ADJUSTING YOUR

EXPECTATIONS

"I can't believe I'm this far behind. I'm never going to get it all done by the end of the month. Everything is falling apart. I haven't exercised in a month and it shows. I haven't mailed out thank you cards yet, and it's been three weeks since the party. I promised to help my sister with her new grant and I haven't even looked at it and it's been on my desk for two weeks. I need a haircut, but I don't have time. I barely have time for lunch and forget breakfast, there is too much to do in the morning. I need a vacation."

Does this sound like you? Terry is not meeting her own expectations and it is stressing her greatly. She feels like she needs to make many improvements, but she does not know where to start. How do you get from where you are currently performing on the cognitive continuum to where you want to be? If your current functioning is equal to or better than your preferred level, and you are not distraught or exhausted, then you are in great shape. If your current level of functioning in the important areas of your life is below what you expect from yourself, such as Terry's, then some kind of change may be necessary. Either you have to change your behavior to get it closer to your goal, as we discussed in the last chapter, or you have to change your expectations or standards to match your behavior. A third option is that you accept the fact that there is a discrepancy between what you want to do and what you are actually doing. You make peace with yourself about it or you make a plan to achieve the goal at another time in your life, when it may be easier to achieve. For example, I would really love to have a house that stays neat most of the time. Unfortunately, I have three sons who are not very concerned about having a neat house. If I wanted to achieve my goal right now, it would mean that I would have to spend quite a bit of time each day cleaning up after my boys. They can create messes as fast as I can clear them, especially dirty laundry. If I spent a great deal of time cleaning my house each day so that it stayed as neat as I might like it to be, it would mean that there were other things that I would not be able to do. For example, instead of writing this book first thing in the morning or in the evening after the kids have gone to bed, I would have to do housework. If I did not want to give up my writing time, I would have to give up something else, such as my exercise time, seeing patients in my office, teaching my class, or spending time with my husband. There are only so many waking hours in the day, and I only have so much energy. I try to allocate my time to the things that are most important to me. In the grand scheme of my life, although I like a neat house, neatness isn't as important to me as writing, exercise, or time with my family. In this case, I have made an adjustment in my expectations for housekeeping to match what is reasonable for me to achieve at this point in my life.

If you find that you are not meeting your own expectations you have to decide where to make the adjustment. The first question to ask yourself is whether or not your standards are reasonable given your life circumstances, resources, and abilities. How do you know if your standards are reasonable? First, you need to be aware of your expectations or standards for yourself. You may already know this and can move on to later sections of this chapter. If you are uncertain, do the exercise in the previous chapter to develop a cognitive continuum for each of your expectations.

Another way to evaluate how reasonable your standards or expectations might be is to ask other people what they think. If you are exceptionally hard on yourself, chances are that you have demonstrated this to other people in your life. You do not have to be a trained clinician to see when a person expects too much from himself. Ask your parents, your friends, your partner, your staff, or your customers. Your children might even be old enough to understand this concept and give their opinions. In general, if you work as hard as you can and still feel bad about it, or feel as though it will never be good enough, then your standards are probably too high. If the schemas covered in Chapter 3 sounded like things you tell yourself, then you may be on the wrong track. If you are making any of the thinking errors that were described in Chapter 5 you may also have a distorted view of what is reasonable to expect from yourself or from others in your life.

If you did not do the exercise in the last chapter on developing a cognitive continuum, you might want to go back and do it. If you did not like that idea, here is another: The question you must answer is, What do I expect from myself? If you are a true perfectionist you should be well versed in the "shoulds" and "oughts" of life. A way that inwardly focused perfectionists beat themselves up is by listing all the things they should do, should have done, or ought to do and have not yet done. Does this sound familiar? What are your shoulds? Outwardly focused perfectionists' lists of shoulds often include other people (my wife should, my kids should, etc.). Inwardly focused perfectionists' lists usually start with "I should . . ."

DEFINING YOUR STANDARDS

How did you decide what your standards should be? You may not be able to answer this question right away, but it is worth taking some time to figure it out. Sometimes perfectionists find that they are troubled because no matter what they do it never seems good enough. If I ask, "For whom is it not good enough?" they do not always know the answer. After giving it some thought they usually conclude that it is not good enough for them and not good enough for other important people in their lives. This is a key point, because it suggests that the standard you may be struggling to meet may not actually be your own. Instead, the standard you have set for yourself may be the standard of some important person in your life, such as a parent or a boss or a spouse. Living your life in pursuit of someone else's expectations is a difficult way to live. If the standards you listed were not yours, it may be time to define your personal expectations for yourself and make self-fulfillment your goal.

If you find that it is difficult to meet your expectations, whether they originally came from someone else or you made them up yourself, then it is time to lower your expectations. I know that this is easier said than done. Susan, Brent's little sister, talked with her therapist about this issue.

Susan: Lower my expectations of myself? Oh great! That will make Dad happy. My bosses are on my back enough as it is; if I try to do less I will be fired.

Therapist: Susan, let me see if I understand what you are saying. When I mentioned lowering your standards, you sounded surprised and upset. What kinds of feelings got stirred up in you at the thought of expecting less?

Take some time to think about this.

- What are your standards?
- What percentage of the time are you able to meet your own standards of performance? Some of the time? All of the time?
- Does it bother you that you are unable to reach the standards you set for yourself on a consistent basis?
- Does it bother you that in order to reach your standards on a consistent basis you have to spend a lot of time and mental or emotional energy? If it does not, skip this chapter and go to the next.

Susan: I have to do what they say or I'll get axed. I'm lucky to have this job and I had to get my brother to help me get here in the first place.

Therapist: Those are very upsetting thoughts. Can you identify the feelings or emotions that are triggered by these thoughts?

Susan: Panic, fear.

Therapist: The panic and fear is that you will get fired if you lower your expectations of yourself?

Susan: Absolutely!

Therapist: I don't know your employer, so help me understand what it is like for you. Has she given you any feedback on your performance?

Susan: No, not really. She hasn't said anything about it yet.

Therapist: What do you think that means?

Susan: I don't know, but it feels very tense when she is in the office. She seems to be very picky about every little detail, from what I have heard.

Therapist: Do you know exactly what she expects from you?

Susan: She expects me to do the job well. I am an administrative assistant and there is a job description for this kind of position. I have done this kind of work before in another company. I was pretty good at it.

Therapist: You have said things about your work that sound like you are waiting to be fired any minute. One error and you are out of there. Is that right?

Susan: That's how it feels. I try not to leave my desk until everything is done, even if I have to stay until seven at night. My boss seems to work all night. By the time I get into the office, my in-box is partially full. I work to empty it and she just keeps filling it. My brother has told me about the people in this company and the pressure to perform. I feel it even in my job. The problem is that I am working later and later and my husband is getting angry. It is a salaried position, so I do not get paid overtime. I am so tired when I get home after forty-five minutes on the road that I can hardly do anything. I have given up exercise at night. Luckily, my husband likes to cook, so I don't have to worry about dinner. But my house is a wreck. I have to spend all weekend doing housework and laundry. My husband and I want to have a baby, but I would never have the time to care for it. (She starts to cry.)

Therapist: I can see why this is so upsetting to you. To work the way you believe you have to is wearing you out and interfering with the other parts of your life. The idea of not pushing yourself is just as scary because you think it will lead to losing your job. Am I getting this right?

Susan: Yes. That's it.

Therapist: Have you talked to your boss about this yet?

Susan: No way. If you complain, you've had it.

Therapist: Sounds like you are boxed into a corner. No wonder you are so upset. What do you think would happen if, at the end of the work day you still had a few things to do, but you left them for the next day?

Susan: I don't know.

Therapist: Do you know what your boss would say about that?

Susan: No. But I imagine she wouldn't like it. She would probably think I was lazy. I don't think she has much of a life outside of the office, and I don't think she would be sympathetic to those who do.

Therapist: What if you asked her if a particular task or project could be completed the next day or if it was important to her that it be finished before you left for the day? If she said it could wait, then you leave. If she needed it right away you stay and work on it. This would communicate a willingness to work overtime if need be rather than laziness. If she does not give you specific deadlines, maybe having everything done by the end of the day was your idea and not hers.

Susan: I suppose you are right. My mom and dad always taught me to do my best, but I guess that would apply to my life outside of work as well. I can't do everything. I'm learning that the hard way.

Susan and her therapist practiced how to approach her boss. She found that getting everything done by the end of her day was not her boss's expectation. The boss thought that Susan was a workaholic and did not try to stop her, although she did think Susan's hours were a bit excessive. The boss helped by telling Susan which projects needed to be done immediately and which could wait a day or two. This helped Susan prioritize her work.

The concept of lowering your standards is a frightening one for many perfectionists. Sometimes the automatic thoughts about lowering standards stir up a lot of emotion. And sometimes these thoughts are dysfunctional, inaccurate, or distorted in some way. The thinking errors we discussed in Chapter 5 would apply to lowering standards as well. The main thing that stirs up so much emotion around lower standards is fear of the consequences. Shown are some common automatic thoughts about lowering standards. Which ones do you believe?

If a thought about changing standards fills you with emotion, it may keep you from adjusting your standards to more realistic levels. If your standards are too high, which means that you have tried and you cannot consistently reach them without a lot of work and distress, you will not feel better until you adjust them to make them more realistic. You can always increase your standards later if you find that the circumstances of your life have changed and you are able to take on more or do more with your time. Perhaps later in your life you will find yourself with more time, more skill, a better assistant, a new technology that helps you, or you will learn something new that improves your performance.

To help you explore more thoroughly your reactions to adjusting your standards you can use Schema Exercise Number 1 from Chapter 4, where you examined the evidence that supported your thought and the evidence against your thoughts. Here is a brief summary of how to evaluate the evidence for your automatic thought and some examples of how our four perfectionists worked through their ideas. Get out a piece of paper and divide it into three columns, like the example shown. At the top, write down the idea from the list of automatic thoughts about lower standards that you want to explore. Choose the one that bothers you the most or that arouses the most emotion in you. If it is in the form of a question, rewrite it as a statement. For example, change "What if we get

SELF-ASSESSMENT

Automatic Thoughts About
Lowering Your Standards

Pick out one or two of the statements below that you most strongly believe. Perhaps you can restate the idea in your own words to make it fit your circumstances. What kinds of feelings are stirred up by these thoughts?

Remember that for this exercise we are referring to "feelings" as emotional reactions such as sadness, anxiety, dread, or anger rather than ideas or thoughts like the ones on the list. Use the 0% to 100% scale from Chapter 6 to rate how strongly you believe the automatic thoughts you picked from the list below and to rate the intensity of the feelings you are having about this idea.

1. If I don't push, no one will.
2. It's up to me. If I don't who will?
3. It wouldn't be right.
4. People expect the best from me.
5. I'll lose my job. The competition is fierce.
6. I demand the best from my employees. I can only do the same myself.
7. I won't be able to live with myself.
8. If I don't keep pushing myself, I'll just get lazy.
9. People will talk.
10. Germs will grow.
11. What if someone comes to visit?
12. What if we get audited?
13. It drives me crazy.
14. I can't.
15. If only I can be the best, the fastest, then . . .
16. If only my kids could be the best then . . .
17. If only my department could be the best then . . .
18. When I don't do my best, people think less of me.
19. If you don't expect the best from your kids, they will not give their best.
20. A job well done will be rewarded.

audited?" to "We might get audited." Next to it write down the emotions it stirs up and the intensity of both the thought and the feeling.

Make a list of all the things you can think of that support your idea. These might include experiences you have had or things you have heard other people say. In the second column write down everything you can think of that does not support your idea or that suggests your idea is wrong. This is more difficult to do if you are pretty convinced that your idea is correct. You may have to ask others for their help with this column. Usually, if you take some time and give it some thought you can come up with some evidence to put in this column. Although you will probably be tempted to do this exercise in your head, it will be more helpful in the long run if you write it down. This allows you to compare your points more easily and will allow you to review your work at a later date if a reminder is needed. You can use the form shown as a model.

Automatic Thought:		
Feelings:		
What evidence do you have that the idea is true?	**What evidence do you have that the idea is not true?**	**What would someone else say in this situation?**

Adapted from Basco, M.R., and Rush, A.J. (1996). *Cognitive-Behavioral Therapy for Bipolar Disorder.* New York: The Guilford Press.

When you have finished the first two columns, take some time to examine your list of evidence. When you look at both sides of the argument you may decide that the evidence you came up with does not support your original idea convincingly. You may still believe it a bit, but perhaps the intensity of your belief in this idea has declined. If this is the case, you should also feel a decline in the intensity of the emotion. Rerate the intensity of your belief and of your emotion associated with the belief and mark it on your page. If your belief in this idea is not 100 percent, restate it in a way that makes it more accurate or easier to believe. If you think the idea is altogether wrong, then you will need to replace it with a more accurate view.

When you review the two columns of evidence you might decide that your original idea was, in fact, accurate and that your feelings about it were justified. If it is the case that your belief is true, what is the probability of these consequences occurring? For example, what is the likelihood that you will get audited, that if you do not keep pushing yourself you will just get lazy, that people will talk about you, or that germs will grow out of control? If you can think about this calmly and believe that there is a strong probability that one of these bad things could happen, then you can move to developing a plan for decreasing the chance that it will occur. If the event is likely to occur, how serious are the consequences? If the consequences are likely to be great, develop a plan for preventing the consequences or for coping with them if they occur. In this way you are putting your energy into planning for something real in a concrete way rather than just worrying about it.

Drawing Conclusions

- If the automatic thought is false, change it to make it more accurate.
- If you are uncertain whether it is true or false, get more information.
- If the automatic thought is true, evaluate the likelihood that the bad event will occur.
- If the likelihood is high, figure out how to avoid or prevent the outcome or develop a plan for how to cope with any negative consequences that occur. Turn your fears into an action plan.

If, after you have reviewed your list of evidence for and against your negative thought you cannot decide whether your idea is true or not, then you need more information to help you make your decision. You can talk to other people about their experiences, ask the opinions of loved ones, or try an experiment on your own to test out what will happen if you lower your standards or let down your guard. I know this sounds scary, but it may be the only way to prove or disprove your predictions about lowering your standards to a more reasonable level.

If it was difficult for you to generate evidence for or against your beliefs about lowering your standards there is another way to gain perspective on these ideas. Try to put yourself in the position of an adviser. Pretend that your friend, your colleague, your spouse, or a stranger is voicing the same idea of having to always set high standards. He is unhappy because it creates so much pressure. What advice would you offer him? Put that advice in the third column on your form. After you have done so, listen to yourself and your good advice. Does it change the intensity with which you held the original belief? This is where those ratings come in handy. Rerate the intensity with which you believe the original idea and the intensity of the feelings. Sometimes thinking about these ideas will stir up more emotions. Remember that emotions greatly influence your point of view. You may have to try to calm down and come back to the same exercise later.

Here is how some of our perfectionists responded to the idea of lowering their standards to more easily achievable levels. Joe's perfectionism stresses him emotionally when he thinks about his kids and the standards he holds for them. He looked over the list and chose "If you don't expect the best from your kids, they will not give their best." He changed the wording to fit his view. He said, "If I don't demand the best from my kids, they will not give their best." The emotions he associates with this idea are frustration and anger. He does not like having to make demands, but his children always seem to frustrate him. "They do not listen. If they listened and did what I said, they would be fine. They refuse to follow my advice."

The way that Joe completed this exercise also allows him to compare the advantages and disadvantages of his point of view. His

Automatic Thought: If I don't demand the best from my kids they will not give their best. (100% Belief)

Feelings: Frustration (75% Intensity), Anger (50% Intensity)

What evidence do you have that the idea is true?	What evidence do you have that the idea is not true?	What would someone else say in this situation?
I push my kids all the time and they do well. When I do not remind them to do their homework, they don't always do it. They will do a sloppy job with their chores unless I make them do it right. They are too young to realize the importance of doing your best.	When I was overseas the kids still did well in school. They are smart kids and they like school. Even if I demand their best they do not always give their best. My dad did not expect anything from me and I still turned out OK.	Maria says that there are other ways to motivate the kids besides threatening them. Most kids are slobs at home. It is better for them to want to do well than for them to do it just to please me. It is better to tell them you have confidence in their abilities than to be demanding.

demands may help him to accomplish his goal of getting his boys to do their best, but it also carries several consequences. It creates tension, resistance, and emotional distance between Joe and the boys. Schoolwork becomes a battleground and Joe cannot control his kids' behaviors in the classroom. His strategy might create an unnecessary power struggle between himself and his sons, and this kind of a struggle over schoolwork leaves the boys feeling bad about school. Joe is angry and frustrated with them when it comes to school and housework. They feel his disapproval and respond back to him in a negative way. Once Joe considered the consequences of his automatic thoughts, he was able to restate his original idea to make it more accurate. He says to himself, "I must teach my children the importance of demanding the best from themselves. I need to find a way that does not cause fights and push them away." The next example shown comes from Terry.

Automatic Thought:	"If I don't push myself to do my best, people think less of me." (75% Belief)	
Feelings:	Sadness (70% Intensity), Anger (50% Intensity)	

What evidence do you have that the idea is true?	What evidence do you have that the idea is not true?	What would someone else say in this situation?
When I do a good job the boss praises me and people congratulate me. No one pays attention when the work is just OK. When you make mistakes people talk about you behind your back. When you look bad, no one ever forgets. Whenever I did anything wrong my ex-husband would throw it up in my face.	Some people like me who do not work with me. My kids like me even when I make mistakes. Some people hate you for being perfect. Being perfect can be intimidating for others. When I do things perfectly some people do not recognize it and some people still do not like me.	People should like you for who you are and not for what you do. Maybe there are other reasons that people do not like you. Maybe always trying to be perfect is what makes people not like you. There is nothing wrong with not being perfect.

Terry reviewed the evidence for and against her automatic thought, and concluded that it might be an oversimplification of what is really going on in her workplace. Perhaps there is no association between how perfectly she performs and how much people like her. She has always had trouble making friends. In the past she coped with the loneliness by getting lost in her work. This turned out to be very rewarding, because she got a lot of positive attention from people for doing a good job. She became the sweetheart of the department very early in her career for being spunky and smart and confident in her abilities. She worked very hard in a system where people had gotten away with minimal effort for many years. She shaped up her department and that won her the admiration of her boss. But that was years ago and, while she has continued to be successful, she has had a lot of trouble in her personal life. She really is not very happy, feels isolated from others, and is not always certain what she does to push people away. She says to herself that people do not like her because she is serious about work and makes them look bad. While she may be partially right, she knows in her heart that she is hard on people and that creates tension in their relationships.

Here again, Terry is not only questioning the accuracy of her self-statement about lowering her standards and lightening up on others at work, but she is also examining the personal consequences of keeping this view of others and letting it affect her behavior toward them. While Terry's rationalization for her behavior may be perfectly valid, there may be personal consequences she must face to maintain this position. If other aspects of her life were more satisfying, Terry could probably better tolerate isolation from others at work. Since her divorce she has been lonely. She was right in her issues about her ex-husband Steve and their marriage. But she has figured out that there may be more to life than being right. At work she seems to have the same problem. She makes it her mission to prove that she is right. She often succeeds in this venture, but the reward may be loneliness.

June's perfectionist thoughts center on her home these days. She has been depressed for some time. When she considers lowering her standards around housekeeping, she immediately thinks, "What if someone comes to visit and the house is a mess? Rather than looking at the evidence of this happening or not, June's therapist helped her by having June imagine the consequences that she fears:

Therapist: So your biggest fear about lowering your housekeeping standards is that you will do this and someone will come to visit, unannounced I assume?

June: That's right. I would be so embarrassed.

Therapist: June, sometimes things seem scarier than they really are when you only think of them in general terms or when you do not think them through to the end. To get a better handle on this, let's imagine that it really happened. What would be the worst-case scenario of someone coming over when the house is a mess?

June: The worse case would be someone who does not know me very well and would tell others that my house is a mess.

Therapist: Like who? Give me an example.

June: Mrs. Sanders from Sissy's high school cheerleading program. She is nosy and often gossips about the homes of other parents. She has complained to me about the condition of another cheerleading mom's house. That woman works full-time and has two small children in addition to her high school daughter. She does the best that she can given her schedule. Mrs. Sanders went by her home to pick up the order form and money for the Christmas fund-raiser and apparently caught Mrs. Sharp on a bad day. At the board meeting she was telling everyone about the mess in Mrs. Sharp's house and the children running around. I was embarrassed for Mrs. Sharp and a little put out by Mrs. Sanders.

Therapist: So your fear is that Mrs. Sanders would do the same to you?

June: Yes, I suppose that would be the worst.

Therapist: This might sound like a dumb question, but what would be so bad about that?

June: The other women seem to love that kind of gossip. They tell their daughters and the girls develop bad attitudes.

Therapist: Did your daughter develop a bad attitude about Mrs. Sharp's daughter after that incident?

June: No, of course not. Sissy is a nice person. She knows better than to believe simpleminded gossip. She and Laura Sharp get along well. Sissy knows that Mrs. Sharp works hard and does not have the time on her hands that I have to do all the little extras around the house.

Therapist: Are there any other girls on the cheerleading squad that think like your daughter?

June: I suppose so, though I'm not certain. Sissy hangs around with about five other girls. They are all very nice and respectful. None of them seem mean or hateful in the least. Sissy complains about Ellie Sanders. She apparently has a mouth like her mother's. All the girls work well together, but Ellie and a few of the others do not socialize much with Sissy and her friends.

Therapist: Now I am confused, June. Help me out here. You started off saying that one of the things you worried about was that if Mrs. Sanders saw your house in some sort of disarray, she would tell the other mothers and they would tell their children and their children would be ugly with Sissy. Did I get that right?

June: Yes, that's right.

Therapist: But you are telling me that the majority of the girls on the squad are your daughter's friends and would not treat her badly just because Mrs. Sanders talked badly about your housekeeping. So what is the problem?

June: I see why you are confused. I guess that is not so much a problem. I just don't like the idea of people criticizing me or talking about me behind my back.

Therapist: If you keep your house just right by setting very high standards for yourself, does that mean that you will prevent people like Mrs. Sanders from ever talking badly about you behind your back?

June: Well, when you put it that way, I guess not, but I don't want to give her any reason to gossip.

Therapist: Is keeping Mrs. Sanders from gossiping important enough to make you work as hard as you do and to be unhappy with yourself when you cannot keep up?

June: You know, now that I think about it, I don't really like Mrs.

Sanders and I really don't care what she thinks. People who are my friends would never talk about me behind my back. If my house were a mess they would be concerned about me and would ask if they could help with anything. I don't know why I waste the energy trying to please people like Mrs. Sanders. She has no business being nosy or talking about people anyway. Who knows how she runs her household?

June's therapist pushed her to examine her fears about lowering her standards. When she thought them through, they did not seem all that frightening. That is often the case with scary automatic thoughts. They seem horrible on the surface, but in reality they are either unlikely to occur or are actually preventable or manageable. June restated her original fear in a way that seemed to fit for her: "I need to keep my home in a way that is comfortable for me and for the family. I know that even if I did less, I would never allow the house to get completely out of control. I do not really care what people like Mrs. Sanders say about me. I do care what my family thinks of me and I do care about myself."

Another approach to evaluating the accuracy or validity of scary automatic thoughts about lowering your standards is to examine the logic surrounding your conclusion. Does your logic hold? Here is an example from Brent's struggle with perfectionism. You may remember that Brent has trouble going out on a limb with new ideas because he is fearful of rejection or humiliation. He only tends to share ideas publicly that he is pretty certain will be well liked by those who matter in his company. He does this by checking out his ideas with colleagues, friends, and family members before he says a word. He has unique ideas at times that he thinks would work, but he does not share these with anyone. Sometimes he is so overwhelmed with anxiety over the whole thing that he cannot bring himself to utter a word about his ideas. He thinks that he can compensate for being weak in creativity, with accuracy and attention to detail. He thinks that if he consistently does good work, he will eventually climb the corporate ladder. He has been with the company for some time now and his advancement has been minimal. He has watched others advance ahead of him who have been with the company less time, which really angers him. He attributes their success to their willingness to play politics, snuggle up to the big boys, and basically fill their brains with "bullshit." He thinks that his superiors are not always smart enough to see a con job when it is thrown in their face, and this makes him sick. He is not about to lower himself to kissing up to anyone just to

---

Automatic Thought: "I can't do less. Only a job that is well done will be rewarded." (90% Belief)

Feelings: Anxiety (60% Intensity)

---

1. If this is true, does it also mean that a poorly done job is never rewarded? *No. I have seen poor work rewarded because the person kissed up to the boss.*
2. Does doing less always mean that you are not doing a job well? *No. Every piece of work coming out of my department is done well.*
3. Is quantity as important as quality in your company? *Yes. The dollar is the bottom line. More work usually means more money for the company.*
4. If you could not do more, but still wanted to get ahead, what would it take? *It would take one great idea that made the company a lot of money.*
5. Are you capable of coming up with that one great idea? *Yes. I think so. I have the ideas, I'm just afraid to get shot down.*
6. If you did less would you have more time to come up with that one great idea that would get you ahead? *Maybe.*
7. What would be more valuable to you, doing your work perfectly yet feeling stressed and not really getting ahead, or doing fewer tasks but focusing more energy on quality and creativity? *Getting ahead is the goal. I've tried to get there through hard work. It hasn't really paid off. Maybe it is time to take a chance.*
8. What would be the consequence of taking that chance? *I might fail.*
9. What would be terrible about that? *It would be painful. I would be embarrassed. I would not get ahead.*
10. Would it likely lower your position with the company? *No. I have been here long enough to have seniority even if I am not climbing the ladder. This company is loyal to its loyal employees. My position is pretty secure. It would just be embarrassing.*

get ahead. He thinks that hard work will earn him a seat with the "Execs." When Brent gets passed over for promotion, he tells himself that he just has to work harder. Eventually his hard work will pay off and he will be rewarded.

Brent's idea about working hard and receiving rewards makes sense to him, but it is not always the way that things work in his company. In fact, many people believe that hard work will lead to rewards. When the rewards are not forthcoming they tell themselves that the personal reward for having done a good job is sufficient. While this may be true some of the time, if you are working hard for someone else, you usually want something in return.

To review, these exercises were designed to help you evaluate your thinking about achievement and performance. In the last chapter you worked on the error of oversimplification or black and white thinking. You then defined your expectations on the cognitive continuum. This helped you to expand your view from oversimplifying your self-evaluation as success or failure, perfect or not, to a view where you could see the shades of gray between complete success and complete failure. You selected areas of performance that were important to you and defined points on your continuum of performance from 0 percent success to 100 percent success. You marked your current level of functioning, your preferred level of functioning, and a level that was OK, one that you could live with. If your actual performance was not at your preferred level, or even at the OK level, or if you were only achieving your goals with considerable stress, you had to decide whether or not you needed to lower your expectations or change your behavior. Many perfectionists have trouble with the idea of changing their standards or expectations for the reasons listed in the self-assessment (e.g., "It wouldn't be right. I can't. I couldn't live with myself.") The exercises in this chapter were designed to help you challenge your thinking about performance. The next step is to reexamine your cognitive continua from the last chapter. Look at your ratings of what you prefer to achieve and what you find OK. Revise these ratings if needed. The ultimate goal is to have a better match between what you expect and what you can accomplish. If you marked your preferred levels at 100 percent success in all areas, you need to take another try at lowering your expectations. This is particularly true if you are feeling downhearted, anxious, or depressed about your performance. Reread Chapter 3 on schemas that drive perfectionism and Chapter 5 on thinking errors. Get some feedback from a therapist or counselor if you continue to feel bad or if you develop any other symptoms of depression.

If you have decided that it may be worthwhile to lower your standards, it may be easier to do so a little at a time. Some perfectionists deal with oversimplification problems by swinging in the opposite direction (e.g., "I can't do it all, so I will do nothing"). It would be another error of oversimplification if you swung to the other end of the continuum. The goal is to live life in the gray zone. That is where most nonperfectionists live. It is a more peaceful place. You can be satisfied with yourself and with others. You can make mistakes and forgive yourself. You can be creative without fear of rejection. You can let people get close to you, see your weaknesses, and help you compensate for them. This is how to get started.

SETTING PRIORITIES

Perfection takes a lot of time and energy, both physical and emotional. You will have to choose when it is important to give an all-out effort and when it may be better to ease into the gray zone. What you will be doing is turning on your perfectionism when it is most useful and turning it off when less necessary, in order to conserve energy. How do you decide when to turn it on and off?

In the last chapter you listed all your important areas of performance. These were the ones you rated at SAT or UNSAT. Use that same list or make a similar one. You might want to add any daily responsibilities that are important but were missing from your original list. These would include daily responsibilities in each of the domains of your life (e.g., work, home, hobbies, etc.). The next step is to rank order the items on the list in terms of how important it is to perform perfectly in each area (e.g., brain surgery ranks highest, neatness of your desk ranks lowest). To help you along with your rank ordering, it may be useful to indicate for each item the level of risk to you or others for *not* being perfect (e.g., brain surgery ranks high, keeping your car clean ranks low). Use high (H), medium (M), or low (L) to rate the risk of *not being perfect* for each item. High-priority items carry the greatest consequences or risks if not performed perfectly. For these items the greatest amount of perfectionist energy should be used. Items that are lowest in priority or have the lowest risk are those that should receive the least amount of perfectionist energy. The rankings on your list will vary over time depending on current activities and responsibilities. It may be helpful to reevaluate your priorities every three to six months, depending on how rapidly your life changes. Shown is a portion of Terry's list of responsibilities and her rankings.

Terry was not rating work as being more important to her than her children. She is ranking the relative need to get it perfect because the consequences for not doing so at work would be very high, whereas not being perfect in playing with her kids would be relatively low.

Terry's List and Rankings

	Risk for not being perfect	Ranking of need to get it perfect
Caring for my children	M	3
Playing with my children	L	7
Supervising staff	M	6
Reporting data to the executive board	H	1
Writing reports	H	2
Staying caught up with laundry	L	11
Looking attractive	M	5
Sending out thank you cards	L	12
Getting a haircut	M	8
Exercise	M	10
Eating regularly	L	9
Helping my sister with her grant	H	4

Terry will adjust her effort so that the two work items get a lot of her energy and the rest of the time she will try to live in the gray zone. Practically speaking, she will spend less time in the morning trying to get her makeup and hair "just right" and spend more time caring for her kids. She will worry less about trying to get things just right with her staff, and spend more time focusing on the tasks. This will probably improve her supervisory skills, because Terry's staff members feel her intensity and get stressed. If she relaxed, the work environment would be better. When she evaluated the idea that "I must be perfect for people to like me," she concluded that people would probably like her more if she stopped trying to be so perfect. She also decided that her thought "If I don't push, no one will" may not be entirely accurate. She does have a lot of self-motivated people on her staff. "Maybe," she considered, "I should try treating them like my children, where I give praise and encouragement and they do well on their own." Thinking through her assumptions about work has helped her to decide how and when to use her perfectionism. Because she is not altogether certain that she can lower her guard with her staff, she will try to do it in steps. She will start with the ones who seem to be the most self-motivated, the perfectionists on her staff. She knows that there are some, such as her secretary, who would slack off if left to their own devices. She will experiment with how to loosen up with them.

STEP-BY-STEP

If even after you adjust your standards you are still not functioning at the level you prefer, make a plan for achieving your goals. The simplest way is to take a large task and break it down into smaller steps. You then try to do one step at a time. If you think of that cognitive continuum, you are trying to slowly move yourself up the continuum toward your goal, your OK level at first, and then your preferred level, by taking one step at a time. For example, if your goal is to achieve 70 percent success in getting organized and you are at 25 percent, figure out how to get yourself to 30 percent, then 50 percent, then 60 percent, and so on. You will then need a plan for how to stay at 70 percent once you get there. The stress from being burdened by the problem can immobilize you, especially if you oversimplify and see the problem as one big ugly mess. The inability to accomplish the goal can make you feel more distressed or depressed, and those feelings lower motivation and energy. If this happens, use the exercises in this chapter to get back on track.

SAFETY CHECKLIST

If it is your nature to work hard and put in a lot of hours, it may be difficult for you to slow down or to lower your standards. If this is the case you may need to develop a safety checklist to set limits on yourself. The safety checklist is similar to a contract you make with yourself. The first item on the safety checklist may be to set a time limit on tasks. How many hours are needed to complete the task and how many will be allocated each day for the task given your other responsibilities and time limits. Decide when to call time-out and say it is good enough for the day. Another way to think about it is to set limits on how many days per week you will work late on your project or how many family activities you will miss each month. Make a commitment to yourself and stick to it.

Second, try to take care of your basic needs so that you will have the energy to do the work. For example, get a full night's sleep. This is tough for those who get a burst of energy and creativity at night. Remember that the ability to do the job is within you; it is not really dependent on the time of day. Maybe you are more creative at night because you are more relaxed, it is quieter, and the phone is not ringing, or maybe it is because you have had a good meal and feel satisfied. If any of these are the case, find a way to arrange for these same circumstances during more reasonable working hours. Another way to take care of your basic needs is to eat. For example, set limits on how many lunches will be missed per week and stick to it ("I will miss ___lunches/week"). If you have more energy you will be able to be more productive. The thirty minutes you use to have a quick lunch will be time well spent. You can skip it, but your productivity will likely be lower and your frustration and irritability will likely be higher.

If you are a perfectionist, you are probably very good at structuring yourself and making certain that you get your work done. You are probably highly motivated and committed to doing well. All you have to do is put your well-being on the list of things to do. Mark it as a high priority and make the time to take care of yourself.

8

PERFECTIONISM AND
GETTING ALONG
WITH OTHERS

Perfectionism is very much a state of mind that influences actions and emotions. It is the way that perfectionists view themselves ("I'm never good enough"), their future ("I will never be good enough"), and the world ("If I am imperfect, I will be rejected"), which includes other people ("No one cares about their work. I'm better off doing it myself"). Situations or experiences can stimulate these thoughts, especially those in which the perfectionist feels that he is being watched or scrutinized by others. These automatic thoughts of perfectionists leave them feeling bad, rejected, guilty, embarrassed, angry, or a combination of these things.

One of the most stressful areas in the perfectionist's life can be interpersonal relationships or interactions with others. Why is this the case? Because the drive for perfectionism or the avoidance of failure often relates back to fears of what other people will think. This is especially true of inwardly focused perfectionists.

The high standards, inflexibility, and difficulty in trusting others that outwardly focused perfectionists experience can often cause difficulty in relationships, upsetting others and creating conflict. This tension places a barrier between people, creating emotional distance. This was evidenced in a study at the University of British Columbia, where pain patients who were married to outwardly focused perfectionists rated these partners as being unsupportive. Because their mind-set is that others may not be good enough, the focus is on others rather than on themselves. For this reason, outwardly focused perfectionists may know when things are not going well in a relationship, but they may have difficulty seeing their role in the problem. This chapter is designed to help perfectionists see how their views of themselves, of the future, and of others influences their interactions with the people in their lives. The next chapter of this book was written for the other people in your life who are not perfectionists, to help them understand you. You can read it yourself and then share it with others in your life.

In Chapter 5 the concept of thinking errors was introduced. The two thinking errors that seem to cause the most trouble for perfectionists in their interactions with others are oversimplification and mind reading.

EMOTIONAL LABELING

Oversimplification was covered more fully in Chapter 5 on thinking errors. In this section we will discuss how oversimplification can cause relationship problems. Because outwardly focused perfectionists expect a great deal from others, they are quick to notice and judge their behaviors. This is particularly true when the actions of others do not meet their own standards. Although they are not usually trying to be mean, they can appear judgmental or critical. From their perspective they are only trying to call it as they see it. Criticisms of others are often in the form of an emotional label, a type of oversimplification of the facts. A label is a word or expression that categorizes the other person in some way. For example, an emotional label may be "He's a jerk," "She's irresponsible," or "They are clueless." They do not take into account the person and the circumstances; instead, situations are taken out of context. Words that express extremes or absolutes can be part of the criticism, such as "He's *totally* wrong," "It *won't* work," "They have *no* idea," or "It is *absolutely* ridiculous." These are called emotional labels because they are often more emotional than logical. You might find that you use these labels when you are really angry, but when you calm down these labels no longer seem to apply. If you use emotional labels in an argument, they are likely to make the other person feel bad or to anger them. The typical argument goes something like:

"You are such a _____."
"No I'm not."
"Yes you are."
"You are wrong. You missed the point altogether. This is what happened . . ."
"I know what happened and you are _____."

You can fill in the blank to represent your favorite argument. The recipient of the criticism usually goes on the defensive. Sometimes the best defense is a good offense, so a counterattack ensues.

Emotional labels should be avoided as much as possible, because they are oversimplifications of the facts, are rarely accurate, and can be quite hurtful. In particular, you should avoid using emotional labels for the important people in your life or those with whom you must get along. So what should you do instead? There are two parts to an emotional label. There is the event that precipitated the label and there is an emotional reaction to the event. For example, you got angry (emotional reaction) because someone cut you off in traffic (event) so you call them a "dirty rotten @!#&%" (the emotional label). Another way to express your feelings about the event is to address the emotion and the specific event directly and omit the emotional label. So when someone upsets you, you tell them that they upset you and you tell them what they did that upset you. "I am so angry with you right now! You missed dinner and didn't bother to call me ahead of time." This is better and more to the point than something like "You are so inconsiderate and self-centered." In the first example the person knows exactly what she has done to upset you. In the latter, the listener does not know what you are talking about and, furthermore, thinks you are absurd. Instead of apologizing, the listener wonders, "What is *your* problem?" When you use emotional labels you invalidate your own complaints by magnifying the criticism to the point of sounding ridiculous. Then, when you are not taken seriously, it fuels your anger.

The other problem with emotional labeling is that it does not give you any direction. How does anyone fix something like being "self-centered," a criticism that is too vague to help the listener figure out what to do about it? "I'm angry because you were late again" tells the listener that she needs to do something about being on time or calling ahead when she will be late.

To Get Along Better with Others

1. Avoid using emotional labels to express yourself.
2. If it sneaks out of your mouth before you catch it, apologize for the comment and follow the steps below.
3. Tell the person what emotion you are experiencing. Some examples are: "I am angry with you." "You scared me." "That really hurt my feelings." "I'm upset with you." "I am so frustrated right now."
4. Tell them what they did to upset you. "You are ignoring me when I am talking to you." "You didn't call like I asked you to." "You were not home when I needed you." "You will not take better care of yourself."
5. It also helps if you give the person a chance to respond or explain.
6. If you want people to change their behaviors, tell them what you want them to do. "You owe me an apology for that." "I want you to go back and do what you promised to do." "Next time I want you to call if you cannot make it home on time for dinner."

MAKING ASSUMPTIONS AND
MIND READING

Perfectionists expect a great deal from others just as they expect a great deal from themselves. Their expectations of others seem reasonable to them because they are based on their own standards of performance. Since people usually do not discuss their standards with others, each person just assumes her standards are the same as everyone else's standards. That seems logical doesn't it? In the absence of any contrary information you assume that people think the same way you do. This is where it starts to cause problems for outwardly focused perfectionists. Because you assume that there is a universal standard of performance, you take it personally when your expectations are not met. Specifically, the perfectionist assumes that the other person knew what he was supposed to do but chose to do otherwise. For example, you might think "He just doesn't care," "She is trying to irritate me," "She is stupid," or "He is not trying hard enough." In contrast, the inwardly focused perfectionist will assume that the other person's actions had something to do with his own failures, (e.g., "I must not have told her explicitly enough," "I'm not a good parent; I didn't help my child enough," "I should have done it myself"). These are all good examples of mind reading or making assumptions about what other people are thinking. Where problems worsen is when the perfectionist acts based on his inaccurate view of the situation.

So what is the alternative to mind reading? Ask questions instead of making assumptions. This sounds so simple, but there is a reason people rely on mind reading instead of talking. The fantasy that many

---

Take time to think about this.

Since people usually do not discuss their standards of performance with one another, they just assume that their standards are the same as everyone else's. When your expectations are not met, you may take it personally. The assumption is that the other person knew what he was supposed to do but chose to do otherwise.

people have is that because they have known their partner, their boss, their spouse, their friend, or their child for such a long time they know how they think. On some occasions, this may be correct. People, however, change their minds, their views, their opinions, and their preferences over time. What they like today they may not like a month from now or a year from now. New experiences (and age) shape your opinions, your tolerances, and your needs. So even if you guess correctly some of the time, you will be wrong the rest of the time. If you do not ask questions, how will you know if you are right or wrong?

An even more troublesome and conflict-producing interaction that starts with an attempt to mind read is when the person whose mind you are reading tells you that your assumptions or guesses are wrong and you disagree. Instead of acknowledging that you made an error by trying to read their mind, you tell them you are right and know their thoughts or intentions better than they know their own. In communicating this you are suggesting that they are either lying to you or that they do not have the psychological insight or intelligence to know their own thoughts. In my clinical work and in my research on couple communication I have watched lots of couples argue, and have seen firsthand how mind reading and insisting you are right are great ways to start a fight.

This chapter covers some typical scenarios in which perfectionists have difficulty in their relationships with others. Brent has trouble finding a wife. Joe's son is misbehaving in school. June has a problem with her friend. Listen for how misinterpretations of people's actions, emotional labels, and mind reading seem to cause problems in relationships.

LOOKING FOR THE RIGHT MATE

Brent's friend Jessica understood his loneliness. She fixed him up with one of her old friends from high school. Jessica was certain that her friend Valerie would be a perfect match for Brent. Beautiful, bright, fun, and quickly climbing toward partner in her law firm, Valerie was a great person. They organized a double date with Jessica and her fiancé present to make sure all went well. Everything seemed fine, but afterward Brent never called Valerie for a second date. When Jessica asked, Brent had several excuses, mostly having to do with Valerie's faults: "She's too full of herself. Have you talked to her about getting a nose job? I'm sure she can afford it."

Jessica knew Brent well enough to be direct with him: "Brent, I care about you a lot, but you definitely have a problem. Valerie is perfect for you. You have a hang-up about successful women. They threaten you. I think the woman you are looking for does not really exist. You need help, and you better get it before you find yourself alone, organizing your closet into retirement."

Brent was hurt, but he knew deep down inside that Jessica was right. She was not the first person to accuse him of having problems. The others had been people who couldn't even manage their own lives, so their advice was worthless, but Jessica was a friend. She liked Brent despite his eccentricities, his flaws, and his weaknesses. ("She's probably right. I'd better get help now. I don't want to be alone.")

When Brent talked with his therapist about his date and what Jessica had said, the therapist asked Brent to imagine the date with Valerie. She wanted him to try to recall the emotions he felt when he was around her. What were the turning points in the evening? How did Valerie make Brent feel about himself? At first Brent thought these were weird questions, but he knew that his therapist sometimes went the long way around the barn to get to the door, and the trip usually served a purpose.

Brent closed his eyes and pictured Valerie.

Therapist: Tell me what you saw, what you thought about, and how you felt that evening.

Brent: We met at Jessica's place. I knew that I was the last to arrive because I saw a new BMW parked outside and assumed it was hers. Al answered the door. Jessica and Valerie were in the living room. Jessica was pouring a glass of wine. Al and I shook hands and he showed me to the living room, where Jessica made the introductions. I was feeling excited and nervous. My thought was, Wow, she's beautiful. Conversation came pretty easily. She was an interesting person and seemed very comfortable with me. That made me feel comfortable with her. She was from a small town two counties over from where I was born, so there was lots of conversation about home and what we missed most about the changing of the seasons and the holiday times.

Therapist: It sounds like things got off to a good start. When did you remember beginning to feel uneasy about her?

Brent: It was after the drink and appetizers were ordered at the restaurant. Jessica told a funny story. Al told another and everything was going fine. Valerie asked me about my work and seemed very interested. I downplayed my role in the company, as I usually do, and she said something like, don't sell yourself short. It sounds like you have done well for yourself. I asked her about her job, and that's when I started to feel my neck tighten and my stomach churn just a little.

Therapist: Do you remember the feelings you were having and the thoughts that were going through your mind?

Brent: I didn't think much of it at the time, but now I remember it was like a flash. I could picture us at dinner after we were married. I had on an apron and was serving the dinner while Valerie chatted with some bigwig from a company that had once turned me down for a job. I was the little househusband with the dreary life and the low salary and Valerie was jetting all over the world, now having become senior partner of her law firm. I was proud of her on one level and embarrassed and angry on another. That was when the evening changed. After that, every time she said something about her work it sounded like bragging. Actually, it sounded like she was putting me down. And that little comment about selling myself short sounded very patronizing in retrospect. I am a gentleman, so I watched my tongue and acted very interested. Jessica really wanted this evening to be a success and I did not want to disappoint her.

Therapist: Now that you have had time to think about your initial reaction, what do you make of it?

Brent: I think this woman would never want me. I can't begin to keep up with her. My salary will never be close to hers. My job will never be as exciting. I'm sure she has a lot of men following her. She has no reason to settle for me.

Therapist: You look very down as you say this. How are you feeling right now?

Brent: Lonely, hopeless, sad.

Therapist: What part of all of this makes you feel the worst?

Brent: I'll never find the right girl. I need to stop kidding myself. The ones I want would never want me. The ones that want me are just not my types. I'm destined to live alone. And the sad part about it is that I'm really a nice guy. I would take good care of a wife and family. I don't know what's wrong with me.

After discussing these events, Brent and his therapist concluded that Brent probably made several thinking errors in his interpretation of the events of that evening. He made errors of fortune-telling and mind reading by making guesses about what Valerie thought of him and about what a life together might offer. He also fell into his old pattern of self-criticism and self-doubt. Taken together this all amounted to a rejection of Valerie. He was reminded of something he had heard a guy in the elevator say. "It is better to reject quickly and protect your manhood than to wait to have the door slammed in your face. You lose the girl, but you keep your dignity." Brent remembered that when he first heard this it made a lot of sense to him. He thinks this is what he did with Valerie and perhaps what he had done with other women he had dated. Brent hated to have to admit this to his therapist as much as he hated admitting it to himself. It made him sound like a heartless and gutless jerk.

Therapist: Those are pretty strong labels. Are you sure you deserve them? Isn't part of the problem that you are entirely too hard on yourself?

Brent: Yes, I know. I know.

Therapist: Is there anything that Valerie did or said that gave you the impression that she was interested in you despite your prediction about her feelings?

Brent: Jessica claims that Valerie called her after the dinner and told her that she liked me and thought we would get along well together. She said she thought I might be the kind of guy who would like her for who she is rather than hate her for what she does. How's that for a real knife through the heart?

Therapist: Before you bleed all over my carpet, tell me what you think you should do about this?

Brent: I should stop being a jerk, first of all. Valerie was proud of her accomplishments and had the right to brag a bit. Actually, it was Jessica who pushed her to tell about her recent accomplishments in the courtroom. She was reluctant to bring it up herself. She never insulted me or anything like that. She seemed genuinely interested in what I did for a living. I probably need to give her the benefit of the doubt. I should ask her out and try to find out what she thinks rather than assuming I know her thoughts and feelings. I may still get rejected, but if I keep this "strike first and run" philosophy of dating, I will probably be alone for the rest of my life. That would be worse than rejection from Valerie.

Therapist: I think you are on the right track. Jessica sounds like a good friend. She was honest with you even though she knew the words would hurt you. It sounds like you took criticism from her without feeling devastated. What do you think that means?

Brent: I guess it means I am tougher than I think. I can take the truth. Actually there is probably nothing anyone could say to me that would be worse than what I say to myself.

We choose our mates not only for what they are like, but for how they make us feel about ourselves. If a successful partner makes you feel like a failure by comparison, you will shy away from that type of person. Brent is a good example of the struggle between wanting a partner who makes him feel good about himself and wanting a partner who is an independent and successful person. He does not want someone who is dependent, yet he fears someone who is independent. This conflict in needs led to loneliness because Brent could not find anyone who met all of his expectations.

Interactions with people stimulate emotions and ideas. If you have a particular vulnerability, such as thinking you are not good enough,

---

Take time to think about this.

We choose our mates not only for what they are like, but for how they make us feel about ourselves. These self-perceptions will affect your actions in the relationship. For example, if a successful partner makes you feel like a failure by comparison, you will shy away from that type of person. Here are some things to think about.

♦ How does your partner make you feel about yourself?

♦ What kinds of interactions with him make you feel good about yourself?

♦ What kinds of interactions with him make you feel bad about yourself?

---

it will be stimulated by situations that feel threatening. Brent felt threatened by Valerie's confidence and success. He did not see her; he saw himself as compared to her.

As an inwardly focused perfectionist, Brent's difficulty in finding a partner had to do with how women made him feel about himself. Outwardly focused perfectionists can have a slightly different take on relationships. They may have trouble finding someone who meets their expectations. A guy in Brent's office had this difficulty. Jerry was in his late thirties, had never been married, and lived alone with his cat, Gerdie. He was looking for a "perfect 10," while women saw Jerry as being more like a 6 ½. The 10s usually refused to date him despite his attempts. Even after several rejections, he refused to give up the pursuit. He knew that someday he would find a beautiful girl, fall in love, and live happily ever after. Brent and the other guys thought he was nuts. Several of the women in the office thought Jerry was cute and occasionally asked him for a date, but he declined politely. He was not in a hurry to find a woman and he did not mind being alone. He was comfortable waiting for the right one. The funny thing about Jerry is that he was not easily deterred. He was kind and thoughtful and had some moves for getting the really beautiful women to date him. He caught them at vulnerable moments, like after a fight with a boyfriend, and he would be kind and thoughtful and they would go home with him after work. The other guys were always amazed and envious when this happened. Jerry did not have the low self-esteem of an inwardly focused perfectionist. He had the high expectations of the outwardly focused perfectionist and was willing to risk being alone rather than compromise his standards.

It is normal to fantasize about the perfect romance, the perfect lover, and the perfect life together. Starting in our adolescence we read stories about romance, we watched movies about romance, we saw people in love gazing into each other's eyes and we wanted some of that. We were socialized to believe that it is possible. But is it possible to find the perfect mate? I don't know. Perfect is probably in the eyes of the beholder. What Jerry saw as perfect were women that Brent had dated and hadn't liked. What Brent thought was perfect at age twenty-two is different than what he thinks is perfect at age thirty-two. Joe thought his wife was perfect when he found her at age nineteen. He still occasionally thinks that she is perfect, and sometimes she is, yet at other times she infuriates Joe. That is probably the nature of most intimate relationships.

LEAD, FOLLOW, OR GET OUT OF THE WAY

June and her girlfriend Cindy volunteered to organize the Parks and Recreation Department's annual Fourth of July picnic. This was a citywide event with entertainment, food, and fireworks. The local Chamber of Commerce would organize and fund the fireworks display, but June and Cindy had to organize the rest. When you give June a task she does a great job, no question about it. She takes charge and she makes things happen. June had organized the last three Fourth of July picnics and was a real pro at it. She had never shared the responsibility for the picnic with anyone else, and she was looking forward to working with her good friend Cindy. Cindy was excited at first, but soon became frustrated with the whole thing. June had a clear picture in her mind of the right way to do things. She told Cindy her plan, but Cindy had a few ideas of her own. This is when it became tense. June had considerable experience in organizing large events. Cindy was a beginner by comparison. June knew why all of Cindy's ideas would not work because she had tried several of them over the years and watched them fall apart. She tried not to discourage Cindy, but she really did know what was best. Cindy became resentful of June's refusal to take her suggestions seriously and got even angrier when she realized that in several instances June was absolutely right. "I hate it when she is right," she said to herself. June tried to be patient with Cindy and tried to respect her point of view, but working with her was making the job harder and taking more time. Cindy was not experienced enough to take the lead in coordinating the activity. She had strong opinions and did not take well to doing things June's way, so she was not a good follower. June really wanted Cindy to get out of her way and let her take care of things so they could meet their deadlines. Finally, June took it upon herself to take charge and make things happen. One evening she made phone calls, ordered food, and arranged the entertainment without asking Cindy what she thought. As a concession, she was planning to tell Cindy that she could go ahead with one of her own ideas for an activity at the picnic. It was something that would be fun if it worked and not really missed if it failed.

The next day, when June and Cindy met, June gently told her what she had done. As predicted, Cindy was angry, but controlled it well. June enthusiastically told Cindy that she could organize the softball game and the sack race.

"Oh Yippee," Cindy said to herself sarcastically. She conceded to June and gave up her efforts to influence the events of the picnic. She organized the two games, stayed away from June, and had a terrible time at the picnic. June had a good time and received a great deal of praise, which she graciously shared with Cindy.

June felt Cindy's coldness when she tried to talk with her. June thought Cindy was mad because she did not get her way about how she organized the food line. She thought it rather petty of Cindy to have a tantrum over such a small matter. After all, June explained how these things worked. When all was said and done, June had shared the praise with Cindy even though Cindy did very little of the actual work. June did value her friendship with Cindy and felt bad when Cindy did not return phone calls and stopped coming to the Women's Club meetings.

When you are used to being a leader it is hard to stop and let someone else take the lead. It actually takes some self-control to be a follower. You have to fight the urge to take over or tell the leader how to do his job. You have to be willing to make concessions. I am a natural leader and I have two partners that I work with, both of whom are natural leaders. We are all intelligent people and we all have opinions about how things ought to be done. So how do we manage to get along and get the job done? How does each of us deal with the frustration that June felt when she tried to work with Cindy? First, we recognized the need for leadership and selected a leader from among ourselves without a lot of discussion. We chose the most senior of the three of us in terms of age and experience. The second thing we did was to place as much value on maintaining our relationship as we placed on the tasks at hand. That meant that while we may have all wanted to do things our own way, we put more effort into being respectful of one another's ideas than into getting our own way. We each gave a little here and there and when we disagreed we deferred to our leader. When I joined this group, I was the youngest and least experienced of the three, so it was easy for me to go along with the other two. I was raised to be respectful of my elders and so I took my proper place in line. (My schema about age and respect guides my actions.) As time has gone on and I have gotten more experience, I have grown more comfortable in asserting my ideas and maybe even being a little pushy. Of course, my partners have had numerous opportunities to watch me work and have come to trust me. If I feel strongly about something I push harder. They always listen and sometimes let me take the lead. When they do not agree it is not the end of the world.

What June did not notice while organizing the picnic was that something was happening to her relationship with Cindy along the way. She was so focused on the task that she did not realize that she was losing a friend in the process. Sometimes it is more important to preserve a relationship than to be right or to have your way. Although it may seem as if there is a right way and a wrong way to do things, it is seldom that simple (is this starting to sound familiar?). Just because it is different does not mean that it is wrong. It may be scary to take a risk and do something differently than you had been accustomed to in the past. If things go wrong, the perfectionist feels at risk for getting blamed or being embarrassed. That is how June felt about

---

What to Do When it is Not Your Turn to Lead

---

1. Recognize that it is hard to not be in charge.
2. Put effort into being a good follower.
3. Respect the role of the leader and do your part to support this person.
4. Make concessions when possible, but be assertive if you feel strongly about something.
5. If you place value on the relationship as well as the task, be mindful of how your behaviors affect others. It is not OK to just "speak your mind" or to "just be honest," or to "call them as you see them" if you know it will hurt the feelings of others or damage the relationship.
6. Take time to think, measure your words, and use tact.

---

the picnic. If one of Cindy's plans had gone wrong, June would have looked bad to others. June is very sensitive about how others perceive her and does not like to take risks with her reputation. Of course, if you asked June she would acknowledge that she had taken risks by trying new things over the years and all had turned out pretty well. She could have taken chances with Cindy's ideas and preserved their friendship along the way.

ARE YOU A SLOB OR AM I TOO PICKY?

Perfectionists sometimes catch themselves being hard on others, but are confused about which one of them is wrong. They know they can be too picky on the one hand, and notice details that others overlook. On the other hand, sometimes other people do poor quality work and deserve criticism. How can you know if you are being too critical? In most cases, the best strategy is to talk to the person you are observing. Tell him what you expect, what you prefer, or what you will demand, depending on the situation. If he cannot or will not comply, then you have to negotiate a solution, find someone else to do the task, help the person to meet your standards, or do it yourself. If it is important to make something turn out "just right" it will usually be best to find someone who can work at your level or do the task yourself. If you are buying a service, this will usually cost you more money. Quality work takes more time, and time is money.

A friend, who has some characteristics of both inwardly and outwardly focused perfectionism, wanted to have his house painted. He inquired at the local paint store and received names of several painters who frequent this store. "This one is a perfectionist," the store manager warned, "and the highest priced of the three." Although my friend values perfectionism, he had a budget to consider, so he hired someone else on the list. The first painter took his deposit, worked a day or so, and never showed up again. After several weeks he was forced to hire another painter. According to my friend, this new one had apparently never learned to stay between the lines and smeared paint on the shingles of his house. When my friend confronted the gentleman, the response he got was a sharp criticism: "You are so anal. No one can please you. I quit! You can have the paint. Find someone else to finish the job."

Not having been there myself, I have no way of knowing how big of a slob the painter was or how "anal" my friend was about the work. I think anyone would fuss if someone left paint on the shingles of the house. As a personal rule, I try not to practice psychology on my friends or relatives. But if I did, I might have explored whether he had seen the second painter's work in black and white terms. To do so I might have gotten my friend to list his expectations of the painter. He would probably have said something like "I expect him to do a good job and to complete the job on time." If I pushed him to be more specific, he probably would have made a list that included neatness, protecting his garden, cleaning up after himself, using quality products, punctuality, speed, craftsmanship, and politeness. I would have asked him how the painter fared in each of these areas on a continuum such as the ones discussed in Chapter 6. I would have asked him to rate his expectations of the painter on the continuum from 0 percent to 100 percent perfection in each area as well as levels that would be tolerable. After comparing the painter's actual performance against my friend's standards he could conclude whether or not he was being too picky or too "anal." Rather than oversimplifying the painter's performance as "poor" or using emotional labels such as "crook" or "lazy," this exercise may have helped my friend to identify specific things the painter did that he did not like. He could then give the painter specific feedback and instructions.

The question of what is reasonable to expect from others is tricky because the answer is usually subjective. Your expectations of others will depend upon their role in your life. For example, if you are paying for a service, such as a painter's services, you may have different expectations than if a friend had volunteered to paint your house. What you might expect from an employee may be different than what you expect from your spouse. The role determines the goal. You can see from these examples that the vulnerabilities of the perfectionist affect their interpersonal relationships. When things are not going well with others it is easier to see what the other person is doing wrong than to see your own faults. This is true for both types of perfectionists. Nonperfectionists expect themselves to make mistakes, so when they do it does not hurt quite as much, although it never feels good to hurt someone else's feelings. If you expect yourself to never make that kind of mistake, it will feel like a personal failure when you inevitably do make a mistake. The mistakes themselves may not be all that important. What is important is how those mistakes make you feel about yourself. If your emotions run high, they will likely influence how you handle interactions with others.

Unfortunately, high emotion has a way of bringing out the worst rather than the best in each of us. Know your vulnerabilities and fac-

---

How to Cope With Nonperfectionists

1. Acknowledge that you are a perfectionist and details are important to you.
2. Define your expectations. Be specific. How will you know if your expectations are met?
3. Discuss your expectations up front.
4. If the other person cannot or does not agree to meet your expectations, negotiate a solution. Find someone else to do the task, help with the task, or do it yourself.
5. If they agree to meet your expectations, but do not, give feedback and instructions, help with the task, or find someone else to finish.

tor those into the equation when you are trying to understand why your interactions with others are not going well. Think of it this way. Your underlying views or beliefs (schemas) about being perfect are like filters. Your communication with others will pass through this filter. Sensitivity filters such as perfectionism will color how you interpret the things that other people say. For example, you might hear criticism of your idea when someone else is offering a different opinion. Perfectionism is a filter that will also affect the words that come out of your mouth. You may intend to say one thing, but the filter of perfectionism will make the words come out differently by affecting your tone of voice or your choice of words. Joe wanted to communicate to his kids that it was important for them to always try to do their best. His perfectionistic filter made the words come out sounding like criticism or disapproval. Perfectionists can learn to become aware of their beliefs so that they can keep them from filtering their communication with others and distorting either how messages are sent or how they are received.

PERFECTIONISM AND PARENTING

I am sure that by this time you have figured out that you share some characteristics of perfectionism with your parents. This is probably not a coincidence. Dr. Randy Frost and his colleagues at Smith College in Northampton, Massachusetts, studied perfectionism in parents and children and found that mothers' perfectionism and fathers' criticism of imperfection was associated with perfectionism in their daughters, passing from one generation to the next. Although perfectionism can serve you well in a lot of areas in your life, including parenting, it can also cause you grief. You are reading this book because you want to get a handle on the times when your perfectionism gets the best of you. Therefore, you will want to think about whether or not you want to pass your perfectionist standards on to your children. Understanding how your perfectionism can affect your interactions with your children will help you to decide when you need to tone it down. Following are some examples of how the vulnerabilities associated with perfectionism, such as fearing rejection or humiliation from others or setting standards that are difficult to reach, can affect how you act toward your children and perhaps cause you to send the wrong messages.

When Your Kids Let You Down

Joe got a call from Sergio's school counselor. It seemed that the group of "delinquents" his son hangs out with had gotten into trouble at school. It was not yet clear how Sergio was involved in the situation. Joe and his wife, Maria, were asked to meet with the school counselor. Joe was so angry he thought he would explode. He politely agreed to the meeting and then walked outside slamming the door so hard it nearly fell from its hinges. To himself, he said: "Wait until that @#%$&! comes home, I'm going to beat the crap out of him. My sons do not, absolutely do not, get in trouble. It will not happen as long as that boy lives in my house. I do not care what Maria says, this time I'm going to beat some sense into that boy. And if those little creeps he hangs around with come near my home, they will know my fury."

Joe's emotions were strong and influenced his thinking about how the situation should be handled. Before the boys came home from football practice, Joe had managed to calm himself down. He spoke to his wife, and she talked him into listening before reacting: "All right Maria, but this is it. If Sergio is involved in gangs or drugs, he will hear from me no matter what you say. Man to man."

Joe, Maria, and Sergio met with the school counselor. Sergio's friends were caught smoking marijuana in the boys' bathroom. Sergio was not seen smoking and swore that he was there, but was not using drugs. The counselor said that Sergio was a good kid, but was easily influenced by kids who have problems at school, including those using drugs. After talking with Sergio, she had concerns about him. He seemed depressed to her. She thought he needed to be seen by a psychologist and that the whole family should be involved. Joe did not understand what his boy's friends had to do with depression and why he should have to be the one who goes to counseling. "There is nothing wrong with me," he thought. The school counselor patiently explained that she thought that Sergio was having trouble communicating with Joe. She believed that he was afraid of Joe and said that, if this were not remedied, Sergio would be in for bigger trouble in the future. She referred the Martinez family to a psychologist in town with experience in working with the families of troubled youth.

Joe's heart sank into his stomach. The school counselor confirmed his deepest fear. His mule-headed Marine Corps ways had hurt his children. He felt a great deal of shame. His automatic thoughts followed from his fear of failure and his schema that he was supposed to be a better parent than his dad had been. He hugged his son as they left the meeting, but said nothing. When they got home he skipped dinner and went to his workshop, where he stayed up half of the night. His wife knows that when he is like this he needs to be left alone, but she had never seen such despair in him, and so she began to worry as much about her husband as she did about her son. A week later they reluctantly saw the psychologist to begin work.

This whole event was more disturbing to Joe than to his son or his wife. To Joe this was personal because it meant that he had failed as a father. (This is a good example of an oversimplification.) Part of him knew that every time he was hard on the boys, he should lighten up, especially with Sergio. He knew that Sergio was different. He was more sensitive than the older one. He was weak in Joe's eyes, and he hated that part of his son, just as he hated that part of himself. Sergio made Joe feel like he had failed. Usually when Joe feels bad, he comes out fighting. When the counselor first called Joe to give him the news about Sergio, Joe took it in the stomach. A heavyweight champ could not have delivered a harder blow. His initial reaction had been anger, but his real feelings were disappointment and guilt. He was disappointed in Sergio. It seemed to Joe that Sergio had done this "to him" on purpose. After all the lectures that Joe had given, after all the warnings, Sergio had done this just to spite Joe. This made Joe angry, so when Sergio walked through the door that day Joe exploded. Sergio had taken it like a man, just as his father had taught him. He said yes sir and no sir. He knew that there would be no way to convince his dad that he had not done anything wrong, so he decided not to try.

Both Sergio and Joe were having a silent conversation, each reading the other's mind. Both made assumptions that proved incorrect. Each reacted off their emotions rather than their logic.

Joe's reaction of isolation after talking with the counselor was fueled by his feelings of guilt and the thought that he had let his son down. He had failed at being a father. ("If I had been a good father, my son would never have done this.") He felt so bad for his son that he sat in his workshop and cried to himself. He thought about going back into the service. He thought the boys would be better off without him. He thought about moving out and letting Maria raise the boys, washing his hands of all responsibility to them. He knew how to be a Marine. He did not know how to be a father. He had failed. Joe's oversimplification did not lead to reasonable solutions to Sergio's problem.

Sergio met with the psychologist first so that she could try to evaluate him for symptoms of depression and to establish an alliance with him. The school counselor had said that Sergio was a sensitive kid and needed an ally. When the family met with the counselor, Joe had his guard up. He was not about to lower himself by falling apart like some "sick bay commando." After all, he was a proud man. For Joe, talking to a psychologist was like losing his pride. Only "sickos" see a shrink. (This is a great example of emotional labeling.) In the back of Joe's mind he knew that he needed help, that he was not as strong as he thought he was, and that he was probably going to break down and cry right in the middle of this lady's leather couch. "Oh God," he thought. He could picture them bringing in the straitjacket and wrapping him up.

The therapist turned to Joe and said, "Mr. Martinez this must be especially hard on you."

"What do you mean?" questioned Joe.

"You are obviously a proud man with very high expectations for yourself and for your family. When someone in the family does something wrong, parents often feel that it was their fault, that they had failed in some way. That has to hurt inside."

There she went and did it. She unplugged the faucet of his tears and they began to stream down Joe's cheek. "Damn it, why did we have to come here?" he thought to himself trying to maintain his composure. "Suck it up, Martinez. Don't lose it," he tried to tell himself.

"You know Miss, er, Doctor, you hit the nail right on the head. This thing is killing me. I'm sorry to break down like this, but I love my son and I feel like I have failed him. I have been hard on my boys. I want them to turn out right, to have a good life. Maybe I just pushed so hard he went right over to the other side."

"Is that what you think this is all about?" she asked.

"I know my son and I think that's what is going on."

"It's not quite that simple, Mr. Martinez," the doctor replied. "Sergio is a complicated kid and he has some complicated problems. I know you want to help so let me try to explain."

The doctor went on to explain that Sergio was in the wrong place at the wrong time. She did not believe that he used drugs of any sort, but she was troubled by his choice of friends. Sergio had told her that when he is around them he feels good about himself, whereas at home he does not feel very good about himself. He feels that he has failed his father and that no matter what he tries he can never be good enough. This comment hit Joe like a blow to the head.

"My Sergio is a good boy," Maria interjected.

"He is a very good boy," Joe added. "He has always been very smart, very polite, and hardworking. I am proud of his accomplishments. He has good grades and his teachers have always said good things about him. At home he helps out, does his chores, and never complains. How could he think he wasn't good enough?"

The doctor went on to explain that while Sergio takes criticism very hard, he usually doesn't hear praise when it is offered. Certain that he has let his father down, Sergio has given up, taken the easier path, and hangs out with guys who are worse off than him. By comparison, Sergio is in great shape. Unfortunately, these boys were dumb enough to try to smoke pot in the bathroom and got caught. Sergio was actually on the scene to try to stop them, but he got caught with the rest of them. The school counselor was right about Sergio looking depressed. He was mildly depressed and needed a bit of counseling, probably with his father, to straighten out all the misunderstandings. Joe needed to tell Sergio that he was good enough. Sergio needed to tell Joe what he was saying or doing that made Sergio feel bad. Each agreed to stop trying to read minds and to start sharing their thoughts and asking questions. And they all lived happily ever after? Well, it was not that simple, but with work they were able to help both Sergio and Joe feel better about themselves and each other. Again, in this scenario, trying to read minds rather than ask questions led to misunderstandings. Joe oversimplified the problem as "I am a failure" as did Sergio. Both needed to learn to look more closely at the problem. Sergio helped Joe figure out how to be a better dad by giving him feedback on how he came across to others. Joe's intention was to motivate his children and push them so that they could excel. He never intended to make them feel bad in the process. Joe had to figure out how to accomplish his goals as a father in a way that worked for his kids. He had to talk to them.

Joe's emotions, tendency to jump to conclusions, mind reading, and negative self-schemas initially interfered with his ability to handle this problem with his son. For such a level-headed, methodical,

---

When Your Emotions Get the Best of You

Even if you are generally a levelheaded person, emotions can interfere with your logic. Take time to calm yourself before you try to handle an important problem, especially if it involves other people. While you reduce the intensity of your emotion you give your logic a chance to help you with the problem. Here are some ways to reduce the intensity of the emotion.

1. *Get some air.* Take deep breaths to lower your heart rate (don't hold your breath and count to 10).
2. *Walk away.* Physically remove yourself from the situation that is upsetting you.
3. *Get physical.* After you walk away and take a few deep breaths, do something that lets you expel some of the physical energy. Here are some ideas: do a chore like sweep the floor, dig a ditch, wash the car, or take out the garbage; exercise—take a walk, a swim, or a jog; hit a punching bag if you have one; take a broom, a tennis racket, or a pillow and beat your mattress (make sure no one gets in the way).
4. *Get quiet.* Leave the scene, listen to soothing music, stare at the fish tank, lie down and close your eyes, take a bath, go outside and look at the stars.

and logically minded person, Joe reacted very emotionally. When emotions flare, logic takes a backseat. Before Joe could use his head he had to calm down. When he was able to do so, he was able to help his son and himself.

Emotional reactions to bad events or tense interactions with others are stimulated not only by the events themselves, but by the meanings attached to the events. Joe's perception of his son's problem at school changed as his emotion changed. Anger led to blame of his son. Self-criticism led to guilt. Both emotional reactions led to plans of action that were unhealthy and would not have helped to cope with the real problem. If your take on events changes dramatically and each view is believable at the time it occurs, you should stop and ask yourself if your emotions are governing your thinking. If so, to have an accurate view of events you have to reduce the emotion. If you do not, you will draw the wrong conclusions and take the wrong course of action. Sometimes these actions, which are intended to help you cope with the problem, actually make things worse.

Praise for an Action Versus Acceptance of the Person

If you watch perfectionist parents with their children you can see that their children's performances in school, in dance class, or on the playing field stir up a lot of emotions. The young girl scores a goal and her mom and dad go wild in the stands. Another child misses a free throw and everyone can see the disappointment on his father's face. A fourth grader forgets her lines in the school play and Mom is embarrassed. You are probably wondering if this is just part of normal parenting. It is. The difference in the lives of perfectionists is that when your child does not do well you may feel responsible.

A child's failure can be an emotional experience for the perfectionist parent, especially if it occurs publicly. Remember that events themselves are not as important as your interpretation of events. When your child does well, perhaps you interpret this as evidence that you are a good parent, and when your child does poorly as evidence that you are a bad parent. Your sensitivity to what others think of you may kick in when others comment on your child's performance. Perhaps when your child receives praise from your peers it makes you feel more accepted. When he performs poorly, you may mistakenly assume that others are scrutinizing your parenting skill.

Remember that your thoughts and your feelings greatly influence your actions. If you are troubled by your child's mistakes or her failures, your most likely reaction may be to withdraw emotionally from her, if only for a short while, as you think it over. Even if you offer words of support and encouragement, a sensitive child will sense your emotional withdrawal and may interpret it as rejection. Because automatic thoughts and the accompanying emotional reactions can evolve quickly, you may pull back from her before you have had time to think through how she will perceive your reactions. Children are very sensitive to the emotional reactions of their parents, no matter how well you try to hide them. To avoid this trap, you have to watch and think about your reactions to your child's achievements. The goal is to love the child for who she is and not for what she does.

From your child's perspective, if you hold back emotionally when he fails and hug him enthusiastically when he succeeds, he will learn to associate good performance with love or affection and poor performance with anger or rejection. It does not take long for a child to try to figure out that if he does things well, it will lead to more positive interactions and fewer negative ones. In some families, children might even avoid things in which they know they will not excel in order to avoid the rejection they think will follow.

Take time to think about this.

When a child does well, perhaps you interpret this as evidence that you are a good parent, and when he does poorly as evidence that you are a bad parent. Perhaps when your child performs poorly in front of others it seems as though others are scrutinizing you. The discomfort you feel may cause you to withdraw emotionally from your child. He may sense this and feel rejected.

How To Give Praise

"You are such a good boy. Mommy loves you very much." "Good girl!" "You are such a big girl." Do these forms of praise sound familiar? They are common ways that parents reinforce their children for a job well done. The only problem is that these expressions say nothing about the job that was done; they are merely comments about the child. Without intending, parents' praises of their children can sound like love or acceptance of the child rather than a praise of the action that occurred. Expressions that are specific to tasks are things such as "That was a great catch at the bottom of the second!" "Thank you for remembering to put away your plate." "Nice job on your spelling test." "You handled that situation really well." "It was kind of you to share with your brother." "Good job!" To practice unconditional acceptance, deliver praise when the child does something you like. Save your expressions of love and acceptance for another occasion. Try not to tie the two together.

Parents can often forget to express their love or affection toward their children on a regular basis. Big events, such as big successes, a winning game, report card day, or graduation make people feel emotional and remind them of how much they love their children. Dr. David Burns, author of the best-selling book *Feeling Good: The New Mood Therapy,* has observed that perfectionist parents often use love and approval as rewards for superior performance. It is OK to express love at these times as long as you express love and acceptance the rest of the time as well. When a child does poorly and is feeling bad about it, expressions of love and affection can help to mend hurt feelings. Spare the kid the lecture on performance, hard work, and the future and just show her your love.

Encouragement Without Criticism

Most parents want their children to do well. Remember that perfectionists have very high standards for themselves and for others.

Thinking that they are not good enough themselves will motivate parents to want their children to be better, smarter, stronger, or more experienced than them. There is an unwritten rule among parents that in order to get your child to do her best you have to push her. If she does fairly well, but you know she is capable of doing better, you push a little more. Unfortunately, some children mistake this kind of encouragement for criticism. They hear the part of the message that is evaluative ("You could do better," which means you are not good enough now) and they miss the praise and encouragement part ("You are so smart. I know you will continue to excel"). If your child is sensitive to criticism she can develop "tunnel vision" at an early age (see Chapter 5 on thinking errors) and miss the positive part of your messages. Some examples of the messages parents send to motivate their children but that are often received as criticism by them are "I know you can do better," "Practice makes perfect," and "Don't get overconfident just because you got an A this time."

Try to avoid giving your child mixed messages. Separate giving praise from giving criticism or suggestions for improvement. Sometimes it is better to just give praise than to try to use the event as an opportunity to teach, coach, critique, or motivate the child. For example, instead of saying, "That was good, but . . ." just say, "That was good." When praise is accompanied by a critique or by "helpful advice," the child hears criticism. The critique cancels out the praise in their minds. There are other ways to motivate a child. In the section following entitled "What is the Answer?" we will discuss ways to help children set their own goals and motivate themselves.

Humility Is a Virtue

Perfectionists often have strong ethical, religious, and moral values. These are generally passed on to their children in the form of lessons or by setting good examples. There are many families that believe that humility is a virtue. There is nothing wrong with being humble. However, sometimes, as parents teach their children the value of humility, they accidentally teach a less positive lesson about self-esteem. Here is how it works. Some people, including perfectionists, see humility as being the opposite of pride (i.e., pride is bad and humility is good). When teaching this to their children, some parents oversimplify the concepts and give children the wrong message. Children often interpret things in very concrete or literal ways. So when you tell them that pride is bad and humility is good, some will come to believe that if they feel good about their accomplishment this is pride, and therefore it is bad. They also may come to believe that the opposite is good, for example, downplaying their achievements, taking note of only their weaknesses, or being self-critical. For some parents, while teaching the value of humility you may inadvertently discourage attention to achievement. Thereby, good work may not only go unnoticed, but may even be punished.

Add to this confusion a family value of hard work, effort, and success. Mix it all together and you send confusing messages to children. It goes something like the following: "It is important that you do your best in school and achieve high marks. But it is not OK to boast or brag, so do not run home bragging about that perfect score on your spelling test. I will punish you if you do this. I will also punish you if you do not do well in school. It is OK to be self-critical. We can talk about your faults. It is not OK to talk about your achievements." This may sound like an exaggeration, because these sentiments are not usually communicated as directly as this. They are, however, implied in the various verbal and nonverbal messages that parents send their children.

I have met many perfectionists who learned these rules as children and dealt with them by quietly achieving as if it were breaking a family rule. They ended up with an uncomfortable mix of self-confidence in some areas and great self-doubt in others. They are still trying to get things "just right" so that their parents will accept them, praise them, and feel good about them. If you talk with their parents, their parents will sometimes say, "Of course we are proud of our child. We have always been proud." They had the rules of humility and pride straight in their minds, but when they tried to teach these fairly complicated rules to their kids, the message that was heard was, "There is no way you can make us feel good about you. You will get negative feedback about doing well and about doing poorly. You will never be good enough."

I believe the mistake that parents make is one of oversimplification. Humility is a complicated concept. Applying it to a child's life and experiences is not that easy. Humility and pride are not two sides of the same coin, not black and white concepts. They must be taught without losing the more important message of parental acceptance of a child, unconditional love, and the value of good self-esteem.

There is another way that the value of humility held by parents can be a problem for their children. Some people who have high-achieving children deal with their personal need to be humble by being critical of their children in front of other people. They either balance bragging about their children with criticism of their children or they only criticize. Some parents talk about their children's weaknesses in front of others with the hope that the listener will respond with a compliment of the child. This feels comfortable to a parent because it is not prideful if someone else praises you or your child. You can act humble in response and this will keep you from violating the "pride bad–humility good" rule. This strategy might not be so bad if your children did not hear it or know that you did it. However, kids are very smart. They pay attention even when you think they are not listening. If they did not hear the criticisms directly from you, it is certain to get back to them if you criticize them often enough in public places. It is bad enough for a child to receive criticism from her parents. It is doubly hurtful when the criticisms are shared with others.

Some parents do not teach about humility in such a direct way; rather, they teach it only by example. Depending on how the parent handles their own achievements, children can either get a healthier understanding of humility or another confusing message. Here is where it gets complicated. In some environments pride is not only adaptive, it is the path to advancement. If you do not promote yourself, others will not take notice of you and reward you for your successes. You have to let others know that you have a great idea, have done well, have made them some money, or that you have been recognized for your achievements. Advancement and success are based on such things.

It will be useful to your children to learn this at some point in their lives. How do you teach self-promotion and humility at the same time? When is a child likely to understand and be able to apply these concepts? Perhaps the time to teach these concepts is when the child can apply them to her day-to-day experiences. For example, self-promotion may not be necessary in elementary school, but what happens when your child gets into high school and wants to run for class president? That may be a time when self-promotion is essential. The same is true for humility. It is much easier to teach about this complicated concept when there is a specific situation to which the child can apply the lesson. For example, when your child does exceptionally well or earns an award and his friends do not, you would want to teach him to feel good about it, but to not use the achievement to be hurtful to others. In this case, self-promotion that is used to criticize peers is not adaptive and will create problems for your child ("I made the team and you didn't, ha ha ha").

Another way to teach about humility is to help your child understand the continuum of behaviors that range from self-criticism to

---

Things to Avoid as Parents

1. "That was nice, but I bet you could do better"
2. Criticism of the child rather than the behavior, ("Bad boy")
3. Always associating praise with love or acceptance and criticism with anger or rejection.
4. Threatening loss of affection for poor performance or failure.
5. Threatening punishment for failure, ("If you fail that test . . .")
6. Making acceptance of the child contingent upon good performance.
7. Taking children's failures personally. It does not mean you are a bad parent.
8. Holding back affection when a child has made a mistake.
9. Redoing your children's chores (e.g., remaking the bed).
10. Criticizing them to others or in front of others.
11. Confusing good self-esteem with lack of humility or prideful behavior.
12. Hiding your weaknesses and errors from your children.
13. Consistently try to improve upon or criticize their appearance.

prideful boasting that hurts others. Over time, help her to pick the right response to match the circumstances.

WHAT IS THE ANSWER?

I am not suggesting that praising or punishing a child is wrong. It becomes a problem when the punishment or rejection is severe, when the approval and praise is hard to come by, and when the child is particularly sensitive to these things. That sensitivity could have been there from birth or could have been shaped by early childhood experiences of rejection or punishment. So what do you do about it?

You can do a lot of things to make a child feel good about himself. Children usually come to see themselves as their parents see them. Tell them that you have confidence in them and they will come to have confidence in themselves. Tell them that you will love them no matter what they accomplish and they will come to love themselves no matter what they accomplish. Tell them that they are more than just good enough. Tell them that they are terrific. I may be oversimplifying the matter a bit, but I think that this part of parenting can be easy to accomplish. You just need to deliver these messages convincingly and consistently. Children will hear your inconsistency. They will believe what the tone in your voice suggests, not the words coming out of your mouth. Does this mean that you cannot push your children to exceed? Not at all. The message just needs to be delivered separately from messages of acceptance and love. "I know you can do it" is a message of confidence. "You had better get a good grade" is a threat.

I believe that parents can help their children develop realistic views of adulthood in general by letting their children see their imperfections. When you as the parent make a mistake, admit it, particularly if your mistake was with your child. Much of what is learned from parents is through modeling. This is another way of saying that kids learn from example. Show them how to cope with imperfections, mistakes, errors, and blunders, including how to accept responsibility for their errors. Show them that you can screw up, fix it, and everything can work out OK. Show them that you can make mistakes and still be a good person. Although adults seem to have all of the answers, they are just further along in learning and experience than their children. Most parents want to help their children avoid the mistakes they made as kids or young adults, so they give lectures or advice. However, most of the best lessons children learn from adults is through example. Talk less and show more.

Children will ultimately need to learn to set their own standards rather than spend their adulthood continuing the struggle to be good enough for you. Sometimes this does not happen until they are out of college and on their own, but there is no reason why you must wait until adulthood to begin teaching them. If your child sets a standard for herself, the motivation to succeed will be internally driven. This is more powerful than being driven by fear of rejection or punishment by you: "I had better do well or my parents are going to kill me." If the child has a personal goal, then he has a reason to work hard and succeed. This can be developed as simply as saying "What do you plan to get on your spelling test this week? What do you need to do to get that grade? Is there anything I can do to help you reach your goal?" If your child does not reach her goal, help her set a more reasonable goal, such as an improvement over the previous week. You might want to hear your child say that the goal is to get a perfect score on the test. For some kids, this is a reasonable goal. For others, it may not be. Help your child set a goal that can realistically be achieved. It is OK if it is a little high. You have to start somewhere. It is also OK if it is a little low if the child knows that the task is very difficult. For example, my sixteen-year-old son might set a goal of getting an A in at least three of his eight classes and nothing less than Bs in the rest. For him this is reasonable. My husband and I will listen to his goals, and if we think he is capable of doing better we might counter with "What would it take for you to get an A in four classes?" For him it usually means less time on other school activities and with his girlfriend and a little more time studying. If he is convinced that it is worth his effort to go for that extra A, then he is doing it for himself rather than to please us.

If your child comes home with a grade lower than you expect or prefer, chances are that he is not very happy about it either. The traditional approach is to tell the kid he can do better, deliver a punish-

---

Things to Do as Parents

1. Give praise for accomplishments. Say "Good job," not "Good boy."
2. Express love and affection frequently, not only when the child has performed a task successfully.
3. Pay attention to your own self-consciousness. When a child has a problem, keep the focus on him. It is not necessarily about you.
4. When you have to scold or correct your child, keep the focus on the action. Make sure the child understands that you love and accept her regardless of any mistake she might make.
5. You have to give negative feedback, give it privately and give the child a chance to correct her behavior and try again. Reward improvements.
6. Encourage your child to feel good about his accomplishments.

---

ment (restrict TV time), increase study time, and monitor progress. If you want to encourage your child to set standards and goals, ask him how he feels about the grade. What would have been more satisfactory? What would he have to do to raise the grade? How can you help? Express confidence rather than anger. Remember what it was like to be a kid with a bad grade you had to show to your parents. Remember what it was like to be put on the second or third string when your dad was a starter. Remember that most kids care about how they do in school, in sports, with friends, at piano lessons, or in scouts. Support achievement and avoid making it a battleground or a power struggle. Kids come to believe about themselves what their parents believe about them. Communicate directly that you believe in their abilities. Move the emphasis from having them reach your standards to having them reach for their own.

9

LIVING WITH

PERFECTIONISTS

Maria, Joe's wife, prides herself on being a patient woman, but sometimes Joe gets on her nerves. Joe and Maria decided to change the wallpaper in their home. Maria got referrals from several of her friends and neighbors who had had similar work done in the last year and selected a local contractor with a good reputation for quality work and efficiency. The contractor measured the rooms and gave Joe and Maria an estimate of the cost of the work and the timeline for completion. Trying to please his new customers, the contractor gave them an overly optimistic time projection for completion of the work and a cost estimate that assumed their walls would not require any unusual preparation time or effort. These turned out to be two big mistakes that caused everyone a great deal of grief. Joe has a few basic rules for work that he expects everyone to follow. They include: "Do what you say you are going to do," "Always be honest in

your estimates of time and cost," and "Do not inconvenience the cus-
tomer any more than is necessary." Although these may all seem like
reasonable rules, when taken too literally, and inflexibly, they created
friction not only between the wallpaper hanger and Joe, but also
between Joe and Maria. When Joe first found out that the job was
going to cost more because the removal of the old paper damaged the
plasterboard beneath, he was upset. He assumed that the reason for
the damage was poor quality workmanship.

Maria was usually the messenger of bad news, so she always got to
hear Joe's initial angry reactions. "I thought you said these people
could be trusted," he snapped at Maria. "I thought your friends said
these guys knew what they were doing. These guys are trying to rip
us off."

Although she knew he was really angry with the workers and not
with her, he had a bad habit of blowing his top with her and then
calming down and speaking rationally to the real target of his anger.
In this case, she tried to explain that the original paper had been
glued directly to the plasterboard without any wall preparation, and
that had caused damage when they tried to remove the old paper, but
all he heard was that she was defending the contractor.

The contractor apologized when Joe confronted him and explained
that sometimes "these things happen." This was not an acceptable
excuse. In Joe's mind you either do what you promise or you don't,
simple as that.

The first estimated date of completion of the work came and went
and every additional day Joe's frustration grew. He was tired of the
mess, having strangers in his home, and workers not showing up when
they said they would. He threatened to fire them multiple times, but
Maria pleaded with him to let them finish the job. They argued over
the wallpaper so much that when the job was finally done neither one
of them could enjoy their home's new look.

"No one is ever good enough for him," Maria complained to her
mother over the phone. "I knew we were in for trouble as soon as the
contractor said, 'No problem. We should be able to get it done in a
week and a half.' Once you make Joe a promise, you had better live

up to it. I felt sorry for the young workers. They were so afraid of Joe that they would get nervous and do something wrong, like trip and spill water on the floor, just as he was walking through the door. I swear I will never hire anyone to do work in this house again."

Maria gets frustrated trying to help Joe calm down when things like this happen. She would say that dealing with him is harder than dealing with the wallpaper hangers, the mess, the delays, and the extra costs. From the beginning, Joe had doubts that the wallpaper could be hung as quickly and as cheaply as the contractor had originally estimated. Despite this, he expected the contractor to keep his promise. Joe felt that he had the right to be angry. Maria felt as though she had the right to be frustrated and angry with the workers as well, but Joe never let her have her turn. She felt attacked by Joe whenever the subject of the wallpaper came up because the whole project had been her idea. Instead of agreeing with Joe that the workers were a problem, she went on the defensive.

Perfectionists can be tough to get along with sometimes. The high expectations, attention to detail, and adherence to rules and structures of outwardly focused perfectionists can cause tension and conflict in relationships, while the insecurities and self-doubt of inwardly focused perfectionists can cause problems with others in different ways.

"Don't worry, honey, it's not that big of a deal. All you did was make a little mistake. It could have happened to anyone," Brent's mother tried to console him. "You don't understand, Mom," he replied. "It made me look like a total idiot in front of everyone in my office."

"Now Brent," she said in her most motherly tone, "I'm sure that not everyone thinks you are an idiot. You are very well respected by everyone in your office. You are being entirely too hard on yourself. You know how you can get."

"You're probably right, Mom. I have to go now. I'll call you next weekend."

Brent's mother hung up the phone knowing full well that Brent did not believe a word she had said. He never does when he gets into these states. She feels so frustrated because she wants to console him and knows that if he would only listen to her and *believe* what she said he would feel a lot better. She knows that he will spend the weekend beating himself up for his latest mistake, put more time in at the office to avoid any new ones, and eventually calm down. He will never notice that few people really cared about the small error he made and even fewer will notice that he is working harder to avoid future errors. She knows that he is a very intelligent and hardworking person and that he is too hard on himself. In his heart of hearts he knows this too, but when he gets caught making a mistake, no matter how insignificant it is in the grand scheme of things, he sees himself as a failure. Brent's mom never knows how to help him when he worries like this.

This chapter is different from the others. Its goal is to provide some tips for getting along with the perfectionists you encounter at home and at work. If you are the perfectionist you may want to share this chapter with your loved ones. If not, this chapter may help you to look at yourself from another person's point of view. If you bought this book to help you better cope with the people in your life who make you feel like you are not good enough, then this chapter should provide you with some insights. The first part deals with the special relationship issues in living with outwardly focused perfectionists, while the second half provides tips for living with inwardly focused perfectionists. If you are uncertain if your loved one is a perfectionist, fill out the test in Chapter 1 called "Am I a Perfectionist?" as you think he might answer. The scoring rules will help you decide the degree to which he is a perfectionist, the type of perfectionist, and the areas where his perfectionism is most likely to show.

LIVING WITH OUTWARDLY FOCUSED PERFECTIONISTS

I am attracted to outwardly focused perfectionists because they are self-motivated, organized, driven, hardworking, and intelligent. They have self-confidence, take initiative, and set high standards for themselves. I appreciate their leadership and their ability to get a job done. When they expect a lot from me they imply that they think I am capable of great things. Outwardly focused perfectionists are assertive and strong, yet they have noticeable vulnerabilities. All of the outwardly focused perfectionists I have known turn their perfectionism toward themselves on occasion. They can need guidance and reassurance, and their self-esteem is not always strong. They are as hard on themselves as they are on others. They feel bad when they make mistakes and worry that everything will fall apart if they do the wrong thing or lose control. I sympathize with the insecure part of them and feel motivated to provide support and encouragement when their self-confidence is lacking.

Disapproval

Somehow I have managed to surround myself by outwardly focused perfectionists throughout my adult life. Most have been a source of both joy and tremendous frustration. These perfectionists have had very high standards for others, and that includes me. When I do not get things just right, at least by their definitions, they notice. Sometimes they comment ("You forgot that one"). Sometimes they get mad at me ("How could you have forgotten something so simple?"). Sometimes the disapproval is silence when you expect a response. Sometimes it is actually delivered as a halfhearted compliment ("That's nice, honey"). Outwardly focused perfectionists can be very disapproving if you do not meet their standards, but the disapproval can be communicated in ways so subtle that it leaves you wondering if it is just your imagination and not really disapproval at all. Overt disapproval, while potentially more painful at first, is a little easier to deal with because it is out in the open and it gives you something concrete to address. Usually the criticisms that hurt the most are those from people you really care about. Their opinions of you matter. Sometimes this makes their criticism sound not only like disapproval, but like rejection of you rather than rejection of your idea or your actions.

"You said you were going to take care of this for me. If you don't really intend to help me, don't offer next time. I should have done it myself," Terry scolded her ex-husband when she picked up the girls and found that he had not called their daughter's coach to find out the time and location of tomorrow's soccer game. Because it was said in an angry or tense tone, Steve got the message that Terry was angry and disappointed in him once again. Her second comment, "I should have done it myself," came across as an insult such as "You are not capable of taking care of things." She was not interested in hearing any of Steve's "excuses." He always seemed to have a new one, but the bottom line was always the same. He did not do what he had promised and she would have to take care of it herself.

One way to cope when you have been criticized or are feeling disapproved of is to say to yourself that the other person is wrong. She was being too fussy or too intolerant. You can justify your actions or your ideas ("I tried to reach the coach with no luck, and I had planned to try again later in the evening when he was more likely to be home") or you can take some pleasure in knowing that you are right and refuse to take their disapproval personally ("I do put out a lot of effort to help with the girls. Terry is just in one of her moods"). You can even get angry with her for expressing her disapproval ("She has no right to jump on my case"). While these methods may give some immediate relief, they are not totally satisfying, and they do not usually help to stop this kind of interaction from recurring.

A more productive way to cope with disapproval from your perfectionist friends or family members is to try to understand their way of thinking. Perhaps when you have these kinds of upsetting interactions it is not really about you, but a problem with them. Maybe they are feeling frustrated themselves, under pressure, stressed, rushed, or tired. Understanding this will help you to not take their disapproving comments so personally and will help you avoid responding in an equally hurtful way. In the previous example, Terry had been running late to pick up the girls from Steve's house and had a lot to do before the evening was over. A late morning or afternoon soccer game for her daughter the next day meant that she could catch up on some much needed sleep. An earlier game meant spending time tonight getting her uniform, water bottle, and cleats prepared and rushing around early in the morning with no real breaks until tomorrow afternoon. The thought of more to do after a very hectic week was more than

Terry could bear today. So by the time she drove up Steve's driveway to pick up the girls, she was tired, tense, and needed a break. When she found out that Steve had not helped out by getting the information they both needed about their daughter's game it was like the straw that broke the camel's already tired and overburdened back.

Despite what Terry thinks, Steve is interested in helping her with the girls and he wants to be supportive of Terry. He hates fighting with her, especially in front of the children, but he gets so angry when she says things such as "If you don't really intend to help me, don't offer next time" that he instinctually wants to respond with a defense or a counterattack, even though he knows that just makes things worse. In the past those strategies would only lead to more conflict and ill feelings. In this example, Steve tried to see the big picture before he responded to Terry's criticisms. He knew that when Terry felt backed into a corner or when she was exhausted and overwhelmed, her words came out sounding harsher than she would have wanted. He tells himself not to overreact.

Outwardly focused perfectionists do not consciously seek out conflict with others, but sometimes their emotions get the better of them and they react in ways that can start a fight. They feel disappointment when things do not go the way they think it should, but instead of communicating this directly they sometimes strike out at you if they think that you are partially to blame. They do not always realize how critical or how hurtful their words come across. If you give them the benefit of the doubt that they did not intend to be so harsh, then that feedback can be very helpful to them. You can pose it as a question, such as "Did you realize how critical you sound?" or "Are you really that mad at me or did you just have a bad day?" You can also give them feedback in the form of a statement, such as "When you said it was all my fault you really upset me" or "It hurts my feelings when you talk to me like that." Even more effective is feedback that acknowledges your contribution to the problem. For example, Steve said to Terry, "I'm sorry you are angry that I do not have the information on the game right now. You can call the coach yourself if you would like, but I do not mind trying to reach her again and calling you

> ### Take time to think about this.
>
> Outwardly focused perfectionists feel intense disappointment when things do not go the way they think it should. While they do not consciously seek out conflict with others, sometimes their emotions get the better of them and they sometimes strike out at you if they think you are partially to blame. Before you counterattack, consider the following options:
>
> 1. You may sometimes hear disapproval when there is none.
> 2. She may not have intended to communicate disapproval.
> 3. She may not have realized that her disapproval was showing.
> 4. She did express disapproval, and she was right to do so.
> 5. She did express disapproval, but she was absolutely wrong!
>
> Think first. Calmly let her know that you were offended by her comment and try not to counterattack.

later. Is there anything I can do to help with the girls in the mean-time?" All of these strategies can be helpful in stopping a conflict from erupting if they are delivered in a nonattacking manner.

"The Best Defense Is a Good Offense"

My husband has all of the positive attributes of an outwardly focused perfectionist and some of the negative ones. He has tremendous self-confidence, but there are times when his self-esteem takes a beating. If I point out one of his weaknesses, the inwardly focused perfectionist in him feels hurt and the outwardly focused part of him gets mad. There-fore, if I am angry with my husband for something that he has said or done I only bring it to his attention if it is something that is really important to me. I do not point out all of his shortcomings, and he does me the same favor. When I do raise an issue, I try to be very careful to not hurt his feelings. I do not want to make him feel attacked. If he doesn't feel attacked, he doesn't have to defend himself.

People can feel attacked even when they are not actually under attack. The attacks that are easiest to identify are those that are direct, that come with harsh words or actions, or that leave an obvious scar. These include sarcasm or disapproval, or other forms of criticism. In day-to-day life, these types of attacks are not as common as the more subtle or indirect attacks. People who walk around with some self-doubt, or believe that underneath it all they are not good enough, are more sensitive to personal attacks than others. (If your feet are already sore you are going to be more sensitive to pebbles in the road.)

When people feel attacked they respond in a variety of ways. Some retreat and some defend or counterattack. Outwardly focused perfectionists are more likely than inwardly focused perfectionists to defend themselves by counterattacking. Problems arise when they misread a situation and are not actually under attack, yet respond in a defensive manner. The defensive or counteroffensive behaviors usually elicit the same reaction from the other person. For example, if I yell at you, you will probably yell back at me. Leading marital communication researchers, such as Gayla Margolin, Ph.D., of the University of Southern California, and John Gottman, Ph.D., of the University of Washington, call this communication pattern *negative reciprocity*. Their research has shown that this type of interaction is more common in couples with unsatisfying relationships than in couples who report having a happy or satisfying marriage. Negative reciprocity can quickly escalate into a fight.

The trick to stopping this type of conflict is to avoid starting it in the first place. If your perfectionist is sensitive to feeling attacked, try to communicate your message in a nonattacking or nondefensive manner. Here are twelve communication rules that may help.

"Why Don't You Trust Me?"

Maria, Joe's wife, has been helping her co-worker Dennis with a project at work that, if successful, could open the door to a promotion for him. Maria likes Dennis and would like to see him succeed, so she agreed to help, despite some reservations. In the past, Dennis has asked for her advice, but did not follow it. Rejecting her advice did

Communication Rules

1. Try to be calm when you start the conversation. This will give you greater control over what you say and how you say it.
2. Try to catch the other person when he is not angry so you are less likely to put her on the defensive.
3. Think about how your message will be heard before you speak.
4. Talk about one problem at a time.
5. Be specific so the other person knows what you are talking about. Give a recent example of a time when the problem occurred.
6. Avoid extreme words like never, always, every time, can't, or won't. These are usually not accurate and will keep the listener from taking you seriously. Make your point without distortion.
7. Do not use hurtful words, insults, or name-calling.
8. Keep the tone of your voice low. You do not have to be loud to be heard. Even if your words are nonattacking, yelling and other angry nonverbal displays will keep the listener from hearing your message.
9. Listen carefully when the other person speaks instead of using the time to plan your next response.
10. Consider the possibility that you are wrong.
11. Be creative and flexible in trying to find a solution. Think about how each of you can contribute to resolving the problem.
12. If the conversation is going badly, call time out and try to discuss it again another day.

not really bother Maria, because she believed Dennis was capable of making his own decisions. However, when he would reject her suggestion and then later follow the very same suggestion when another person gave it, Maria would get really steamed: "He should have listened to me in the first place." This is one of Maria's pet peeves. Dennis is a perfectionist in his work, and as such has difficulty trusting the advice of others. He is afraid of making a wrong decision and the resulting embarrassment or failure. Therefore, when he needed guidance, although he trusted Maria greatly, he would seek several people's opinions and look for a consensus before he would act.

Dennis once again asked Maria for advice. When she gave it, he hesitated a moment and then told Maria that he would give it some thought. This usually meant that he was not going to follow her advice. Maria was annoyed for a while, but dropped the issue, knowing that some people learn from experience rather than instruction. She cannot protect Dennis from making a bad choice any more than she can keep her children from occasionally making bad choices, despite her warnings. A week later, Dennis came back to her with the same issue and told her that he was going to follow the advice of his boss, Mr. Peabody. Maria wasn't crazy about Mr. Peabody, so when she realized that the "great suggestion" he had given Dennis was the very same suggestion she had offered, she nearly hit the ceiling.

Although Maria did not say a word, she thought to herself, "Oh great! You'll take that dope's advice, but you won't listen to me! You won't trust me, but you'll trust that moron." She felt angry and disgusted, but could only mutter "Whatever" as she turned in her chair and began rustling through a pile of papers. Dennis sensed her annoyance and left her office.

As usually happens with automatic thoughts, this event also made Maria think about the other times that Dennis did not seem to take her seriously. Her anger got more intense, and she started to think that he really did not value her ideas and, even further, when he has followed her advice it was probably only because someone else told him to do so: "To think that I have wasted my time on that ungrateful brat. He wouldn't know a good idea if it stared him in the face. I may not have as much education as him or his boss, but I know what I am talking about. Peabody hasn't had an original idea in the last five years. He probably remembered how well my project turned out and gave the same advice. I ought to give them both a piece of my mind."

At this point Maria had another emotional shift and a new set of cognitions: "Maybe he was right. Maybe I'm not all that smart. Maybe my ideas are not as good as others. Maybe I'm too uneducated to know the difference." She felt a combination of sadness and embarrassment.

Maria took an early lunch to get away from the situation so that she could calm herself and figure out how to handle this problem. She and Dennis would be working together for some time and they had to be able to get along. Maria knows that when she gets upset she can sometimes jump to conclusions. She had been through some therapy in the past and knew that the way out of the upset was to take a closer look at the conclusions she had drawn and decide if they reflect the situation accurately. She got out her pad and did something similar to Schema Exercise Number 1 from Chapter 4. First she wrote down all her negative automatic thoughts about this situation with Dennis, and next to them wrote down the feelings she had experienced. She knew that the first step was to make herself look logically at her negative thinking. She knew that when she became angry about one thing it was very easy to think of a dozen other things that made her mad. It was easy to reinterpret past experiences (receiving thanks from Dennis) through her angry point of view ("He was insincere"). Was there any evidence to support her negative view? Based on her personal experiences, input from others, and her past interactions with Dennis she figured out that her negative thoughts about herself and about Dennis were inaccurate for the most part. After she felt calm, she was still left with one complaint: that he had rejected her advice once again, yet had accepted the same advice from someone else without acknowledging his change of view (e.g., "I rethought it and I think you are right"). Because Maria knew that she would be working with Dennis for some time, she would have to find a way to work out this problem.

Outwardly focused perfectionists have a difficult time placing trust in others when the stakes are high. With Dennis and his new project, the stakes were very high. His lack of trust in others and his fear of looking bad in front of others made him act very cautiously. Maria knows this about Dennis, and reminding herself helps her to be sympathetic to his feelings. She knows that there is nothing wrong with getting second opinions or being cautious about taking advice before acting. The reason this particular interaction with Dennis was so upsetting was because it tapped into one of her pet peeves about not being trusted. She goes through this kind of thing with her husband, Joe, all the time, and it always seems to get her upset.

The bottom line here is that disapproval from the important people in your life can hurt. However, when this happens there are several things to consider. First, it is possible that, because of your own sensitivities, you sometimes hear disapproval when there is none. Second, it is possible that the perfectionist did not intend to communicate disapproval. Third, he may not have realized that the disapproval was showing. Fourth, it is also possible that he did express disapproval, but was absolutely wrong! To fix the problem, you first have to know which one it is. Taking time to talk about it is the first step.

Maria went back to the office and told Dennis that she had been upset with him. He had known something wasn't right, but he had no idea that he had upset Maria, and he felt very bad about it. Dennis reassured Maria that he trusted her very much, but that he would sometimes get conflicting advice from other people who seemed to know what they were talking about. He was not experienced enough to know the difference between good advice and bad advice, and he had not yet learned that sometimes very knowledgeable people can give bad advice. Maria understood Dennis's position because she had been there once herself. They talked about what to do to avoid another misunderstanding and agreed that Dennis would tell her when he was uncertain about her ideas or when he was getting conflicting advice. Maria agreed to tell Dennis when he was getting on her nerves, so that they could resolve the problem immediately.

Maria had a misconception about relationships. She thought that if a person trusted you he should take your advice. If you take her logic a step further, it would mean that if Dennis liked and trusted her then he should accept her advice, even if it was not any good. Even Maria would acknowledge that this did not make any sense.

If you read between the lines you can see that coping with this situation required Maria to be willing to speak up about what was bothering her. She had to take the chance of finding out that she was wrong, which takes some guts. It is much easier not to discuss an issue, stay mad, and silently assume that you are right. In discussing this issue with Dennis she also had to be willing to trust that he was telling her the truth. And, most important, she had to be able to admit to him that she was wrong in her assumptions about him and take some responsibility for the problem. Dennis had to be willing to do a few things as well. He had to listen to her complaint, which did not feel very good. He had to consider the possibility that she was right and that he had been a jerk about rejecting her advice and yet taking the same advice from someone else without acknowledging her contribution. Most important, Dennis had to be able to respond to Maria in a nondefensive manner. This can be very hard for some outwardly focused perfectionists. We will discuss this more in the next section.

"No Matter What I Do It Is Never Good Enough"

Coping with parents. Outwardly focused perfectionists set very high standards for others without even trying. If your parents are outwardly focused perfectionists, perhaps they have always seemed like a model of how you should act, or perhaps they have told you how you should act, even if they do not follow their own advice. In Joe's case, he may not always give direct instructions, but his boys watch him and know that they are supposed to be like him. Sometimes they try to be like him. Sometimes they resist being like him. Sometimes they just give up the fight, saying, "What's the use?" Joe cannot help the fact that he knows how to do things the right way; he simply has had more life experience than his boys. He has already made the mistakes that his children are now making. The problem with having perfect parents such as Joe is that you may never get a chance to see them make a mistake when you are young. At least, when you were a kid, your parents seemed flawless. When they criticized your mistakes or made you redo your work until you got it right, they communicated that errors were unsatisfactory, reinforcing the message that people should not make mistakes. To make mistakes is wrong or stupid. Therefore, since you, like all other kids, could not help but make mistakes, you concluded that you must not be good enough.

If you are an adult now and your parents are still telling you how you ought to be, you may still be getting the message that you are not good enough. If you are not a perfectionist yourself, your self-esteem may be strong enough to ignore this kind of input or to fight off their criticisms or disapproval. But if you still have trouble coping with your parents, perhaps it would be helpful to understand their motives.

Parents like Joe have adult-sized expectations for their children because they think that if they expect a lot from their children then their children will come to expect a lot from themselves. The flip side of this argument is that if you do not expect a lot from your children, they will not expect much from themselves. Joe is trying to instill in his boys the drive to do their best but, despite his good intentions, the way that Joe is going about conveying his message is creating tension between him and his boys that is damaging their self-esteem. Joe's direct and subtle criticism of the boys makes it clear that they are not meeting his standards. Because his disapproving remarks or looks are frequent, and he is not as generous with praise, the take-home message for his boys is that they are not good enough. Joe isn't out to hurt his kids' feelings; he simply does not always realize that his messages are hurtful or annoying. Perhaps your parents are a lot like Joe. Consider the possibility that their intentions were to encourage you rather than to be mean.

If your parents are still living, you can try to ask them what they think of you and your accomplishments in life. Share the idea that their criticisms or disapproving comments have given you the message that they do not think you are good enough. Give them a chance to tell you how they feel about you. The conversation can start with some feedback to them about their criticism, such as "Do you realize how critical it sounds when you say things like that?" or "I get the impression that you do not approve of me or my actions. Am I hearing you right?"

Of the depressed people I have treated, the children of perfectionists have the toughest time feeling good about themselves. As adults some have continued to try to meet their parents' standards. Despite doing quite well for themselves, they never get or hear the approval or praise from their parents that makes them feel that they are finally good enough. This leaves them occasionally unhappy with themselves or with their lives and sometimes feeling depressed. Interestingly, when I have talked with the parents of my depressed patients I have found that they greatly admire their children and are very proud of their accomplishments. They see their children as being more than just good enough; they think their children are wonderful adults. So how is it that my patients have missed this fact? It probably has something to do with the way the parents treated their children and the way the children heard their parents' remarks. For example, some parents assumed that their children knew they were pleased or proud of them and did not think their children needed to be told so, an incorrect assumption. Some parents thought that if they praised too much their children would stop trying to excel. In some cases, praise was given, but the child did not hear it or rejected or invalidated the praise ("He's not really proud of me; he's just saying that to get me to do something for him"). When I have helped adult children and their parents talk to each other about these issues, they usually resolve the problem. The parents get a chance to talk about their intentions and goals of parenting. The adult child gets the approval he has sought all through life and can now focus on setting his own standards and achieving those goals.

Sometimes, in the course of these discussions, the adult child comes to realize that his goals are different from his parents' goals. This is an important revelation, because it helps each person to understand the other's point of view. It helps explain to the parents why their child does not seem to do things the way they expect. It helps the child to understand this distinction so that she can pursue her own goals without feeling the burden of knowing that her parents will not approve.

Coping with partners. The perfectionist who is never satisfied with your performance may be a spouse or partner. Your self-esteem may be fine. The problem you may have in getting along with your perfectionist is that his expectations of you and your expectations of you may not be the same. If he gets upset with you when you do not meet his expectations, then you have a different kind of problem than the boys have with Joe. It is not usually the case that your partner says to you "You are not good enough" or "That wasn't good enough." Usually the way that you know is that he criticizes what you have done ("This soup is too salty"), corrects you ("Don't do it that way"), compares you to himself unfavorably ("When I was in charge of the bills they always got out on time"), redoes your work ("Let me do that"), or insults you in general ("You are so irresponsible").

These things happen in all relationships. Most of the time they can be worked out or ignored. They interfere with relationships when they happen excessively or when they hurt your feelings. A person who complains about you is not very pleasant to be around. Even if you know that they are wrong or that they do not really mean it, it is still upsetting. This kind of behavior creates emotional distance between people. If you and your partner value your relationship, you have to find another way to deal with complaints. If these kinds of problems are the rule in your relationship rather than the exception, marital counseling might help. With persistent conflict, it is difficult for one person to make significant changes in the relationship all by herself. Counseling helps to get both people to look at their contributions to the problems and to make changes.

If the problem is infrequent but bothersome, there may be some things that you can do to change the pattern of the communication so that it is not as hurtful. The first thing to do is to look for a pattern in the complaints or the criticism. Is there something that you do that your partner consistently complains about? Do you usually put too much salt in the soup? Are you often late in paying the bills? Although you may be hearing a complaint, perhaps there is a legitimate problem that needs correcting. Chances are that there is something about your partner's behavior that bothers you as well. For example, when she uses your car and returns it without gas or criticizes you in front of others. If changes are needed on both parts there may be room for compromise. If you change something, such as consistently using less salt when you cook, then perhaps your partner will change something, such as talking to you about concerns when no one else is listening. This kind of compromise is called a quid pro quo. It means something like "if you scratch my back, I'll scratch yours." Donald Baucom, Ph.D., from the University of North Carolina, and Norman Epstein, Ph.D., from the University of Maryland, in their book *Cognitive-Behavioral Marital Therapy* suggest making quid pro quo agreements as one way of helping couples resolve conflict and have more satisfying relationships.

When some people get frustrated with criticism from their partners they say to themselves, "No matter what I do it is never good enough. So why bother trying?" They get angry, and then they give up. If this is you, you may have already figured out that giving up on trying to

---

Negotiating a Quid Pro Quo

To negotiate a quid pro quo with another person you need to know what you want them to do or change and what they want you to do or change. A structure for the agreement is as follows:

I agree to _____

if you agree to _____.

The action you fill in the blank should be specific enough that both you and your partner will know when the change has been made. For example, "I agree to clean up after the dog if you agree to remind me without getting angry." Another example is "I agree to let you relax after work for forty-five minutes before I ask you to do anything if you agree to help me bathe the children and put them to bed."

---

please your partner does not usually make things better. You may get some temporary satisfaction ("I'll show him"), but the complaints may continue and you may become more distant from your partner. Some people go the other route and try to change themselves or their behaviors to please their partner and to avoid criticism and conflict. This can work on occasion if you are willing to make such changes, but there are two big problems with this approach. Not only do you risk losing yourself in the trade, but people change over time and what they want from a partner can also change over time. Even if you change yourself to avoid irritating your partner today, you will have to continue to make changes as her preferences change. It is very easy to get caught up in the wishes of an outwardly focused perfectionist and confuse their goals with your own. If you have not already done so, you need to set your own standards of performance to determine what you expect from yourself. If you need some help, return to Chapter 7, "Adjusting Your Expectations." When you have finished defining your own standards, share them with your perfectionist partner. This may help to open up a discussion about what is reasonable to expect from each other.

There is another solution somewhere between giving up altogether and changing yourself completely to comply with your partner's wishes. Think about all of the things that you do that bother your partner or that might not be "good enough" in her eyes. Make a list in your head or on paper, then take the list to your partner and explain that you keep getting the message that you are not good enough, and that this message is hurting your feelings and making you feel emotionally distant. Most people fear losing their partners and are motivated to maintain the relationship. Show your partner the list and tell him that you are willing to make changes in a few of these areas, but not in all of them. Ask him to choose the things that are most irritating. If you agree with the ones that were chosen, tell your partner that you are willing to make some changes in those areas if he is willing to get off your back about the others. It is kind of like a quid pro quo, but you are not asking your partner to do something for you, you are just asking your partner to keep the complaints to himself. Explain that the consequence of continuing to be critical is that the relationship will suffer more and more over time. If you cannot do this intervention on your own, find a marital therapist who can help.

If your partner cares about you, she probably only wants the best for you. Pushing you to do better may be her way of being encouraging and supportive even though the manner is emotionally hurtful. If you explain how her words affect you, your partner will probably be motivated to change rather than continue to hurt you. Because most people are not tuned into how their actions or words affect other people, you need to provide feedback so that she has a chance to explain and an opportunity to make changes. Always try to give her the benefit of the doubt that she has your best interest in mind. Work from this positive perspective before blaming and criticizing her for her blaming and critical words.

Dealing with Criticism

When you hear criticism listen for the message of concern. Acknowledge his good intentions and give him feedback on how the criticism affects you. Try to hear the caring statement and ignore the criticism. If the criticism is persistent, try setting limits on the criticism (e.g., "This has to stop," "I won't listen to you when you are being critical," or "Calm yourself and then tell me what the problem is with kinder words"). See "Setting Limits" in the section below for more ideas.

"I Hate It When You Are Right"

Outwardly focused perfectionists are great at taking charge, organizing a project, assigning tasks to others, and supervising the process. They know how to do things. They know how to think. And they usually have an idea about how to do it right. He is not afraid to tell you when you are doing something the wrong way. The correction can be gentle and instructive or harsh and critical. You can resist his directions and guidance, but you may find that things do not work out just as he predicted ("I told you that would not work"). Outwardly focused perfectionists can anticipate trouble before it occurs because they are good with details and are very organized. If you do not take his advice and later have problems, chances are that he will not be very happy with you. Joe tells his boys that if they do not put a drop cloth down before they open the paint can, it will spill out onto the patio floor. "We can do it dad," Sergio replies. Joe says, "Fine. Do it your way," and waits and watches. When the kids spill the paint, as predicted, they are angry with their dad rather than with themselves. Why? Because he told them so and they hate the fact that he is always right.

Sometimes this is so bothersome that in order to cope you may refuse to follow the directions your perfectionist suggests. You can either change some element of the directions or do the opposite. If it all works out you can feel proud of yourself for having asserted your individuality and succeeded. You have proven that this perfectionist's way is not the only way. Problems can arise when his way would really have been a better or more efficient way of doing things. You may have cost yourself more time, energy, or money in proving that you can do things your own way. Perhaps it is worth it, or perhaps it is not. Next time you reject directions from your perfectionist ask yourself if you hate the idea because it is his idea or if you think you really know a better way to do things. The motivation should be to accomplish something important rather than to spite him or prove that he is wrong.

Here are some other ways to cope. When you are faced with a task to do and your outwardly focused perfectionist is nearby ready to give instructions, tell him that you would like to figure it out for yourself

---

Coping with Outwardly Focused Perfectionists

When you are faced with a task to do and your outwardly focused perfectionist is nearby ready to give instructions:

1. Tell him that you would like to try to figure it out for yourself first. If you need help you will call.
2. Take the instructions as a suggestion rather than as an order. Tell him that you need to think about it and decide how to proceed.
3. Take time to consider whether you are reacting out of emotion or out of logic.
4. If you decide to do things differently, tell him in a confident and assertive voice. He will respect self-assurance.

---

first; if you need help you will call for his assistance. Be assertive about it, not angry or rejecting of his help.

Another method is to take your perfectionist's instructions as a suggestion rather than as an order. Tell him that you need to think about it for a minute (or a day) and decide how to proceed. If it really bothers you that he always seems to have the answers, then you will probably have an emotional reaction when he tries to tell you what to do, which will interfere with your reasoning ability. You need to take a moment (or a day) to calm yourself so that you are confident that you are making a good decision. Take time to consider whether you are reacting out of emotion or out of logic. If you decide to do things differently than your perfectionist suggests, tell him in a confident and assertive voice. He will very likely respect your self-assurance.

LIVING WITH INWARDLY FOCUSED PERFECTIONISTS

In general, inwardly focused perfectionists are eager to please others and to maintain relationships. They fear rejection, so they are particularly sensitive to tensions arising in their relationships with others.

Like outwardly focused perfectionists, they are motivated to do well and take pride in their work. Relationship problems may arise when inwardly focused perfectionists work too hard to please others or to avoid rejection.

Neatness Counts

June is a good example of an inwardly focused perfectionist who tries too hard to please others. They have tried to tell her that she does not have to work so hard, but she will not listen. The kids get irritated with June's insistence on keeping a clean house; their chief complaint is that they feel as though they live in a museum. She expects them to keep their rooms in order, their bathroom neat, and to keep their personal belongings in their rooms.

"She acts like some magazine photographer is going to drop by any minute and everything has to be picture perfect," Sissy would complain to her father.

"I know dear, but it is important to your mom that the house look nice. Just humor her. You know how upset she can get when we make a mess."
"But Dad, who cares if I have stuff under my bed? No one can see it."
"Your mom cares, honey, so just take care of it like she asked."
"This is totally not fair. Sally is allowed to keep her room any way she wants. It's her room. I don't have any space of my own."
"I'll talk to your mom about it when I think the time is right, but for now you have to follow the rules."

When June is busy with her volunteer activities she gives her house less attention than usual. This is perfectly fine for her husband and kids, who, predictably, don't even notice the difference. When the church fund-raiser was complete, June finally had time to attend to detailed cleaning in her home. She was horrified to find how quickly things fall apart when she is tied up with other activities.

Bill came home to find June vacuuming the walls. "What are you doing?" Bill asked in a surprised tone.

"Oh Bill, I was hoping to be finished before you got home. I am so sorry I let the house get so bad. There are cobwebs all over the place and dust on the baseboards that just makes my skin crawl. I've wanted to get to this for days, but I haven't had the time. The kitchen floor was so disgusting I could hardly stand it. I had to use a toothbrush to get between the tiles."

June had been at it since the kids left for school that morning, and she did not look like she would be stopping any time soon. June's husband and children could see the strain on her. They feel bad when she looks tired or when she never seems to have time to play. Her husband tells her to "take it easy"; her children tell her to "chill out," but June does not know how to take it easy or chill out. She needs help from her family to make changes and improve the quality of her personal life. She needs to take care of herself, but she has been taking care of others for so long that she has no idea what it means to take care of herself. In fact, she thinks that taking care of her family is the way to take care of herself.

June and perfectionists like her need three kinds of help from their families. First, they need permission to relax. ("It's OK if you don't have time to do this today, Mom, it can wait.") Some inwardly focused perfectionists do not feel comfortable taking time for themselves, but they will take time for their family members. Her husband can say, "I need us to take some time to relax together. Can we go somewhere on Saturday instead of doing chores?" When he has tried this approach in the past it has worked beautifully. June did not have to feel guilty for relaxing instead of doing chores because she was doing something for her husband. It was fine with her that she was able to relax and enjoy herself as well.

A second kind of help that inwardly focused perfectionists need is assistance with their work. If it is important to June that the kitchen is cleaned before she goes to bed, her husband or kids can take time to help her. This gets the job done faster and allows June some time to relax before bedtime. If the kids know that June is going to fuss at them for having a dirty room, they can clean it up before she reminds them. Of course, you may run into the problem of not doing a job well enough to meet your perfectionist's standards, which we'll explore in the section called "Setting Limits."

A third way to be helpful is to show inwardly focused perfectionists how to relax and have fun. This may sound silly, but I have had many people over the years tell me that they do not know how to relax. You can show them how to relax by scheduling playtime with them and by directing the activity. Keep in mind that they may not have the temperament for sitting around the house, watching television, lying in the sun, or daydreaming. You may have to offer a way to relax that gives them something to do such as taking a walk or going to a movie.

June's son, Skippy, has complaints of his own. June wants him to be well groomed when he goes out of the house, so she sometimes makes Skippy go back in the house and change clothes before he goes to school if she thinks he "looks bad." Unfortunately, June's idea of looking good is different from her son's idea of looking good, so he ends up going to school dances in his Sunday best or going out to play with his friends in clothes that are too well matched for a little kid, and his friends make fun of him. Skippy would never complain, knowing it wouldn't do any good anyway. June doesn't usually bend on these issues.

June, however, is sensitive to what it feels like to be made fun of by your friends. She thinks that she is preventing problems for Skippy by making him dress well in public. She is looking at childhood from an adult perspective. Her intentions are good, and Skippy is too respectful to tell his mother than she is creating problems rather than solving them. He copes by staging small rebellions when he thinks he can

---

How to Help Your Inwardly Focused Perfectionist

1. Give them permission to relax.
2. Assist them with their work.
3. Show them how to relax and have fun.

get away with them. He untucks his shirt when he gets on the school bus and takes off his pullover sweater and ties it around his waist.

Details, Details, Details

Brent is an inwardly focused perfectionist in the workplace and, to some extent, with household tasks. He can sometimes get stuck on details in his work and waste a great deal of time, which, in turn, interferes with progress and irritates his coworkers. Brent has the good fortune to have an assistant, Sheila, whom he trusts. Sheila catches Brent when he is stuck on a detail and moves him to another subject by suggesting that he allow her to tend to the detail or assign it elsewhere. Brent usually does not realize when he is stuck, but Sheila knows it is happening when their conversations seem to take a sharp left turn off the subject that they were on. It may take a minute or so for her to figure out why she is feeling tense and frustrated. If other people are in the room, she can see the glazed looks on their faces as they try to follow Brent. Sometimes Brent catches himself and gets back on the subject. Other times Sheila intervenes.

The inwardly focused perfectionists that I have worked with can get stuck by worrying about one aspect of a larger project. While the issue that they are worried about may be quite important, it is usually more productive to move forward and tackle the parts that you can handle and temporarily leave the issue of concern for another time. For example, an inwardly focused perfectionist might raise an issue of what to do if something goes wrong before you have had a chance to plan out a whole project. A friend of mine and I were organizing a surprise twenty-fifth wedding anniversary party for our neighbors. My friend is somewhat of an inwardly focused perfectionist and is attentive to details. I am less detail-oriented and more focused on having a general plan with details to be filled in at a later time. Usually I delegate the detail work to those who are much better at it than I. My friend was always two steps ahead of me and worried about a part of the plan that I had not yet thought through. For example, she was worried about whether to use plastic or silverware while I was still trying

> ### Take time to think about this.
> ---
> When your inwardly focused perfectionist gets stuck on details, here is how you can help. First and foremost be respectful of her concerns, even if she seems to be jumping ahead with worries. Secondly, keep your eye on the big picture even when your inwardly focused perfectionist loses it.

to figure out the guest list. An inwardly focused perfectionist's fear of making mistakes coupled with her ability to see and attend to details can make her worry about things going wrong long before they are a reality. Sometimes she worries unnecessarily, although there are times that I have missed an important point, and she is insightful enough to anticipate trouble so that it can be avoided. A detail-oriented inwardly focused perfectionist can be a good partner if you can find a way to work together. Here is a plan that I have developed with many of the perfectionists I see in therapy.

First and foremost, be respectful of your inwardly focused perfectionist's concerns, even if she seems to be jumping ahead with worries. This means that you should acknowledge her concern with details and work together to decide if the issue should be addressed right away, should be handled by one of you individually, or should be tabled until a later date. Second, keep your eye on the big picture. For example, if you are planning a big event, such as a surprise party, keep your time frame in mind as you work through the details. Know when you need to send invitations, order food, and chill the champagne. This way, if a detail is slowing you down, you will know how much time to allow before skipping ahead.

Fear of Rejection

The inwardly focused perfectionists who have been most precious to me are those who fear rejection. I told you about one of my favorite ones in Chapter 1, who despite all of my encouragement, could never be convinced that she was good enough in my eyes. People like her

are dear to my heart because they suffer so much. Their self-doubt and fear of making mistakes and facing the consequences is very painful. After many years of working with her and other inwardly focused perfectionists who fear rejection, I have found that you cannot always change their basic schema that they are not good enough. However, you can help change their negative automatic thoughts about themselves and about you (see Chapters 4 and 5) and the negative emotions that accompany these thoughts. This can be accomplished in several ways. The first is to provide positive reinforcement for their accomplishments. You do not have to make a big fuss; acknowledgment of a job well done will suffice. In fact, if you praise too enthusiastically, they will not believe you. It will seem fake or patronizing. My employees were publicly and privately acknowledged for their good work so that their superiors knew of their talents and accomplishments. However, they were never publicly criticized or humiliated.

Second, to help them combat their self-doubt you can communicate trust or confidence in their abilities. This can be said as simply as "I trust you" or can be communicated indirectly. If an inwardly focused perfectionist student asked me how to do something that I knew he was capable of figuring out for himself, I would ask, "How do you think it should be handled?" He would tell me what to do and I would usually agree. I do this with my children every day. I communicate my trust in them by letting them make decisions and by letting them experiment and figure out how to do things on their own. I can give them answers, but encouraging them to think for themselves builds confidence. When they make mistakes, encourage them to analyze the situation for themselves and solve their own problems.

A third way to cope with employees who fear rejection is to give them information so that they understand the importance of tasks, the benefits of completing them well and on time, and any problems they should be aware of. Keep them informed of deadlines and give feedback throughout the process so that they will know if they are on the right track. Information is power. Some supervisors retain power by withholding information, keeping their employees in the dark and

---

Helping Inwardly Focused Perfectionists Who Fear Rejection.

---

1. Provide positive reinforcement for their accomplishments.
2. Communicate trust or confidence in their abilities.
3. Keep them informed. Information calms the nerves.
4. Be honest and direct with criticism, but be gentle and encouraging as well. Give them time to improve and provide positive reinforcement for their accomplishments.
5. Model imperfection.

---

fearful. This control strategy is unnecessary when you are supervising perfectionists.

If you have to give negative feedback or criticism to an inwardly focused perfectionist who fears rejection, be sensitive to their feelings. Be honest and direct with criticism, but be gentle and encouraging as well. Reassure your inwardly focused perfectionist that you trust in their ability to fix a mistake or improve in an area of weakness. Give them time to improve and provide positive reinforcement for their accomplishments.

One of the ways I tried to help the inwardly focused perfectionists I worked with who feared rejection was to model imperfection. This was actually quite easy for me because, as one of my patients put it, "I am one of the most imperfect people she knows." I allowed my staff to see me make mistakes, just as I allow my children to see me make mistakes. They watched as I coped with the consequences, if there were any. They watched me admit to making errors, and they watched me allow others to see my mistakes. When nothing bad really happened to me (no rejection occurred), they learned vicariously that you can make mistakes and it will not be the end of the world. They actually expected me to make mistakes, forget things, or show up late for appointments, and they never rejected me. (I have always expected myself to make mistakes, so when it happens it is never a surprise. On the contrary, when things work out perfectly I am always a little stunned.) These experiences challenged their belief that if a mistake is made, rejection will follow.

Setting Limits

"Enough is enough," Steve huffed as he stormed out of the room. "There is just so much of this that I can take." He had just gone another round with Terry and was in no mood to be supportive, sensible, or patient. "When she was discouraged and fearful of her future I tried to encourage her and tell her she was too good for that company. She said I didn't really understand and dismissed my advice. When she was in one of those moods and critical of every flaw in my character or my appearance, I tried to be patient and change the things that I could just to please her. She inevitably would find another thing to criticize the next time. I try to be helpful, but this is driving me crazy." Steve had tried many different ways to cope with Terry's criticism. He also tried to provide comfort to her when her perfectionism left her with self-doubt, but this always seemed to make things worse rather than better. His frustration with Terry grew over a period of years, until their marriage ended in divorce. They both felt unappreciated and hopeless about the future of their relationship.

If Steve and Terry had sought counseling before it was too late, Steve might have been told to set limits on his anger and on Terry's behavior. With all the attempts that Steve made to address Terry's criticisms, it never occurred to him that she just needed to stop. He needed to be able to say, "Terry, when you criticize me you hurt my feelings. You push me away with your words. I am not trying to ignore your concerns, but you are hurting me and hurting our marriage with your words." Terry would likely have defended herself by saying that she did not intend to be hurtful or to push him away. On the other hand, there were several things that he did that bothered her and that needed to be changed. This type of conversation could have led to a negotiation such as "I'll change the way I complain if you change some things that bother me."

Sometimes the way to deal with hurtful words is to try to make them stop. Before you can make it stop you need to understand why it is happening. I usually start by giving people the benefit of the doubt that they are trying to make an important point and do not really want to be hurtful. Unfortunately, when people feel that they are not able to get their point across or that no one is listening, they sometimes increase the intensity of the message by speaking louder, using stronger language, or repeating themselves. It is usually frustration that can make them increase their volume. To make the angry words or tone stop it can be very helpful to acknowledge the frustration that is being expressed. Here is an example of what Steve could have said to Terry when she was being critical or disapproving: "Terry, I can see that you are really upset. I want to help, but it is hard for me to listen when your words are so angry and hurtful." A stronger approach might be something such as "I know you want to make your point, but I am not going to listen until you calm down." Still stronger is something such as "I'm not going to talk to you right now. When you calm down and stop talking to me that way I will be happy to listen." You must be prepared to disengage from the conversation by getting some physical distance from the person, such as leaving the room.

There are times when it is appropriate to set limits on an inwardly focused perfectionist's behavior as well. If she is stuck on a detail that is interfering with progress you may have to force her to move on to the next step. I had a student who could spend an entire day organizing her desk and files. Usually this behavior was her way of avoiding work that made her anxious, such as writing a paper for a school project. Sometimes I had to set limits on her busy work. I would ask her to write a small part of the paper and give her a specific deadline. Her desire to meet the deadline would overcome her fear of getting started or of making a mistake.

If you are in a relationship with an inwardly focused perfectionist who has self-doubt, you may occasionally find yourself in the position of trying to convince him of his worth or value, like Brent's mom did in the example at the beginning of this chapter. You may have provided encouragement and support when your inwardly focused perfectionist wanted to do something new or challenging. You might have provided comfort and reassurance when he was fearful. You might have even tried to talk him out of some self-criticism. If your perfectionist is typical of many others, you probably have found that your words have had limited impact.

"I can talk to her until I am blue in the face, but she never listens.

When her boss finally notices her great work and gives her a compliment, she is bursting with joy. That really makes me angry. Her comeback to me is always something like, you love me so your compliments don't count. She rejects my compliments and believes wholeheartedly when that jerk she works for manipulates her with praise. I don't get it." In this particular scenario, the helpful husband needs to set limits on himself. He has tried to convince his wife that she is OK, great, good enough for him, but she does not believe him. He gets more frustrated over time as his efforts to console her fail repeatedly. He becomes angry with her boss, whom she defends. That is like adding fuel to his fire. What this well-intentioned husband needs to do is to stop trying to talk his wife out of her negative thinking altogether. It does not work and it makes him angry. Instead, when his wife is upset, he needs to ask her what he can do to make her feel better. It is better for her to talk herself out of her own negative thinking than for him to try to correct her negative views. ("I will not try to talk you out of your negative view this time. Is there anything else I can do to make you feel better?")

As I said at the beginning of the chapter, the perfectionists in my life are all sources of joy, but they are also challenges. I greatly value them, and therefore it is worth putting up with some of the quirks that their perfectionism brings. (They seem to be willing to put up with mine as well.) You have heard the expression that you have to take the bad with the good. That is what it is like in getting along with most people, perfectionists included. The benefits you receive from your relationships with them can greatly outweigh the difficulties.

When their perfectionism seems to get in the way of the relationship, try to identify the source of the problem and work with them to fix it. Take time to consider how your own sensitivities or reactions may contribute to the problem. In good relationships, both people are generally willing to make changes for the benefit of maintaining the relationship. Most relationships will change over time. To keep up you must periodically take time and make efforts to change things for the better. If your efforts to mend relationship problems have been unsuccessful, it may be time to bring in a counselor or marital therapist to coach you and to referee discussions.

1 0

MAKING CHANGES
THAT LAST

PROGRESS CHECK

If you have taken time to work through each of the exercises in this book, it is time to check your progress. On the following page is the perfectionism scale you filled out in Chapter 1. Complete it again and check your scores against your original answers.

Items 12, 14–18, and 21–24 are marked with a ✔. Together they represent your score on inwardly focused perfectionism (IFP SCORE). Items 4–9, 25–27, and 29 are marked with a (♦) next to them. This is your score on outwardly focused perfectionism (OFP SCORE). Add all thirty items together to get your total score. How does this score compare to your original one? If your score is now less than thirty then you probably have little to worry about. Keep up the effort to monitor perfectionism creeping back into your thinking when you get upset. If your score ranges from 31 to 60 you still have a mild case of perfectionism. When you are stressed your perfectionist char-

Perfectionism Check-Up

Below are some ideas that are held by perfectionists. Which of these do you still see in yourself? To help you decide, rate how strongly you agree with each of the statements below on a scale from 0 to 4.

0	1	2	3	4
I do not agree		I agree somewhat		I agree completely

__ 1. I have an eye for details that others can miss. (D)

__ 2. I can get lost in details and forget the real purpose of the task. (D)

__ 3. I can get overwhelmed by too many details. (D)

__ 4. ◆ It stresses me when people do not want to do things the right way. (R)

__ 5. ◆ There is a right way and a wrong way to do most things. (R)

__ 6. ◆ I do not like my routine to be interrupted. (R)

__ 7. ◆ I expect a great deal from myself. (E)

__ 8. ◆ I expect no less of others than I expect of myself. (E)

__ 9. ◆ People should always do their best. (E)

__ 10. I am neat in my appearance. (A)

__ 11. Good grooming is important to me. (A)

__ 12. ✔ I do not like being seen before I have showered and dressed. (A)

__ 13. I do not like making mistakes. (M)

__ 14. ✔ Receiving criticism is horrible. (M)

__ 15. ✔ It is embarrassing to make mistakes in front of others. (M)

__ 16. ✔ Sharing my new ideas with others makes me anxious. (C)

__ 17. ✔ I worry that my ideas are not good enough. (C)

__ 18. ✔ I do not have a great deal of confidence in myself. (C)

__ 19. I'm uncomfortable when my environment is untidy or disorganized. (O)

(cont.)

Perfectionism Check-Up (cont.)

__ 20.   When things are disorganized it is hard for me to concentrate. (O)

__ 21. ✔ What others think about my home is important to me. (O)

__ 22. ✔ I have trouble making difficult decisions. (S)

__ 23. ✔ I worry that I may make the wrong decision. (S)

__ 24. ✔ Making a bad decision can be disastrous. (S)

__ 25. ◆ I often do not trust others to do the job right. (T)

__ 26. ◆ I check the work of others to make certain it was done correctly. (T)

__ 27. ◆ If I can control the process it will turn out fine. (T)

__ 28.   I am a perfectionist. (G)

__ 29. ◆ I care more about doing a quality job than others do. (G)

__ 30.   It's important to make a good impression. (G)

_____ TOTAL SCORE

_____ IFP SCORE (✔)

_____ OFP SCORE (◆)

D = Detail-oriented   C = Confidence is low
R = Rules and structure   O = Organization and neatness in the environment
E = Expectations are high   S = Self-doubt
A = Appearance   T = Low trust of others
M = Mistakes are avoided   G = General

acteristics are probably more likely to show. If your score is from 61 to 90 you have a moderate level of perfectionism; that means it can still cause you trouble. Scores higher than 91 suggest a level of perfectionism that needs a lot more attention. Add up your scores on the subcategories as indicated by the letter after each item. Transfer your scores to the grid at the end of Chapter 1 along with your initial ratings. Note the similarities and differences. The characteristics that are rated the highest should get more attention than the characteristics rated the lowest. After you have taken time to work on more of the exercises, take this test again to check your progress.

PRACTICE, PRACTICE, PRACTICE

Out With the Eight-Track Tape and In With the CD

Old schemas are like old tapes that play in your mind. Your job is to recognize them when they influence your view of things. If they are negative schemas that leave you feeling distressed in some way, take time to look at them more closely. Evaluate their accuracy and make adjustments or replace them altogether to make them more accurately reflect your reality. Your new, less perfectionist, schemas should not arouse the same degree of discomfort in response to stressful events as your old schemas did.

One of my patients described this process as taking out her old eight-track tape that played the old negative schemas about herself and replacing it with a new compact disk that played her updated self-view. This takes some practice, but it is well worth the effort. With some work your old schemas may just disappear forever or stay so far in the background that they no longer affect your life.

Below is the list of schemas about perfectionism that you rated in Chapter 3. If you decided that they were not altogether accurate you probably changed them to better fit your personal experiences. Next to each of the schemas below is an example of how June, Brent, Terry, or Joe changed their schemas to make them less perfectionistic. This may help you in making changes to your own.

It is a good idea to monitor your perfectionist schemas regularly to assure that they are not taking control of your life again. Some people do this once each month in the beginning, then every six months, and finally once each year or at times when they are feeling more distressed. When you get upset, ask yourself if you are playing the old eight-track tape instead of your updated CD. Stop yourself, make changes, and try again.

Restating Perfectionistic Schemas

Perfectionistic beliefs	Modified beliefs
I must be perfect or I will be rejected.	I need to do the best job I possibly can.
If I make a mistake it will be horrible.	Everyone makes mistakes sometimes. Deal with it and go on.
If I do it perfectly then I will be accepted.	I want to be accepted for who I am and not what I do.
I must be perfect or I will be embarrassed.	A little embarrassment doesn't hurt. It just means you are human.
If I make a mistake I will be humiliated.	Most of the time no one else really cares.
When I get it right I will finally accept myself.	I need to find a way to accept myself and my shortcomings now.
When I achieve perfection I will find inner peace.	This is not the way to inner peace. Finding comfort in who I am will calm my nerves.
If I do it perfectly then it will be rewarded.	You can be perfect all the time and never get the rewards you really want. If you want a reward find a quicker and more direct way to get it.
If others do not approve of me then I am not OK.	My worth is not dependent upon the opinions of others. What matters most is what I think of myself.
If I make a mistake then I am worthless.	No, I'm not.
I'm not good enough. I must keep trying.	I'm just fine. I'm doing the best I can. It will have to be good enough for now.
I must be perfect or others will disapprove of me.	Everyone is entitled to their own opinion. If the disapproval really bothers me I can talk to them and resolve the problem. *(cont.)*

Perfectionistic beliefs	Modified beliefs
If I do it perfectly then everything will work out right.	I can do my best, but there are a lot of things that can go wrong that are beyond my control. It is most important to adapt and go on.
I'll never be good enough.	If you look at the facts, I am already plenty good enough.
If others approve of me then I must be OK.	Approval from others feels good.
If I do it perfectly then everyone will notice.	I've done many things perfectly and no one noticed. It hurt my feelings because I put too much value on their opinions.
I must be perfect or I will fail.	Failure is a big word. I work too hard to really fail. Things might not always turn out my way, but I am not likely to completely blow it.
Things should be done the right way.	I like having things done my way, but I guess other people have the same right.
There is a right way and a wrong way to do things.	With some things this is true, but there are obviously many ways to skin a cat.
It is possible to do things perfectly.	This is true, but it takes a lot of time and effort. Sometimes the effort is worth it and sometimes it is not.

Collect Data

The best way to make lasting changes in your perfectionist schemas is to continuously collect data that support your new view and refute your old view. Taking an example from the previous list, you have to make note of all of the times that it turned out to be true that "I can do my best, but there are a lot of things that can go wrong that are beyond my control. It is most important to adapt and go on" and it turned out to be untrue that "If I do it perfectly then everything will work out right." It can be helpful to keep a continuous log of events that confirm your new view (e.g., "I'm just fine. I'm doing the best I can. It will have to be good enough for now") and disprove your old view (e.g., "I'm not good enough. I must keep trying"). Review the list from time to time if you have doubts about yourself.

Self-monitoring

In Chapter 5, on thinking errors and automatic thoughts, you learned about distorted views that can affect your emotions and your actions. It takes some practice to be able to identify negative automatic thoughts when they are occurring. Your cue will usually be a sudden change in your emotions, for example, from neutral to upset, happy to angry, or from feeling content to feeling sad. Practice writing down your negative automatic thoughts when you feel your mood changing. Use the exercises in Chapters 3, 4, and 5 to help you evaluate their accuracy and reduce the distortions that may be affecting your mood and your actions. Once you get the hang of it you will be able to do these exercises in your head without having to write them down. However, when you are extremely upset, it is better to write down your thoughts and work through the exercises in a systematic fashion.

RELAPSE PREVENTION

"Here We Go Again"—Know Your Vulnerabilities

Even after you have made changes in your perfectionist schemas and actions you will still have times when you fall back into your old way of thinking, particularly during times of stress. To prepare for these times you need to know your vulnerable points. With Brent it was with women, for Joe it was with his boys, for Terry it was when she was being scrutinized by her boss or felt like her ex-husband was not helping her, for June it was when she was overcommitted and overwhelmed. What are your vulnerability points? Is there a connection with your hormonal fluctuations? Does the time of year make a difference? Is it when you are tired or hungry? Is it when you have to interact with your parents? There is probably a pattern to when perfectionism causes you the most grief. Find the pattern and prepare for the next time it occurs.

Develop a plan for avoiding vulnerable situations, when you are not at your best. Have a backup plan for times when you are unexpectedly confronted with situations that always seem to set you back. Practice monitoring your emotions and your negative automatic thoughts even before these events occur. Watch for your tendency to have an overly negative view when things are going wrong and counter it by making the logical part of you do more of the work and the emotional part of you do less.

"Priority Checks"

If you tend to get overwhelmed from time to time with the demands of work, home, family, friends, and your personal life, you may find that part of the problem is that you lose perspective on what is most important. Ideally, you would want to allocate more of your physical, emotional, and psychological energy to the things that are most important to you and allocate relatively less energy to the things that are least important. Unfortunately, small and less important events can nag at us and consume more time and energy than they are worth in the grand scheme of life. Losing perspective can mean that you have allowed small annoyances to interfere with other aspects of your life. Here is a way to regain perspective when you are overwhelmed.

The question you will be addressing is "Am I spending my emotional energy wisely?" First, make a list of all the things that have consumed your emotional, physical, or psychological energy in the past week. Second, rank order the items in terms of how much energy they have consumed, with the number one assigned to the item that received the greatest amount of energy and the last number assigned to the item that received the least. It can be helpful to estimate what percentage of your energy went toward each of those items. Third, rerank the items in terms of their importance to your life. Ask yourself, "In the grand scheme of my life, how important is each of these things to me?" Rank the most important item as number one, the second most important as number two, and so on. Now compare your rankings. An example is shown.

Your rankings of energy allocation and importance should be relatively similar. If they are not, you will need to adjust your attention to each item accordingly. For example, a project being overdue received a much higher ranking in terms of energy consumption than its rankings in terms of importance. This person seems to be wasting energy on something that is not worth the amount of time and energy it is given. It is not uncommon to find that a conflict with another person that you rated as being relatively low in overall importance still nags at you, like the example of a friend not inviting you to a party. Here the importance

Activity or event	Rank of energy consumed by this item in the last week	Rank of importance of the item to my life
Garage door broke.	6	6
Project is overdue.	1	5
Child is slightly ill.	2	1
Garden is overgrown.	5	7
Friend did not invite me to her party last week.	3	8
Haven't had time to exercise.	7	3
Have gained five pounds.	8	4
Feel overworked and need to rest.	4	2

was the lowest, but it got the third most energy of the week. It is easy to slip into this pattern. You might find yourself talking to others about the incident over and over again or ruminating about it instead of getting a good night's sleep. This consumes both your time and your emotional energy. The more you talk about it the madder you get. When you give it too much attention or energy you are giving less energy to something else that might be more important. You only have so much energy to use in a day and so many hours to use it in. To make sure your expenditure of energy is in balance, you have to take stock periodically to make certain that your higher priorities in life are getting the most attention.

PITFALLS IN THE PATH TO IMPROVEMENT

Making changes in the way you look at things is not easy. It takes a great deal of effort to counter old thoughts, old ideas, and old habits. Remember that there are many advantages to perfectionism that you will want to maintain, while lowering the volume on the perfectionism in the areas that cause you grief. This means that you cannot approach perfectionism in an all-or-nothing fashion; you have to use it in moderation. It serves you well and so it will be difficult to control it when it is not needed or when it has the potential to get you into trouble. Below is a brief summary of the kinds of things that can interfere with your progress in controlling your perfectionism. Plan for them, watch for them, and take corrective action when they appear.

Coping with Frustration

If you are used to getting quick results when you attack a new problem, you will probably be disappointed with this book. The results you need to make permanent changes in your life will take some time. It takes time to put these exercises into practice at work, at home, and with other people in your life. You will have to struggle with each until you find an answer. You will inevitably fall into your old patterns, primarily because you will have some difficulty connecting the

> ### Take time to think about this.
>
> When you reach a discouraging point, resist the temptation to throw the whole thing away and call it a failure. That is your old way of thinking. The new view is that progress exists on a continuum and you are slowly moving yourself up the continuum toward a more satisfactory level.

notion of perfectionism to your everyday experiences. The assistance of a therapist or counselor can greatly facilitate your efforts if she understands the model from which we are working. Share the book with her and ask her to help you follow along.

If you generally put a lot of pressure on yourself to succeed, as many perfectionists are accustomed to doing, you will probably get frustrated too easily. Remember that improvement is not an all-or-nothing phenomenon. Progress will occur in small rather than large steps. Set goals for achievement that are conservative rather than dramatic and overnight. If a friend or family member talked you into reading this book, do not promise them that you will be different tomorrow. Ask them to be patient and to not judge your progress in an all-or-nothing way. If you would like, they can help you monitor your emotions, your actions, and your perspective for signs of difficulty.

When you reach a discouraging point, resist the temptation to throw the whole thing away and call it a failure. That is your old way of thinking. The new view is that progress exists on a continuum and you are slowly moving yourself up the continuum toward a more satisfactory level. If you have forgotten how to do this, reread Chapter 6 on developing a cognitive continuum.

Getting Others to Cooperate

There are a few things that are frustrating when you try to make changes that involve other people. One is that their perfectionism can get in the way and the other is that getting along better generally requires effort on both parts. It is not easy to get others to change unless they see a good reason to do so.

The most complicated scenario is when you are an inwardly focused perfectionist and your partner is an outwardly focused perfectionist who does not see anything wrong with his or her views or actions. You can try to adjust your schemas about feeling good enough, but if your partner is critical, openly rejecting, or intolerant of your mistakes, you will have a tougher time believing your own self-talk and ignoring his comments. If it is more than you can handle, call upon a marriage counselor to be the referee.

Another complicated scenario is when you and your partner are both inwardly focused perfectionists. If you begin to feel stronger and more confident, it can be intimidating for your partner. To avoid difficulties, try to involve your partner in your self-improvement plan. Share your new thoughts, ask for assistance in monitoring when your perfectionism is in full swing, and share your progress.

WHEN TREATMENT IS NEEDED

If your perfectionism is only one symptom of a more troublesome problem with depression, anxiety, or eating disorders, you will likely need some professional assistance to make changes. Some of the symptoms of concern were mentioned in Chapter 1. If you have any, consult your doctor or a mental health professional for an evaluation. The signs to look for are extreme changes in mood that linger for days or for weeks. Anxiety can interfere with your functioning by keeping you from doing things you need to do or would like to do. Eating disorders affect your weight, your health, and your self-concept. All of these can consume a great deal of your mental and physical energy, and that is what keeps you from being able to manage your life, your work, your home, or your family.

Many people enjoy reading self-help books but are not crazy about seeing a mental health professional. As with those in any profession, mental health professionals such as psychologists, psychiatrists, social workers, and counselors vary in their level of training, skill, and experience. Some are better than others, and it is not always easy to pick the right one to meet your needs. There are a few rules of thumb to follow. Make sure your mental health professional has a license to practice. While this does not guarantee that he or she will be skilled, at least you know that there is a larger professional organization that has overseen their training and has tested their knowledge to some degree. Second, research from studies of both psychotherapy and medication treatments shows that your relationship with the practitioner can have an impact on your degree of recovery. You should feel comfortable with your clinician so that you can participate in treatment actively. If you do not feel at ease you will be less likely to attempt and benefit from any suggestion they make. You can get a feel for a person by interviewing him on the phone. Ask about his credentials, fees, hours, and his estimate of how long treatment will take.

Sometimes you have to have a few visits before you will know if you can work well with the therapist. Try a few sessions and if not satisfied, shop around for a new one. Be an active consumer or get your family or friends to help you choose. Do not stick with a clinician just because you do not want to hurt his feelings by discontinuing treatment. I call these mercy visits when you come to the doctor because you feel sorry for him.

If you start therapy and do not get what you need, tell the clinician. Set goals for treatment and evaluate your progress along the way. Your therapist should be willing to do this with you and take constructive

---

Questions to Ask Myself

Why do I have to be perfect?

Do I really have to be perfect to get what I want in life?

So what if I am not always perfect?

Who says I have to be perfect? Are they right?

What do I actually get if I am perfect?

Do I have to be perfect at everything?

When is "good enough" a reasonable standard?

Reminders About Perfectionism

People should accept me for who I am, not for how perfectly I perform.

There is usually more than one "right way" to do something.

Perfection is a matter of opinion.

Perfection is overrated.

Strive to do your best rather than to be perfect.

To be imperfect is to be normal.

Things are rarely black or white. Look for the shades of gray.

I can live without complete approval from others, but I need to approve of myself.

What is more important is what I think of myself.

---

feedback if therapy is not turning out the way you planned. You are paying for your care, so demand good service. The more active you are the quicker you will begin to feel better.

If you are truly a perfectionist you are probably highly motivated to do things right. This characteristic will no doubt help you to be successful in controlling your perfectionism. However, it will take practice to make positive changes in your thinking and actions. Shown on the opposite page are some questions to ask yourself that will help you combat your perfectionism. Copy them down and put them in your wallet. Review them from time to time.

The bottom line messages to fight perfectionism include those in the box above. Copy them down and keep them handy. When you are stressed-out, review the list and try to talk yourself out of an unrealistic demand to be perfect.

Being an imperfect member of society, I can personally guarantee that it is possible to have a great life even if you are not perfect. Redirect the energy consumed by trying to be perfect toward relaxing and having some fun. Free yourself from the chains of perfectionism and have a good ("good enough") life.

Where to Call for Help

For referral for treatment or for more information,
we recommend these organizations:

Center for Cognitive Therapy
University of Pennsylvania, Philadelphia 90104
(215) 898-4100

Center for Cognitive Therapy
1101 Dove Street
Newport Beach, California 92660
(949) 646-3390

Institute for Rational Emotive Therapy
45 East 65th Street
New York, New York 10021
(212) 535-0822

National Alliance for the Mentally Ill
2101 Wilson Boulevard, Suite 302
Arlington, VA 22201
800/950-6264

National Clearinghouse for Alcohol and
Drug Information (NCADI)
P.O. Box 2345
Rockville, MD 20857
800/729-6686

National Depressive and Manic Depressive Association
53 West Jackson Boulevard, Room 618
Chicago, IL 60604
(312) 642-0049 312/939-2442

National Foundation for Depressive Illness
20 Charles Street
New York, NY 10014
800/248-4344

National Institute of Mental Health and the D/ART Program
Public Inquiries Branch, Room 15C-05
5600 Fishers Lane
Rockville, MD 20857
800/223-6427

National Mental Health Association
1021 Prince Street
Alexandria, VA 23314-2971
(703) 684-7722
National Mental Health Information Center
800/969-6642

Obsessive Compulsive Foundation, Inc.
P. O. Box 70
Milford, CT 06460-0070
(203) 878-5669
(203) 874-2826
(203) 874-3843 (for OCD Developments)

University of Texas
Southwestern Medical Center at Dallas
Department of Psychiatry & Psychology
5323 Harry Hines Blvd. MC 9070
Dallas, Texas 75235-9070
(214) 648-3300

For additional reading on related issues, we recommend the following books:

Don't Panic: Taking Control of Anxiety Attacks, by R. Reid Wilson, HarperCollins, New York, 1996.

Feeling Good: The New Mood Therapy, by David D. Burns, Avon Books, New York, 1980.

How Good Do We Have To Be? A New Understanding of Guilt and Forgiveness, by Rabbi Harold Kushner, Little, Brown & Company, New York, 1996.

Mind Over Mood, by Dennis Greenberger and Christine A. Padesky, Guilford Press, New York, 1995.

The Feeling Good Handbook, by David D. Burns, Penguin, New York, 1989.

The Highly Sensitive Person: How To Thrive When Love Overwhelms You, by Elaine Aron, Broadway Books, New York, 1997.

The Joy of Imperfection, by Enid Howarth and Jan Tras, Fairview Press, Minneapolis, 1996.

Ultra-Solutions: How to Fail Most Successfully, by Paul Watzlawick, W. W. Norton & Company, New York, 1988.

Worry: Help and Hope for a Common Condition, by Edward M. Hallowell, Random House, New York, 1998.

INDEX

Acceptance and approval
  From yourself, 59, 104–105
  From others, 14–16, 21, 45, 76–78,
    80–83, 103, 105–109
  Of others, 209–210
Accomplishment, 45
Advantages of perfectionism, 38–47,
  59–64
Advising others, 122
All or nothing thinking (see oversimpli-
  fication)
Alternative Explanations, 86, 108–109,
  120–121
Anorexia, 6, 32, 34–35
Anxiety, 6–7, 58, 261
Appearance, 23–24, 45–46, 60
Approval (see Acceptance)
Assumptions (see Mindreading, Clair-
  voyant thinking)
Automatic thoughts, 68, 93, 95,
  110–132, 168–169, 178, 186, 210,
  245, 256

Beliefs (see Schemas and beliefs)
Bulimia, 6, 32, 35

Catastrophizing, 85, 119
Children, 7–9
  Positive self-esteem, 43, 76

Let you down, 204–210
And Oversimplification, 130
Clairvoyant thinking, 117–121
Cognitive-Behavior Therapy (CBT), 4, 7,
  112
Cognitive Continuum, 145–162, 164, 260
Cognitive Model, 67
Communication
  Assertiveness, 200, 233, 237–239
  Problems, 191, 196, 202–203,
    231–233, 247–248
  Rules, 228
  Skills, 81, 188–190, 202, 244–246
Confidence
  low, 24–25, 27–28, 45–47, 60
  communicating, 43
Control, 28–29, 37, 41, 50, 51, 53,
  83–84
Core beliefs (See Schemas and Beliefs)
Criticism, 56, 129, 237, 246

Defensiveness, 226–227, 230
Decision-making, 27–28, 57
Depression, 6–7, 32, 35, 38, 59, 68, 85,
  112, 139, 261
Detail-oriented, 19–20, 39–41, 46, 51,
  60, 124, 200–203, 221, 243–244,
  248
Distractions (noise), 53

Disadvantages of perfectionism, 7, 47–64
Disapproval, 223, 226

Eating disorders (also see anorexia,
    bulimia), 38, 261
Emotion, 67–68, 76, 88–89, 93–95,
    111, 122, 146–147, 202, 208
Emotional labeling, 187–189
Examining the evidence (also see
    Changing Schemas and Beliefs),
    114–115, 119, 168–175, 178
Expectations and standards, 4, 40, 51
    Adjusting, 163–185
    Defining your, 147–148, 164–181
    For Others, 21–23, 43–44, 57, 187,
        190, 196, 211–212, 221, 232–234
    Unreasonably high, 5, 21–23, 39,
        45–49, 58, 60, 73
Exercises
    Advantages of Perfectionism, 46
    Advantages of Oversimplification, 131
    Automatic thoughts, 112
    Cognitive Continuum Exercise 1:
        Defining the Problem, 146
    Cognitive Continuum Exercise 2,
        149
    Cognitive Continuum Exercise 3:
        Building a cognitive continuum,
        152
    Cognitive Continuum Exercise 4, 156
    Combating Magnification, 115
    Communication Rules, 228
    Coping with Outwardly Focused Per-
        fectionists, 239
    Dealing with Criticism, 237
    Disadvantages of Oversimplification,
        131
    Disadvantages of Perfectionism, 60
    Drawing Conclusions, 171

Generate Alternative Explanations, 121
Getting Unstuck, 124
Helping Inwardly Focused Perfection-
    ists Who Fear Rejection, 246
How to Cope with Nonperfectionists,
    202
How to Help your Inwardly Focused
    Perfectionist, 242
Negotiating a quid pro quo, 236
Perfectionism Is A Problem When:, 7
Point-Counterpoint, 86
Preliminary Goals For Controlling
    Perfectionism, 65
Questions to Ask Myself, 262
Reminders About Perfectionism,
    263
Restating Perfectionistic Schemas,
    254–255
Schemas, 70
Schema Reality Check, 78
Sorting Fact from Fiction, 119
Things to Avoid as Parents, 215
Things to Do as Parents, 218
To Get Along Better with Others, 189
Ways to Cope, 122
What to Do When it is Not Your Turn
    to Lead, 200
When Your Emotions Get the Best of
    You, 208
Your Perfectionism Profile, 33
Exhaustion, 53

Failure, 25, 137, 202, 210
    Fear of, 85
    Setting yourself up for, 48–50
Fantasy outcomes, 78–86, 197
Feedback from others, 114, 164, 225
Fortune telling, 119, 194
Frustration, coping with, 259–260

Goals, 62–65

Humility, 212–216

Interpersonal problems (see relationship problems)
Inwardly focused perfectionism, 2–6, 10, 29–31, 126–127, 164, 190, 196, 250
  Living with, 239–249
  Schemas of, 72–73, 78, 81, 84–86, 105

Jumping to conclusions, 120–121

Know-how, 42

Leadership, 197–200, 238
Loneliness, 191

Magnification, 113–115
Mindreading, 56, 87, 118, 190–191, 194
Minimization, 115–117
Misperceptions & Misinterpretations, 68, 71, 93, 95, 113–118, 129, 231
Mistakes, 24, 45, 46, 49, 60, 72, 84–86, 94
Motivation, 44

Neatness, 26–27, 39, 41–42, 46, 60, 240–243

Obsessive compulsive disorder, 32, 34
Obsessive compulsive personality disorder, 34
Outwardly focused perfectionism, 2–4, 6, 16, 29–31, 127, 164, 187, 190, 196, 250
  Living with, 222–239
  Schemas of, 72–73, 79

Organization, 26–27, 39–42, 46, 50, 60
Oversimplification, 122–162, 187–188
Overwhelmed, 123–124, 138

Parental influences, 10–14, 203–218
  Conditional/unconditional praise, 10–12, 16
  Coping with parents, 14, 232–234
  Differences in goals, 234
  Modeling, Perfect parents, 12–14
  Overprotectiveness, 13
  Punishment, 16
  Things (not) to do, 215, 218
Peace, 79–80, 103–105
Perfectionism
  at home, 41–43, 52–54
  at work, 40–41, 47–52
  in relationships, 6–7, 43–44, 54–57, 129–130, 186–218, 219–249, 260–261; finding a mate (also see loneliness), 55, 191–197
  and yourself, 44–45, 47, 57–59, 61–62
Personality and Temperament, 7–9
Praise, how to give (also see parental influences), 209–212
Priority
  Setting, 181–183
  Check, 257–259
Progress
  Lack of, 53
  Making, 260

Quid pro quo, 235–236

Reinforcement (also see Parental influences), 15–17, 38, 79–81, 209–212, 245
Rejection
  fear of, 244–246

Relapse prevention, 256–263

Relationship problems (see Perfectionism in relationships)

Reward (see reinforcement)

Risk-taking (also see confidence), 51

Rules and rigidity, 20–21, 46, 60, 187, 221

    Ethics, 21

Safety Checklist, 184–185

Satisfaction, 45

Schemas and Beliefs, 3–4, 6, 50, 66–90, 164

    Challenging, 91–109

    Changing, 95–109, 253–256, 261

    Perfectionistic, 43, 59, 71–88, 95

Self-assessment

    Advantages of perfectionism at work, 41

    Advantages of perfectionism at home, 42

    Advantages of perfectionism in relationships, 44

    Advantages of perfectionism for yourself, 45

    Am I A Perfectionist?, 30–31, 251–252

    Automatic thoughts about lowering your standards, 169

    Disadvantages of perfectionism at work, 51

    Disadvantages of perfectionism at home, 53

    Disadvantages of perfectionism in relationships, 56

    Disadvantages of perfectionism for self, 53

    Do I have perfectionistic schemas?, 90

    I must be perfect or else . . ., 76

    If I am perfect then . . ., 79

    Right way and wrong way, 87

    Schema exercise Number, 1, Part, 1, 98

    Schema exercise Number, 1, Part, 2, 101

    Schema exercise Number, 1, Part, 3, 102

    Schema exercise Number, 2, 104

    Schema exercise Number, 3, 105

Self-blame, 58, 121–122, 194

Self-doubt (also see confidence), 27–28, 194, 227, 245, 248

Self-esteem (also see confidence), 15, 21, 85, 223, 232–233

Self-monitoring, 256

Setting Limits, 247–249

Shoulds, 164

Societal pressures, 10, 39

Standards (see expectations)

Step by step, 183–184

Take time to think about this

    Acceptance, 16, 82, 83

    Alternative Explanations, 109

    Approval, 106

    Choosing a mate, 195

    Disapproval, 226

    Expectations, 23

    Experience and Schemas, 96

    Failure, 50

    Making Assumptions, 190

    Making Progress, 260

    Mindreading, 118

    Minimization, 116

    Misperceptions, 93

    Overwhelmed, 124

    Parental reactions, 210

    Reward, 80

Schemas, 50
Standards, 165
Stuck on details, 244
The right way, 87
Therapy and other treatments, 261–263

Thinking errors, 113–132, 164, 168,
    194
Trusting others, 28–29, 39, 44, 46, 50,
    56, 60, 187, 227–232
Tunnel vision, 121–132